Measurement and Analysis of Political Systems

Comparative Studies in Behavioral Science:
A WILEY SERIES

Robert T. Holt and John E. Turner, *Editors*
Department of Political Science
University of Minnesota

The Logic of Comparative Social Inquiry
by Adam Przeworski and Henry Teune

The Analysis of Subjective Culture
by Harry C. Triandis

Comparative Legislative Behavior: Frontiers of Research
edited by Samuel C. Patterson and John C. Wahlke

Mass Political Violence: A Cross-National Causal Analysis
by Douglas A. Hibbs, Jr.

Cross-Cultural Research Methods
by Richard W. Brislin, Walter J. Lonner, and Robert M. Thorndike

Unity and Disintegration in International Alliances
by Ole R. Holsti, P. Terrence Hopmann, and John D. Sullivan

Comparative Social Research: Methodological Problems and Strategies
edited by Michael Armer and Allen D. Grimshaw

Planning and Budgeting in Poor Countries
by Naomi Caiden and Aaron Wildavsky

Politics and Social Equality: A Comparative Analysis
by Robert W. Jackman

Measurement and Analysis of Political Systems: A Science of Social Behavior
by Stephen Coleman

Patterns of Authority: A Structural Basis for Political Inquiry
by Harry Eckstein and Ted Robert Gurr

Measurement and Analysis of Political Systems:

A Science of Social Behavior

STEPHEN COLEMAN

A WILEY-INTERSCIENCE PUBLICATION

JOHN WILEY & SONS, New York • London • Sydney • Toronto

Library of Congress Cataloging in Publication Data:
Coleman, Stephen, 1942-
Measurement and analysis of political systems.

(Comparative studies in behavioral science)
"A Wiley-Interscience publication."
Bibliography: p.
Includes index.
1. Political science—Mathematical models. 2. Political sociology—Mathematical models. I. Title.

JA73.C62 320'.01'82 75-8704
ISBN 0-471-16492-5

Printed in the United States of America

10 9 8 7 6 5 4 3 2 1

SERIES PREFACE

The last decade has witnessed the burgeoning of comparative studies in the behavioral sciences. Scholars in specific disciplines have come to realize that they share much with experts in other fields who face similar theoretical and methodological problems and whose research findings are often related. Moreover, specialists in a given geographic area have felt the need to look beyond the limited confines of their region and to seek new meaning in their research results by comparing them with studies that have been made elsewhere.

This series is designed to meet the needs of the growing cadre of scholars in comparative research. The emphasis is on cross-disciplinary studies, although works within the perspective of a single discipline are included. In its scope, the series includes books of theoretical and methodological interest, as well as studies that are based on empirical research. The books in the series are addressed to scholars in the various behavioral science disciplines, to graduate students, and to undergraduates in advanced standing.

Robert T. Holt
John E. Turner

University of Minnesota
Minneapolis, Minnesota

Preface

This book presents a new view of society and politics. It is a restricted view, but one that explains many social events involving large numbers of people. Although these events may not affect the detail of everyday life, they are, nevertheless, the dominant forces giving structure and direction to our societies. Our approach to the study of social events is from the general to the specific. We begin by showing how to quantify or measure social behavior independently of its social context. Then we apply the measurement principles to the analysis of specific events and processes in national political systems. Substantive areas to be covered include electoral behavior, political party systems, rationality in voting, political change, the origins of civil wars and revolutions, and the effects and limits of uncertainty in societies. In the theory that develops, we make quantitative predictions and test them in a number of case studies. Among political systems analyzed are the United States, India, Japan, and Germany—all with subnational units of analysis. In each of these societies we discover fundamental regularities of structure and change that are a necessary result of the way people acquire knowledge about their societies, a process constrained by inherent human limitations. These regularities or social "laws" form the basis for a scientific theory of collective social behavior.

This book is expressly interdisciplinary, in content as well as in the intended audience. The social theory presented here requires techniques from mathematics, engineering, and the physical sciences, as well as from the social sciences. The reader need not have a strong background in any of these subjects, but a familiarity with statistics and advanced mathematics—up to the level of calculus or differential equations—would be helpful. Whenever possible, technical subjects are explained in nontechnical language. By following our methods of analysis, the reader can easily duplicate the results or extend the study to other cases of interest. This book is meant to be conducive to further research in all of its interdisciplinary phases, from the analysis of contemporary political systems to related theoretical problems in systems analysis, communication theory, and the philosophy of science. The interested reader will find the necessary stepping-stones for expanding the theory that we develop.

Whichever aspects of this social theory may eventually be of practical importance, the book has a nearer goal: to better our understanding of our societies; to know why and how they are, and what that understanding tells us about ourselves. If the book serves this purpose, it will also reflect the understanding, kindness, and shared openness of the many people whose lives have touched mine during the writing of the book and in the years before.

STEPHEN COLEMAN

Minneapolis, Minnesota
February 1975

CONTENTS

Measurement and Analysis of Political Systems

CHAPTER ONE

Orientation

1-1. Introduction

This book began as an investigation into the measurement of social phenomena, with the long-range objective of determining the extent to which social phenomena can or can not be analyzed as an exact science. There has been a long history of argument that except for economic affairs we will never have a true science of social behavior in the sense of a physical science. A frequent assertion has been that human beings are just too variable and unpredictable in their actions for social "laws" to exist, laws that would be comparable with the laws of physical sciences and capable of accurate quantitative expression. This negative viewpoint on the existence of social laws has often carried with it an implicit judgment that to study people in a lawlike or "mechanistic" fashion constitutes an infringement on human individuality or a lack of respect for it. This view may harbor a fear that a scientific or mathematical understanding of social phenomena would somehow bring us away from an understanding of essential human qualities.

All these pessimistic and negative attitudes about the possibilities for a social science are really unfounded. It is true that individual people are not completely predictable. But, as our study of collective social behavior here will show, the *degree* of unpredictability or uncertainty about behavior in a society is itself capable of quantification and scientific prediction for the society as a whole. And large groups of people acting together in societies exhibit average behavioral tendencies that can be approximated by deterministic mathematical laws. The existence of such social laws, rather than obscuring human values and qualities, has the opposite result: it lets us see exactly what it is about people that makes societies the way they are, in at least certain important respects.

As a study of collective social behavior this book moves along two parallel planes. On the first and most fundamental level we have a concern with the technical aspects of studying social behavior. These include the specification of measurement variables and operations; the testing of hypotheses; and the mathematical formulation of dynamic processes. On the second plane we have to consider the implications of the technical theory for our understanding of social events. As an aid to the reader in following these dual themes of the book, we can summarize here the main ideas of each.

On the technical level the most immediate problem is how to quantify or measure social behavior. There have been, of course, many ways in which this has been done in the past, and there are innumerable procedures by which numbers could be associated with social events. But to have an exact science the measurement variables must themselves be directly and necessarily related to observable empirical properties or regularities of the system one is studying. Since the laws of a scientific theory must be stated in terms of the measurement variables, usually as relationships between measurement variables, an arbitrary quantification of phenomena will not ensure the development of a science based upon quantitative empirical laws. How then do we find the right measurement variables? This is a very difficult problem in any science, and only a small number of fundamental measures have ever been discovered. These include the basic physical measures such as length, voltage, and temperature—and the economic variable price—along with a few other basic variables in parallel use in these sciences. Most other measurement variables of physics and other sciences are derived in some mathematical way from these fundamental variables.

A key finding of the research presented here is that there does exist another fundamental measure for social phenomena; this might be considered another dimension of social behavior along with, but separate from, the economic dimension. This new social measure quantifies the dimension of uncertainty or unpredictability in social behavior, but the exact specification of what this "uncertainty" measure is requires a sophisticated mathematical treatment. In effect, people are able collectively to control or organize the state of their society along this dimension, and they do this with a fairly high degree of quantitative accuracy. To measure social uncertainty, we shall adopt a mathematical technique that has a corresponding purpose in communication theory. That is, we can consider social behavior as a form of communication between individuals in a society and then apply the methods used to study conventional electronic or symbolic communication.

Coincidentally, the introduction of this new social measurement variable gives an answer to the perennial question of whether one should analyze social events and behavior objectively, as a remote observer would, or as the social events are seen and understood by the people in the society. The results here indicate that the objective measure of social uncertainty, as applied to social systems as wholes, is equivalent to the subjective way in which people in the society perceive the ambient level of uncertainty about social events.

Once it becomes possible to measure quantitatively the state of a society along the uncertainty dimension, we can begin to analyze change in the society. The existence of the measurement variable allows a precise formulation of what social change is, for the class of measurable phenomena. The technical questions that arise in the analysis of system change concern the ability of a system to maintain an equilibrium at a given state; the effects of interaction between separate social systems or subsystems; and the spatiotemporal diffusion of change across large geographic areas. We make an extensive study of these dynamic properties in contemporary political systems.

Recent studies of systems analysis have shown that various kinds of physical systems—mechanical, electrical, thermal, and so forth—and economic systems can be analyzed with analogous methods. Although each of these system varieties has a different set of fundamental measures, they share a similar pattern of empirical laws, which in turn allows the same mathematical methods to be used in the analysis of each kind. And we are able to extend this commonality of systems analysis to social systems. This also permits us to develop rapidly and economically a theory of social dynamics, simply by retracing the development of analytic methods as used to study the dynamics of physical systems.

Throughout the book we compare the analysis of social systems with that of physical systems. As we have indicated, this has the immediate purpose of allowing the methods of physical systems analysis to be applied to social systems. But in a broader context, this use of analogy between physical and social systems offers a greater insight into what a science involves and how the social theory constructed here compares with physical science theories at various stages of their historical development. This comparison also points out the theoretical and experimental problems whose solutions are most crucial to further development of the social theory. As a whole, this book presents a theory of social and political phenomena that is roughly comparable with scientific theories of physics in the nineteenth century in the methods of analysis and in the kinds of explanations possible for system phenomena.

At this stage of theory development we are primarily restricted to understanding the behavior of systems in terms of aggregate or collective properties of large numbers of system elements. We can formulate satisfactory laws for systems as wholes, but we have a poor understanding of exactly what is happening among the individual system members or elements that is giving rise to the laws. The working out of these details for social systems goes outside the range of this book but will present a continuing challenge to theory construction in social science. Questions of social engineering are also beyond the scope of this book; we do not consider problems related to the design or control of social systems.

Parallel to the development of the technical analysis of social phenomena is its interpretation for our understanding of social affairs. The solutions to technical problems are constrained to follow their own logical development, being dependent on the exact nature of empirical laws and the limitations of mathematics. Yet the technical constraints also impose upon us new, and often surprizing, interpretations of traditional social and political questions. In a limited but well-defined sense the scientific theory provides answers to such questions as: what a society is; why societies are the way they are; how people know what their society is like; and why things go wrong sometimes in societies, leading to conflict, war, or other social pathologies.

The first question arising from the technical analysis of social behavior is how to take measurements of entire social systems, that is, how to measure the state of uncertainty of a society. The mathematical definition of uncertainty requires us to look at a specific class of social phenomena where we can estimate the probabilities of alternative social events. In its various social guises this mathematical measurement operation leads us to examine social conformity, freedom of choice, social structure, and uncertainty in societies. These apparently dissimilar social topics become equivalent from a measurement perspective. We discover, for example, that national elections in political systems constitute measurements of the state of uncertainty of the system. This view of elections contradicts the traditional democratic interpretation and purpose of elections as popular preference rankings of alternative political parties, candidates, or issues. The technical measurement operation thus brings us directly to a new explanation of certain electoral phenomena, including voter turnout and abstention, political parties, political party systems, and the relationships among these. We investigate these relationships in detail.

In studying the dynamics of change in political systems we encounter a different range of social concerns, beyond the electoral phenomena associated with system measurement. The observation of spatiotemporal patterns of change across political systems informs us of the extent and fluidity of social interaction or communication among people in the society. The distribution of uncertainty measurement values across a national political system can reveal the degree to which the system has been cohesively integrated into a single sociopolitical unit, or whether it remains a collection of separate, semi-isolated regions. We find that in certain instances the pattern of measurements can be of predictive value in assessing the likelihood of secession, civil war, or internal strife due to failures in system integration or due to rapid change in its degree.

There are also times when the normal dynamic processes of system change can work in a perverse way and lead to an authoritarian revolution. Apparently, this path of social change results from the breakdown in social structure and communication that can occur when the quantitative level of uncertainty in the society approaches the maximum level that people can cope with. We analyze the fall of the Weimar Republic of Germany and the rise of the Hitler regime as a case study in the effects of excessive social uncertainty. This case study shows that system uncertainty measurements can be used in predicting events of this nature.

Implicit throughout this study of social measurement and dynamics is the conclusion that we cannot immediately explain large-scale social phenomena by individual motives, attitudes, or values, even when these are widely shared in a population. This conclusion pertains to the explanation of discrete social events, such as elections, as well as to dynamic social processes. Just as one cannot infer that an economic depression is the result of a sudden, universal desire among a population for unemployment and poverty, one simply cannot infer that wars, civil violence, or authoritarian revolutions are necessarily the result of widespread popular intention to bring about these social conditions. Nor can one infer that these conditions are inevitable in human affairs because they represent ever-present human tendencies toward violence and aggression. On the contrary, we see that normal human tendencies can lead to unintended results for a society as a whole because of the complex way in which interaction among people takes place. In general, we must conclude that social phenomena involving large numbers of people can only be adequately explained through an understanding of the nature of interaction between people and its effects on individual choice and behavior in a collective, social context.

In every science there is a close connection between measurement, the analysis of systems, and the way one comes to "explain" and "understand" events. What we know depends on how we have acquired that knowledge. Here too, we see that the methods of social analysis have far-reaching implications for our understanding of social and political events. Of course, everyone concerned with social science has questions or problems for which he would like to find answers and has criteria for deciding what a satisfactory answer is. But what constitutes a proper question or a meaningful explanation in a science is *not* self-evident; it is determined both by our observations of the world and by subtle, extrascientific, social conventions about what is legitimately "scientific". At times there may even be alternative scientific explanations for the same events, although one explanation will usually be more widely accepted than others. Alternative explanations imply alternative, and usually contradictory, views of the world.

This book proposes a new view of the social world and a new set of questions and answers for a social science that would apply to a carefully defined and restricted, yet important, class of social events. The analytic methods used here define the problems of interest to social science within the limits of the theory. There may be many other problems people would think worthy of study besides those dealt with here, but that does not mean the problems can or should be handled within this social theory. Nevertheless, we will find that many traditional questions of social science have not been correctly posed and cannot be answered scientifically unless they are restated in the analytic language of this theory. Perhaps the most difficult aspect of this book is the need to reorganize one's thinking about the nature of social and political processes. Although the view of society taken here may seem to be dependent on a methodology adapted from mathematics and physical sciences, it does not mean that this is an arbitrary view of society forced on us by alien methods of analysis. On the contrary, we find a distinct class of social and political processes, continuously going on in the world, for which these methods of analysis are the appropriate ones and for which the measurement variables introduced here are the only ones for studying these phenomena scientifically. If the mathematical techniques for studying physical systems were not available to us, we would still have to invent them in order to explain social phenomena.

In this chapter we review those aspects of measurement and systems analysis that we will need at different stages in constructing a theory of collective social behavior.

1-2. Formalization

The procedure we follow in developing a scientific theory of social behavior is one of formalization. In formalization the trend of theory construction is to develop increasingly abstract representations or models of the phenomena of interest.[1] We can divide the formalization process into three stages: the specification of measurement variables and operations; the introduction of a system model; and, finally, the use of abstract mathematics to describe and predict system phenomena. These three stages have been incorporated in all the well-established exact sciences, including classical mechanics, electromagnetic theory, and thermodynamics. The measurement stage is the most fundamental of the three, since it is our link with the "real world" events that we seek to understand. For this reason we begin our study of social phenomena by introducing a set of variables for their measurement. The measurement variables fix the range of phenomena we will be able to analyze in the subsequent theory. In the next stage of formalization, a system model is introduced. A system model is an abstract, simplified version of a real physical or social system. The model represents the collection of system elements (atoms, people, or whatever) and the set of relationships among them. Of course, we must construct the model in such a way that we can use measurement data with the model to explain real system behavior. The formalization process also calls for the development of abstract concepts from the original measurement variables for the description of system behavior.

Let us consider a simple example of formalization. In electrical theory one begins with basic measurement variables such as charge, current, and voltage. Then a system model is devised to represent a particular electrical system, a radio circuit for instance. And mathematical techniques such as differential equations let us analyze or predict the behavior of the system. Energy and power—formal concepts derived from the initial measurement variables—are used in the systems analysis.

Formalization serves two purposes in our construction of a social theory: first as a research strategy, and second, as a standard by which we can judge how closely the social theory resembles existing scientific theories. We will imitate the formalization procedures that other sciences have used in their development. We have good reason for adopting this strategy. As we shall see, the exact sciences have a great deal in common with one another. They have analogous patterns of measurement variables; they use similar system models; and they share the same methods of mathematical analysis. It is not completely clear *why* exact sciences have this high degree of commonality. But apparently these common structural features are necessary constituents of a scientific theory, and perhaps are necessary to our acceptance of a theory as a legitimate science. In fact, we construct a social theory which is structurally analogous to that in other exact sciences at each stage of the formalization process. In the end, we have a theory that explains social phenomena in a manner consistent with what we have come to expect from exact sciences.

1-3. The Two-Variable Measurement Pattern

The problem in social measurement is to find a coherent set of measures and concepts for the interpretation of social phenomena. We would like to have a well-defined and universal set of measures and concepts that would allow us to analyze and explain everything of interest occurring in a social system. It would be too ambitious a program, however, to try to explain everything about a society; so, we must limit our range of interest to a manageable extent. But we must still explain "everything", in some sense, within this range if we are to have a satisfactory theory. We must have a sufficient degree of closure in the theory so that surprizing or unpredicted events are infrequent exceptions to the general laws or regularities of behavior anticipated by the theory.

The question thus arises, how can we achieve a high degree of closure or completeness in the analysis of social systems? How can we use measurement variables to limit the range of social phenomena we have to explain and yet have satisfactory explanations for phenomena within that range? The methods currently available for social analysis fall far short of the completeness found in well-established sciences. Apart from economics few social events can be explained with a high degree of scientific exactness. In contrast, one can hardly imagine an event in an electrical or mechanical system that could not be fully and accurately explained with the available theory. Recently it has been observed that many of the exact sciences have in common a particular pattern of measurement variables.[2] And apparently a main reason why these sciences have been successful—why they have attained a high degree of closure—is because they all incorporate the measurement pattern. Classical mechanics, electromagnetic theory, and other sciences all make use of a two-variable measurement pattern which is based on the fundamental empirical laws of the science.

A two-variable pattern is a pair of measurement variables satisfying a number of conditions. Along with time-interval measurement, the initial two variables are the most primitive variables for describing system phenomena. We can derive all other measures and quantitative concepts from the initial pair of variables (and time) by forming derivatives, integrals, products, or other combinations of the variables. In this way we are able to generate a coherent set of measures for the analysis and explanation of all measurable phenomena. Of course, what we cannot measure, we necessarily exclude from the range of explanation.

A primary requirement for a two-variable pattern is that one of the initial variables must be on a ratio scale and the other on an interval or ratio scale. We can categorize measurement scales according to how we assign scale numbers to observable phenomena. The most common measurement scales are of four kinds: nominal, ordinal, interval, and ratio. From nominal to ratio the scales become increasingly refined and specific. On both interval and ratio scales the numerical units of measurement along the scale are of equal size; this is not necessarily true of nominal or ordinal scales. On an interval or ratio scale the distance from a value of 1 unit to 2 is just as far as from 2 to 3, or 5 to 6, and so on. (The length of a unit may vary from one scale to another.) The difference between an interval scale and a ratio scale is that a ratio scale always has a fixed or absolute zero point on the scale, whereas an interval scale does not. An interval scale may have a zero point, but we can assign it to any point on the scale; its location does not affect how we would ordinarily make or use interval-scale measurements. In practice, one is usually interested in the magnitudes of *differences* or changes between values on an interval scale, not their absolute magnitudes.

Since a ratio scale has a fixed zero point, it is possible to express any point on a ratio scale as a fraction or multiple of any other. For example, one might say that a given value was twice another, or one third as large as another. Such statements are not meaningful on interval scales. Note, however, that differences between interval-scale values can be compared on a ratio scale; zero difference is a fixed point. Thus we can always construct a ratio scale from an interval scale by taking interval-scale differences.

Measurement scales are important because a scale captures certain prior qualitative laws or properties of the system one is studying, with respect to the quantity or dimension one seeks to measure. For example, even before we have a measurement scale for length, mass, or temperature, we can perform simple operations on the system to identify system states. We can compare, rank order, and add together objects of the same or different length; or perform similar operations with masses on a pan balance. In the case of temperature, one can use the property that objects expand linearly when heated to identify and compare temperature states. A measurement scale can then be constructed if numbers are assigned to the previously identified system states according to a sufficiently rigorous procedure. This kind of measurement is called fundamental measurement, since the scale is constructed directly from observable system properties, not from other measurement variables. Measurement scales also arise when new measures are derived from existing fundamental measures.

The initial pair of measurement variables of a two-variable pattern for an exact science can usually be measured fundamentally, at least in principle if rarely done in practice. Fundamental measurement, however, is not necessary for the use of the two-variable pattern in systems analysis. It is possible that we may have alternative procedures for constructing measurement scales of the same kind or even for the same quantity. In regard to theory construction, one can see that even at the measurement stage of the formalization process important properties of the system and how one studies it are already being built into the theory.[3]

In the two-variable pattern we refer to the ratio-scale variable as a *throughvariable* and to the interval-scale variable as an *acrossvariable.* (Alternatively they may be called "pervariable" and "transvariable.") These terms come from the way these measurements are often made in physical systems. The throughvariable can measure "how much" is in the system, or the quantity flowing through or past a single point of the system. The acrossvariable measures a difference across or between two points of a system, or between the system and some fixed reference point outside it. The measurement of differences implies again the interval-scale requirement. The throughvariable is sometimes referred to as a one-point measure and the acrossvariable as a two-point measure.

Temperature scales (Fahrenheit or Celsius) are familiar examples of interval scales, and temperature is the corresponding acrossvariable for thermodynamic systems. Because temperature is on an interval scale, we cannot say that 20 degrees Fahrenheit is twice as hot as 10 degrees. And since zero degrees is defined by different physical conditions on the Fahrenheit and Celsius scales, the two zero points are not equal. In thermodynamic systems heat can be taken as the initial throughvariable. We can determine how much heat there is in a system on a ratio scale. In electrical systems one measures voltage differences between points in the system, or one measures the amount of current flowing through a point in the system. Voltage (or potential difference) and current are the initial across- and throughvariables, respectively.

In the two-variable measurement pattern we can also classify variables as either "state" or "rate" variables. In general terms, a "state variable" describes the condition or state of a system. A "rate variable" measures the rate of change of a system state over time. The rate of flow of a system quantity is a frequently used rate variable. The state/rate distinction can be generalized to an extensive/intensive categorization of variables. An extensive variable depends on the "size" of the system; an intensive variable does not. If we can obtain the same measurement value through the measurement of only a part of a system as we can through measurement of the whole system, then the variable clearly does not depend on the size of the system; this is an intensive variable. A variable that depends on the number of elements composing a system is extensive. The existence of an extensive variable also implies that one can distinguish a system from its environment. Mathematically speaking, the intensive variable is a derivative of an extensive variable, or the extensive is an integral of the intensive; in other words, given one of the two variables, we can always construct the other from it.

Throughvariables and acrossvariables can be either extensive or intensive (or state or rate variables). Thus it is convenient to represent the four possible combinations in the two-variable pattern as a two by two matrix:

	Extensive	Intensive
Throughvariable		
Acrossvariable		

But not all kinds of systems analysis use the full four variables. Since intensive variables can be generated from extensive variables, or vice versa, only two of the four possible variables are needed to begin system measurement. Examples of the two-variable pattern for thermodynamic, electrical, and translational mechanical physical systems are given in Figure 1-1.[4] Franksen has shown that economic systems analysis is also based on a two-variable pattern, which is shown in Figure 1-1.[5] It is important to observe that a number of different measurement patterns may apply to the same set of physical objects; a physical system may simultaneously have mechanical, electrical, and thermal properties. We show that a number of different measurement patterns can also apply to human behavior, including the economic pattern described here. And in practice one often has to take into account interaction between the various measurement systems for a given set of system elements.

From the matrix pattern we can see how to construct other variables from the initial two or four. Energy is a diagonal product of variables in many patterns, and power is a vertical product of the two intensive variables. These products may then be integrated over the range of one of the variables.[6]

Another highly important property of a two-variable system is that the through- and acrossvariable measurements can be made independently of each other. For instance, one can measure the voltage in an electrical circuit without necessarily knowing how much current is flowing at the time. Or in a thermodynamic system we can make a temperature measurement without knowing how much heat energy is in the system.

The independence of through- and acrossvariables for measurement purposes does not mean that the two variables are completely unrelated to one another. On the contrary, in an actual system the variables may be related algebraically in any of several different ways. And the relationship may change from one part of a system to another. One of the problems in constructing a system model is to incorporate these various relationships. The algebraic relation we are most concerned with in the analysis of social systems is that of direct proportionality between the two intensive variables. This usually appears as a fundamental law in a science. From this law are developed the principal methods for analyzing change in a system. The direct proportionality law states that when an acrossvariable difference exists between two connected regions of a system, there will be a flow of some quantity from one region to the other, and the rate of flow (the intensive throughvariable) will be directly proportional to the difference. In other words, as the difference increases, the flow increases. In thermodynamics this is known as Fourier's law, which gives the rate of heat flow through a conducting material as a linear function of the difference in temperature

		Extensive or state variable	Intensive or rate variable
(a)	Throughvariable (ratio scale)	Heat energy Q	Heat flow dQ/dt
	Acrossvariable (interval scale)	(None)	Temperature

(b)	Throughvariable	Dielectric charge Q	Electric current $I = dQ/dt$
	Acrossvariable	Electromagnetic flux F	Electric voltage $E = dF/dt$

(c)	Throughvariable	Momentum $p = mv$	Force $F = dp/dt$
	Acrossvariable	Distance or displacement x	Velocity $v = dx/dt$

(d)	Throughvariable	Amount of commodity in physical units Q	Flow of physical quantities dQ/dt
	Acrossvariable	?	Price

Figure 1-1. Examples of two-variable measurement patterns: (*a*) thermodynamic; (*b*) electromagnetic; (*c*) translational mechanical; (*d*) economic.

across it. In electrical theory this is Ohm's law for the proportionality of current flow through a conductor to the voltage difference across the ends of the conductor. In each case the rate of flow also depends on the conductivity or resistivity of the conductor, which is usually assumed to be a constant factor and a property of the conducting material. (The "conductivity" is a derived measurement variable in this case, once the two intensive variables are given.) The general algebraic form of the direct proportionality law is thus:

intensive throughvariable = constant × intensive acrossvariable difference

It should be kept in mind, however, that this law (as with many laws of science) is only an approximation of the behavior of an actual physical system; system behavior is usually not as linear as the law suggests. (The constant factor tends to vary over the range of the other variables.)

In the next chapter we introduce a two-variable measurement scheme for social systems that is analogous to the pattern of measurements described above. And subsequently we show how it is possible to analyze a social system with the proposed measures.

1-4. The System Model

As soon as one begins discussing measurement, the concept of system enters in. In a general way, a system is what one measures; it is where the measuring is going on. There is a still closer correspondence, however, between system and measurement. In order to achieve a satisfactory degree of closure or completeness in the explanation of system phenomena, we must have a model that represents measurable phenomena and only those that are measurable.

A system can be defined as a collection of objects or elements (real or abstract) together with the set of relationships among the elements. For an analysis of the system to be possible, these relationships must be measurable or related to measurement variables. This definition of a system is still too abstract, however, to help us analyze any real system. Before we can analyze a system in practice, we need a much more detailed model to represent the system's components and their interrelationships. Because a system model must be specific, it is a constraint on the kind of phenomena we can analyze, in addition to the constraints the measurement variables impose.

The models we use for social analysis are exclusively *macroscopic* system models.[7] A macroscopic system is composed of a very large number of system elements. The analysis of such a system is based on laws or regularities that appear to govern the collective behavior of system elements as a whole. These laws are always statistical and ultimately derive from the simple fact that when the number of system elements if very large, we cannot know what all the elements are doing individually or exactly how they are interrelated. Therefore our knowledge of the system must be based on average tendencies perceived when we observe the elements simultaneously and collectively. The system elements must be considered as indistinguishable or interchangeable from a macroscopic system perspective.

From the difficulties we would have in trying to understand or predict the behavior of any one person, one might certainly conclude that it would be overwhelmingly difficult to explain the behavior of large numbers of people. But in terms of collective behavior this is not so. We find that groups of people show regularities in their aggregate, macroscopic behavior which would not be evident in their individual behavior. Thus we are able to give scientific explanations of collective social behavior without any knowledge about the specific individuals in the society or the complex web of their interrelationships.

The ability to construct macroscopic social laws without reference to individual behavior also implies that social laws cannot explain the behavior of any specific individual. Different laws must be found to explain individual behavior.[8] To distinguish explanation of collective system properties from that of individual system elements, one refers to the first as the macroscopic level of analysis, and to the other as the microscopic or "micro." A knowledge of microscopic system properties may be helpful in understanding macroscopic laws, but it is not necessary to their formulation.

The concept of a macroscopic system has been especially developed in connection with statistical physics and thermodynamics. The micro-level behavior of the elements (atoms, molecules) in a physical system is explained with mechanical system variables, such as velocity and momentum. At the macro level we use the thermodynamic variables, temperature and heat. (See Figure 1-1. The mechanical variables can, of course, also apply to macroscopic physical objects.) The thermodynamic variables derive from statistical properties of physical systems and have no meaning for individual atoms or molecules. Thus macroscopic laws involving thermodynamic variables cannot be reduced to micro-level explanations in terms of mechanical variables alone.[9]

The measurement variables we use to describe macroscopic systems are based on the irreducible statistical properties of the system. Since macroscopic variables are derived as statistical functions, we cannot expect them to be uniformly constant over time in all parts of a system. The description of a macroscopic system is based on average values of the measurement variables.

It may be possible to partition a large macroscopic system into a collection of subsystems where the subsystems are themselves macroscopic systems. In this case it may also happen that the subsystems differ from one another to an extent that the measurement variables have different values in various subsystems. If a system is viewed as a collection of subsystems, we can call it a composite system. If the measurement values of intensive variables are nearly the same in all subsystems, we say that the system is homogeneous; if not, it is heterogeneous. (Extensive variables can be viewed intensively as quantity per unit system, which is to say, as density functions, in determining system homogeneity.) For analytic convenience the subsytems are often considered to be of equal size.

Statistical Equilibrium and System Change. The central concept for discussing the validity and accuracy of macroscopic measurements is *statistical equilibrium*. We can define a statistical equilibrium as the condition of a macroscopic system when we observe no change over time.[10] This is often meant to apply to intensive variables only, an interpretation we will follow here. In macroscopic systems the concept of equilibrium implies that if a heterogeneous system is closed (isolated from its environment), the system becomes increasingly homogeneous over time. Measurement values taken across the subsystems will tend toward their average or equilibrium values. When the values in any subsystem are close to their average values for the system, the system is said to be in a state of statistical equilibrium. The tendency of a heterogeneous system to become increasingly homogeneous is an empirical property that must be verified to hold in an actual system. Thus change will be observed macroscopically in a heterogeneous system until a high degree of homogeneity is attained. A system will remain in an equilibrium state except for small random fluctuations about the mean values of the macroscopic variables, unless it is disturbed by external influences. The values of the macroscopic variables at an equilibrium describe the *state* of the system.

The time during which a system changes from a heterogenous to homogeneous condition, or from disequilibrium to equilibrium, is called the relaxation time or period. As a rule, the length of the relaxation period depends upon the size of the system, other things equal. Thus we will find that a subsystem, being smaller than the system itself, has a faster relaxation time than the system as a whole.[11] As a result, a subsystem may attain a local equilibrium while the system as a whole is still in disequilibrium. When the subsystems of a system are in equilibria, but not the system as a whole, we say that there is a *partial* or incomplete equilibrium (of the system). A system in partial equilibrium must be described in terms of its subsystems and their equilibrium measurement values, or their aggregate properties.

The term partial equilibrium also describes systems when several processes of change can occur simultaneously and semi-independently of one another, possibly at different rates. If one process ceases or attains an equilibrium in advance of another, this situation is also called a partial equilibrium. In other words, homogeneity may hold for one macroscopic property but temporarily not for others. We encounter both forms of partial equilibria in the analysis of social systems.

We can gain some understanding of the importance of equilibrium in system measurement if we recall the distinction between micro and macro levels of analysis. In a macroscopic system our inability to perceive in detail the behavior of system elements at the micro level results in the fact that macroscopic variables are to some extent independent of change at the micro level. A macroscopic variable may be constant over time for a system, yet there will almost certainly be continuous activity at the micro level. For example, a physical object may have a constant temperature, but the molecules composing the object will be in constant motion. It is a characteristic of macroscopic systems that many arrangements of the system elements give rise to the same macroscopic state. But if the system is in a macroscopic equilibrium, there is a high degree of regularity and uniformity in the microscopic processes; they are stationary in time across the system. So even if we do not have a complete knowledge of the underlying micro processes, the macroscopic variables describe a relatively well-defined system condition.

If a system is not in equilibrium but is changing macroscopically, we know much less about the micro processes. We have no definite idea of how the micro processes are changing in relation to the macroscopic changes. And in general we must assume that there would be very many ways that change could take place at the micro level yet result in the same amount of macroscopic change. Consequently, our knowledge of what is going on in a system during a relaxation period is poor. To have a valid macroscopic measurement, we require that a system be in an equilibrium or partial equilibrium.

Equilibrium, measurement validity, and the existence of intensive variables are all closely interrelated. System equilibrium means that an intensive measurement of the system or any macroscopic subsystem will give the same value and be a valid description of the state of the system. But imagine a system in an extreme disequilibrium condition so that no matter how finely the system were partitioned, no subsystems were in equilibrium. As the partitions become increasingly fine, the number of elements in any subsystem would become too few to show macroscopic properties. In this extreme case it would not be possible to make a valid intensive measurement of any subsystem (and its subsystems), and the intensive variable would not exist for that system.

Because we only measure a system at equilibria, we must also discuss change in a macroscopic system in terms of its equilibrium states. If a system is changing macroscopically, we cannot follow the change continuously in time; we must allow relaxation to occur before we make a new measurement of the state of the system. This contrasts with the methods for studying change in classical mechanics. For example, one can follow the position of a moving object continuously in time.

If the state of a macroscopic system, affected by its environment, is changing slowly compared with its relaxation time, we can measure the system at successive equilibria. This means of studying change is known as comparative statics. It is a method of thermodynamics, macroeconomics, and other macroscopic sciences. But again, because of the complexity of change at the micro level, we do not have a good knowledge about the path or way in which the system changes between equilibria. We do not know how the behavior of individual system elements changed. Note also that change in a macroscopic system is nonhistorical: knowing what the current statistical equilibrium state of a system is gives no knowledge of its past history of states, nor does it allow, by itself, the prediction of future system states. To predict a change of state accurately we would have to know the quantitative effect of the environment on the system.

When the state of a system has been changed, one says that work has been done on the system. Work is the quantitative measure of the act of changing the state of a system. Energy is defined as the capacity for doing work, and power is the rate of doing work.

System models: A Typology. Models of macroscopic systems may be classified into several categories. Since there is no standard terminology for discussing system models, we will follow one adapted to our immediate purposes. We shall divide system models into two broad categories: unitary and component. Each of these categories can again be divided. (See Figure 1-2.) The unitary model, which is essentially the type we have been discussing, is appropriate when the system is taken as a whole, as a single unit, for measurement purposes. For a homogeneous equilibrium system one needs only single measurements of the variables to describe the system. If the system is in partial equilibrium, more measurements may be needed, but we are still interested in the system as a unit and what the final equilibrium state will be. For a heterogeneous system we often use single variables to measure the extent of disequilibrium in the system as a whole or to measure other aggregate system quantities without regard to the specific distribution of values among subsystems. Since the final equilibrium state of a closed heterogeneous system is independent of the distribution of values in the subsystems, we may deal with average or total quantities for the system from the beginning.

Unitary system models can therefore be classified as either homogeneous

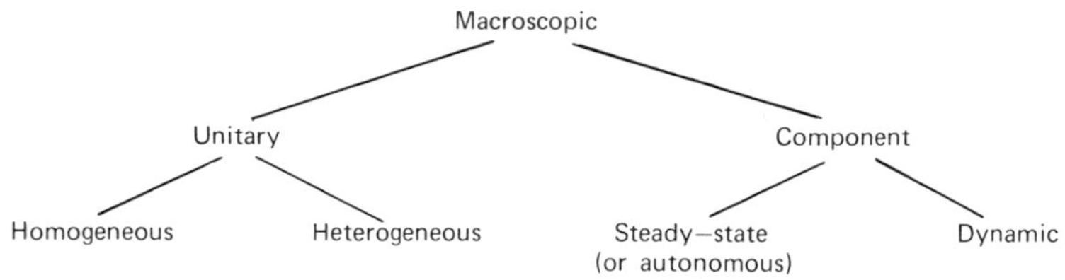

Types of Change

Homogeneous:	Heterogeneous:	Steady-state:	Dynamic:
Random fluctuations about equilibrium values	Relaxation processes; trend toward increasing homogeneity	Time-independent (or time-invariant)	Time-dependent (or time-varying)

Theoretical Questions

Determination or measurement of equilibrium values	Rate of relaxation; amount of disequilibrium; predicted equilibrium state	Transient behavior; stability of systems; controllability of systems; system design (for steady-state or dynamic)

Figure 1-2. A typology of system models.

or heterogeneous. In a homogeneous model the main analytic concern is to determine the state of the system. In a heterogeneous model one seeks to determine the partial equilibrium values or the degree of disequilibrium in order to predict the final equilibrium state and the rate of relaxation. In either case, open systems are studied by approximating them with closed system models.

Systems more complex than unitary systems must generally be modeled as component systems. The need for a more sophisticated model arises when measurement differences or heterogeneous conditions in a system are created and maintained by some external force or constraint that overrides the natural tendencies of the isolated system to reestablish an equilibrium. In such a system one finds that algebraic relationships between through- and acrossvariables, as well as their respective values, may vary from one part of the system to another. The different parts of the system must be represented with different abstract forms, that is, with model components. If this description of a component system seems remote, think of an electrical circuit with its complex arrangement of interconnected components: resistors, capacitors, and so on. Voltage differences and current flow are maintained in the circuit by an external power source connected to the system. If the power source is turned off or the circuit is broken, the system will relax to an equilibrium state.

The law of direct proportionality between the two intensive variables

(Section 1-3) derives from the tendency of heterogeneous systems to become homogeneous. It is the throughvariable flow of some real or abstract quantity, resulting from the difference in levels of the intensive acrossvariable, that produces the required system homogeneity. This quantity diffuses through the system until homogeneity is attained. The amount of flow (per unit time) between two regions of a system is proportional to the intensive acrossvariable difference between the regions at any instant. The direction of flow is usually specified by a separate law of the theory. In most theories flow is considered to be always from the higher-level region to the lower-level region, for levels of the intensive acrossvariable. In a heterogeneous unitary system the rate of flow decreases (exponentially) in time as the system becomes homogeneous. But if the acrossvariable difference between regions is maintained, as in a component system, then the flow between regions will continue unabated. If the difference is constant in time, the flow will also be constant; the system is said to be in a steady state or steady-state equilibrium. Thus we can classify component systems as steady-state or dynamic, depending on whether flow rates are constant or changing in time. (See Figure 1-2.)

A complex arrangement of flows and acrossvariable differences between discrete points or components of a system is called a network. Engineers are usually interested in designing networks that have desirable arrangements or properties. Various mathematical methods are used for the analysis of networks.[12] They call for the solution of sets of equations whose parameters are the values of intensive variables at selected points in the system. If the values of intensive variables change continuously across a system and over time, we may be able to use partial differential equations to find the spatiotemporal distribution of measurement values. Since the two intensive variables are directly related to each other, we can usually analyze a system with only one of the two variables if a sufficient number of its values across the system are known.

In observing the operation of a complex system, we may find that some part of the system is able to cause changes of state in other parts. Or it may happen that a part whose state has been changed is later able to return to its original state by causing a flow to some other part of the system. Flows and changes of state may even take on a oscillatory pattern. The study of state changes is the essence of dynamic systems analysis. Recalling that energy is defined as the quantitative measure of the ability to change a system state, we can interpret dynamic processes abstractly as energy processes. One thinks of system change as energy conversion or source, energy transfer, energy storage, or energy dissipation (out of the system). The formal components used to model a complex dynamic system are defined according to their energy function: one component stores energy, another dissipates it, and so on. Since a change of state may occur for either the throughvariable or the acrossvariable, each kind of change is modeled with a separate component.[13] But the formal components of the model are not necessarily identifiable one-to-one with physical components in the real system. Knowing the behavior of individual components, we may then predict how a system will behave for a given configuration of components.

We can also use an input-output system model to describe how quantities are transformed by the system as they pass through it. But in the simple unitary models of social systems that we use in this study, questions of input-output transformation are of less interest than the nature of what happens inside the system itself. In any case, we must still discover what the right measurement variables are for studying social systems.

Energy is an abstract concept used in conjunction with all physical systems, regardless of the kind of measurement variables.[14] In each science, system models can be constructed with analogous sets of components, defined by their energy function. Energy is also the unifying factor in the physical sciences, since it permits a quantitative accounting of interaction between systems of different kinds, as from a mechanical system to a thermodynamic system. The mathematical method of Lagrange's equations is the common technique for analyzing systems behavior in terms of energy. The Lagrange method provides an alternative to the methods of network analysis, which use intensive throughvariable flows and acrossvariable differences.

A great deal more can be said about the formalization and analysis of complex dynamic systems, but such an extension is beyond the scope of this book.[15] The important point is that the analysis of complex systems stems from properties of simple composite or unitary systems and relies on the same measurement variables. Our objective here is to find the essential properties of macroscopic social systems and the appropriate measurement variables. We are able to do this by focusing on unitary models of social systems. Once we have verified that unitary social systems show the necessary properties, it is a fairly simple matter to extend the formalization to more complex social systems, if necessary. In a few instances, we also show how the analytic models apply to more complex social system models.

In order to model a society as a macroscopic unitary social system, we consider the collective behavior of large numbers of people whom we view as indistinguishable and whom we do not further subdivide and treat as separate groups or classes. We describe the behavior of people in the system with an appropriate set of measurement variables. This model is a considerable abstraction of the complexities of any real social system, but it is possible to model many real systems with this high degree of simplification and still obtain accurate quantitative explanations of social phenomena. We show that unitary social systems have the same kinds of laws and dynamic properties as unitary physical systems.

CHAPTER TWO

Measurement Variables

2-1. *Intuitive Measures for Social Behavior*

Measurement variables in many sciences have originated from simple intuitive ideas or from readily observable phenomena. What we seek are basic measurement variables for social behavior. At least to begin, and in line with our strategy of formalization, we can make use of those readily observable aspects of social behavior that lend themselves naturally to measurement.

Let a social system be a group of people who are interrelated through their mutually perceived behavior and actions. This definition of a social system is general enough so that any measures devised for it would also apply to any real social system. Several measures of collective system behavior appear to be a least hypothetically possible in any such system. In the first place, we could simply count the number of actions or events that that we can observe in the system over an arbitrary period of time. This would be a measure of the total amount of activity going on within the system. It seems reasonable that the amount of activity would vary directly with the size of the population of the system. Some difficulty might arise in deciding exactly what constitutes an action or event, but once events have been identified, there is no problem in counting them. Let us denote this measure of system activity by N.

If we watched the system over a period of time, we would undoubtedly find that some kinds of events occur more frequently or more predictably than others. At any particular time we would have a certain degree of difficulty in predicting what would happen next, depending upon the event probabilities. It seems feasible that a measure could be devised to quantify the predictability of events taken as a set. This would be a second possible measure for the system.

Consider next two systems interacting with each other. In this case a third measure suggests itself. In principle at least, we could count how often events or actions of one system were directed at or observed by members of the other system, or vice versa. This would be a measure of the rate of interaction or rate of communication between the two systems. The general form of this measure would be average quantity of events per unit or interval of time, which is equivalent to dN/dt, the time derivative of the measure N. It also seems likely that some kinds of events would be more predictable in one of the two systems than the other. So if we were trying to predict the effect of interaction between the systems, we might have to take into account differences in the predictability of events in the two systems. This suggests that the predictability measure could be a two-point measurement, the acrossvariable of the two-variable measurement pattern. The measure of interaction between systems dN/dt could be conceived of as a throughvariable flow between the systems; a flow of events or actions; or a flow of communication.

Although these intuitive measures are poorly defined, they indicate that social systems can be analyzed with a two-variable measurement pattern. It is difficult to imagine what additional variables we might use that would neither be related to the ones already suggested, nor require more knowledge about the social system, such as the nature of the events taking place or the identities of system members. Yet if we had to be more specific about the social system we are measuring, the measures would be less generally applicable. Therefore we will conclude, as a hypothesis to be tested, that if social systems analysis can be based on a two-variable pattern, the proposed measures are approximately the right ones.

There remains then the problem of refining our primitive ideas about social measurement. We must define exactly what a measurement consists of and what its quantitative properties are. But these questions cannot be fully resolved without a greater knowledge of the macroscopic properties of social systems. So we must postpone a complete specification of measurement variables until we have a better understanding of the connections between measurement, theory construction, and the behavior of real social systems. For now, we will concentrate on removing the obscurity about the measure of predictability of events.

The counting measure N and its derivative dN/dt are clearly quantitative, but it is not apparent how predictability of events should be quantified. A similar measurement problem arises in communication or information theory. A designer of an electronic communication system must determine the predictability of the possible symbols or messages that may be transmitted, and the rate at which messages are to be sent. In social measurement we are concerned with the predictability of social events and their rate of occurrence. The analogy to communication systems becomes evident if we think of social behavior or actions as messages from one person or system to another. Social communication is more diverse and complex than the messages one analyzes in traditional communication theory. Yet because of the underlying similarity between measurement in a social system and in a communication system, we can generalize measures of communication to social behavior. Moreover, we can develop the measurement of social phenomena from the same formal axiomatic basis established for information theory. As it turns out, a very important contribution of information theory to social science is the concept of *entropy*, a measure of the unpredictability of events. This single measure is the key to the formal scientific explanation of social phenomena.

2-2. *Measurement Axioms; Entropy*

In information theory the measure of information in communication is a measure of the unpredictability of message events. This is a measure we have also proposed for social systems. Although several alternative procedures are available for developing the measure from an axiomatic base, we follow here the method used by Khinchin, but with less emphasis on mathematical detail and rigor.[1]

Consider a finite set of events such that at a given time we know that one and only one of the events will occur, although at other times different events of the set might occur. By observing the relative frequencies of occurrence of each event of the set over a period of time, we could estimate the probabilities of occurrence of each event. (These conditions imply that the probabilities must sum to 1 for the set of events.) The term *event set* will denote a finite set of events together with its associated event probabilities. Every event set describes a state of unpredictability or uncertainty, uncertainty about what will happen at a given time. The question is how to quantify the degree of uncertainty.

There are three properties we would like a measure of unpredictability or uncertainty to have. These are properties that may be used to assess the uncertainty of a situation qualitatively with sufficient discrimination to enable a fundamental quantitative measure of uncertainty. First, for an event set the measure of uncertainty should be greatest when all events of the set are equally likely. When no event is more probable or predictable than any other, this is intuitively the most uncertain situation. Second, suppose that one event set is conditional upon another so that if an event of one set occurs, we have learned something that makes it easier to predict which event in the other set is likely to take place later on. For this case we would want the measure of uncertainty of the later set to be quantitatively reduced by the amount of information gained by knowing what happened in the first set. But to find the total uncertainty of both event sets together we would then have to add on any new uncertainty introduced by the first set. If the two event sets are completely independent of each other, the total uncertainty of both sets together (an event of each set happening) should equal the sum of the uncertainty of the separate sets. This second property tells us how to add uncertainty for two or more different situations. Finally, as a third property of the measure we would require that the uncertainty associated with an event set not be increased if impossible events (events of zero probability) are added to the original event set.

Mathematical notation makes the above three properties or axioms more explicit. Let $S(n)$ be a set of n events such that the probability of the ith event is p_i and $\sum p_i = 1$ for $i = 1, 2, 3, \ldots, n$. Let $H(S)$ be a measure of uncertainty for the set $S(n)$. Then we require that:

1. $H(S)$ has its greatest value when $p_i = 1/n$ for all i.
2. For another set $T(m)$ of m events with probabilities q_j for $j = 1, 2, 3, \ldots, m$ and $\sum q_j = 1$, let $H(TS)$ be the total uncertainty of both sets T and S that results from the possibility of an event of each set occurring. And let $H(S|T)$ be the conditional uncertainty of S given that an event of T will be known before any in S. Then

$$H(TS) = H(S|T) + H(T)$$

If S and T are independent of each other

$$H(TS) = H(T) + H(S)$$

This condition also implies that the uncertainty about S is never increased by knowledge about T.

3. Let $S(n + 1)$ be the set $S(n)$ together with an additional event of zero probability. Then

$$H[S(n + 1)] = H[S(n)] = H(S)$$

Khinchin proves the following important theorem. Let $H(S)$ be a function defined for any integer n and all values $p_1, p_2, \ldots, p_n$ such that p_i is greater than or equal to zero and $\sum p_i = 1$ for $i = 1, 2, \ldots, n$. If for any n this function $H(S)$ is continuous with regard to all the P_i, and if it satisfies the above three axioms, then we always have

$$H(S) = -c \sum p_i \log p_i, \; i = 1, 2, \ldots, n$$

where c is a positive constant.[2]

In other words, the measure of uncertainty must always have this form: a sum of n terms with each term being the product of an event's probability and the logarithm of that probability, the whole sum to be multiplied by an undetermined constant. (Since probabilities are always less than or equal to

1, the logarithm of a probability is always less than or equal to zero; the negative sign before the summation thus implies that $H(S)$ is always greater than or equal to zero.) The quantity $H(S)$ is termed the *entropy* of the event set S.

It is customary to set the constant $c = 1$ and compute the logarithm to base 2. This is equivalent to fixing the size of the units of entropy. In this case the units are called "bits". All reference to entropy in this book will be to base 2. Entropy as derived above is on a ratio scale. The units are of equal size and entropy has the value zero if the only if one of the events in the set has probability 1 while all other events of the set have zero probability. Note also that entropy is a measure based on simultaneous measurement of other variables, the event probabilities, which are themselves comparable on a ratio scale.

The measure of uncertainty can also be derived by a slightly different procedure.[3] Fano begins the derivation by defining the amount of information provided by the occurrence of one event about the occurrence of a second event. That is, he considers pairs of events instead of pairs of sets of events. Subsequently, he defines the self information I of an event expected with probability p as

$$I = -c \log p$$

where c is an arbitrary positive constant, as above. If I is considered a random variable, that is, as a value associated with a random event of probability p, one can calculate the average information for a set of events. If the ith event of the set S is expected with probability p_i, $\sum p_i = 1$, and $c = 1$, the average information is

$$E(I) = -c \sum p_i \log p_i, \quad i = 1, 2, \ldots, n$$

Thus

$$E(I) \equiv H(S)$$

The terms entropy and average information are synonyms.

If we can compute an average information, we can also compute a variance of information in the usual way

$$Var(I) = \sum p_i (\log p_i)^2 - E^2(I), \quad i = 1, 2, \ldots, n$$

Higher moments about the average could also be computed.

The alternative derivations of entropy are all perfectly acceptable, but sometimes it is convenient to think of one or the other as an aid in interpreting the significance of the measurement variable.[4] Fano's derivation has the advantage of leading naturally to the information variance, a concept that is of some interest in the analysis of social systems.

In the analysis of social systems in this book we calculate entropy for finite event sets only. But there may be instances when uncertainty should be computed for infinite sets. This would be the case if the events were not discrete but could assume any value over a continuous range. We can define the entropy of a continuous distribution having a density function $p(x)$ in one dimension as[5]

$$H(x) = -\int_{-\infty}^{\infty} p(x) \log p(x)\, dx$$

The integral is defined only up to an additive constant that depends on the choice of coordinate unit for the probability distribution. If we change to coordinate y, the new entropy

$$H(y) = H(x) - \int_{-\infty}^{\infty} p(x) \log J(x, y)\, dx$$

where $J(x,y)$ is the Jacobian of the coordinate transformation x to y. Thus entropy is on an interval scale for continuous probability distributions, in contrast to the ratio scale for discrete event sets. For the continuous distribution the zero point is set by an arbitrary choice of coordinates. Discussing this situation in information theory, Shannon writes that the concepts of information rate and channel capacity depend on the difference between entropy values, and this difference does not depend on the choice of coordinates, since a change of coordinates would only cause each term to be changed by the same amount.[6] In other words, ratio scales are constructed for information rate and channel capacity by taking differences on the interval-scale entropy measure. The main theorems of information theory for the continuous case are then stated for ratio-scale variables.

In the following chapters we apply the entropy measure to those social situations for which we can estimate the probabilities of alternative events. This use of the entropy measure is based upon prior ideas about how we, as disinterested observers, would perceive the level of uncertainty for an event set. Our intuitive, nonquantitative ideas about uncertainty are formalized in the three axioms or properties from which the entropy measure was derived. To illustrate the possibility of a nonquantitative judgment of a social uncertainty level, as would be necessary to a fundamental measurement, consider an experiment where we would try to predict what would happen in a social system for a given set of events. Our degree of success in prediction over a course of successive events would allow us a qualitative judgment of the uncertainty level, or of changes in its degree.[7] Thus we can treat the entropy measure as a fundamental and objective measure of a social system.

We can use the objective measure to investigate social phenomena without any regard to how people in the society might perceive the same events. But social phenomena are the results of the way people act, and this in turn depends to some extent on their own perceptions about the state of their society. Just as we, as observers, of a social system, can judge uncertainty levels, so might the members of a society be able to make similar, nonquantitative judgments about the degree of uncertainty in their society for specific event sets. If people act on the basis of this kind of knowledge about their society, we might well expect to find evidence of entropy-measurable phenomena in their collective activity.

Common sense would lead us to believe that even if people had a sense of the degree of uncertainty, as they might obtain from their personal success or failure in anticipating social events, it would be a crude sense at best. We could not expect a high degree of accuracy, consistency, or agreement among people in judging, comparing, or ordering uncertainty states. Does this prevent us from maintaining that uncertainty can be a properly defined and measured quantity, yielding an entropy measure applicable to "subjective" perception of a society by its members? The answer we propose is negative: errors in perception or judgment do not make measurement invalid.[8] For example, an imperfect sense of temperature, or of probability, has not hindered the application of measures for these quantities nor reduced their meaningfulness. But we would still have to consider procedures that would lead to unambiguous identification of subjective states of uncertainty. One could, for instance, aggregate individual subjective judgments through an averaging procedure for a number of individuals, possibly over time, or by means of a group decision rule; and this procedure might then largely reduce the bias inherent in individual judgments. This procedure would roughly compare with using a group of people to identify temperature levels, instead of the expansion properties of a physical object, and to construct thereby a measurement scale. We would expect a group of people to consistently give a better judgment of temperature or uncertainty, on the average, than any single individual could, assuming overestimates and underestimates would tend to cancel one another out.

Thus we have two "entropies" to consider in social measurement: an objective and a subjective. In the course of this book our main emphasis is on the objective measure in the analysis of social behavior. We can discover macroscopic laws and develop a scientific theory without any further consideration of how the perceptions, decisions, and actions of people in a society give rise to the observable, objectively measurable, macroscopic patterns. Nevertheless, the empirical findings present strong evidence that the objective entropy, in the particular social situations applied, is a measurement of the same underlying quantity, social uncertainty, that would be measured by a subjective entropy.

2-3. *Properties of Entropy and the Information Variance*

The entropy measure (for finite sets) has a number of properties which are frequently used. We can summarize them here:

1. Entropy is greatest for a set of n events when the probability of each event equals $1/n$.
2. For a set of n events the maximum entropy value equals log n bits; the maximum value thus increases with n. The maximum increases by 1 bit with each doubling of n (each power of 2).
3. The entropy is always greater than or equal to zero. Entropy is zero if and only if one event has probability 1 and all other events of the set have zero probability.
4. Any change in the probabilities that makes them closer to being equal increases the entropy of the set. Thus any averaging of the probabilities increases the entropy.

As an example of entropy computation we will calculate the entropy for an event set S consisting of two events, one event expected with probability .30 and the other with probability .70.

$$
\begin{aligned}
H(S) &= -\sum p_i \log p_i, \qquad i = 1, 2 \\
&= -(.30 \log .30 + .70 \log .70) \\
&= -[.30(-1.74) + .70(-.51)] \\
&= .52 + .36 = 0.88 \text{ bits}
\end{aligned}
$$

The maximum possible entropy for a two-event set is log 2 = 1 bit, which occurs when the probability of each event is ½.

We can easily show the possible entropy values for two-event event sets graphically. We can plot the entropy value $H(T)$ as a function of the probability that one event occurs with probability p (and the other with probability $1 - p$.) See Figure 2-1. The function

$$H(T) = -p \log p - (1 - p) \log (1 - p)$$

The vertical axis of the graph is in units of bits. The horizontal axis is the probability p of the event, multiplied by a factor of 100. The curve attains its maximum at $p = .50$. Note especially that the graph is symmetrical about the vertical line $p = ½$, and that the curve flattens in the vicinity of this line.

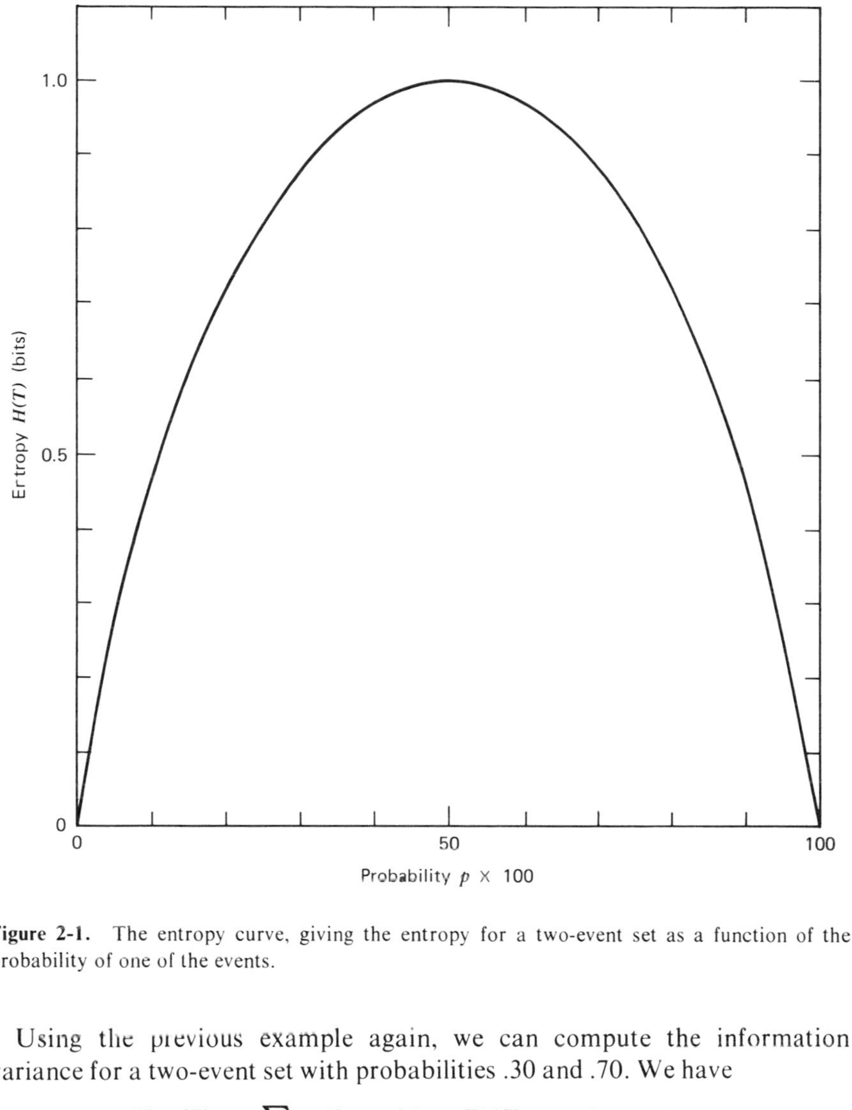

Figure 2-1. The entropy curve, giving the entropy for a two-event set as a function of the probability of one of the events.

Using the previous example again, we can compute the information variance for a two-event set with probabilities .30 and .70. We have

$$\begin{aligned} Var(I) &= \sum p_i(\log p_i)^2 - E^2(I), \qquad i = 1, 2 \\ &= .30(\log .30)^2 + .70(\log .70)^2 - (0.88)^2 \\ &= .30(3.03) + .70(.26) - 0.77 \\ &= 0.32 \text{ bits}^2 \end{aligned}$$

We can also plot the information variance for a two-event set as a function of the probability that one event occurs with probability p. See Figure 2-2. In this graph the vertical axis is in units of bits squared. The curve is symmetrical about the $p = \frac{1}{2}$ line and has two equal maxima at about $p = .08$ and $p = .92$, where the variance is about 0.91 bits^2. The information variance equals zero at the $p = .50$ point as well as the two end points. The general shape of the curve might be described as "M"-shaped, in contrast to the near parabolic shape of the entropy curve (Figure 2-1).

Since the range of the entropy values for a set varies with the number of events in the set, it is sometimes convenient to have a measure that does not vary with the number of events. We can define the redundancy R for a set S of size n as

$$R(S) = 1 - \frac{H(S)}{\log n}$$

Redundancy is 1 minus the ratio of the entropy of the set to the maximum possible entropy of the set. Redundancy is often given as a percentage of the maximum value. The redundancies of event sets can be compared independently of the number of events in the sets. Redundancy is a measure of relative predictability of events, not absolute predictability. In the previous example of a two-event set with probabilities .30 and .70 we have

$$R(S) = 1 - \frac{.88}{\log 2}$$

$$= 1 - .88 = 0.12 \text{ or } 12\%$$

This is a low redundancy, implying that the predictability of events in that set is low.

2-4. *Social Entropy*

Now that we have specified the measure of uncertainty of events, we can begin to see how the variables fit into the two-variable measurement pattern. The measures N and dN/dt for quantity and flow of events are most like throughvariables when interaction between systems is considered. The variable N is proportional to the population size of the system and is therefore an extensive variable. The variables N and dN/dt are on a ratio scale, which conforms with the scale requirement for throughvariables. With N and dN/dt classified as throughvariables, entropy must necessarily be an acrossvariable. To demonstrate this conclusively, however, we need experimental evidence for the proposition that differences in entropy levels between social systems must be used in determining the rate of interaction or flow between the systems.[9] The fact that entropy differences are used in in-

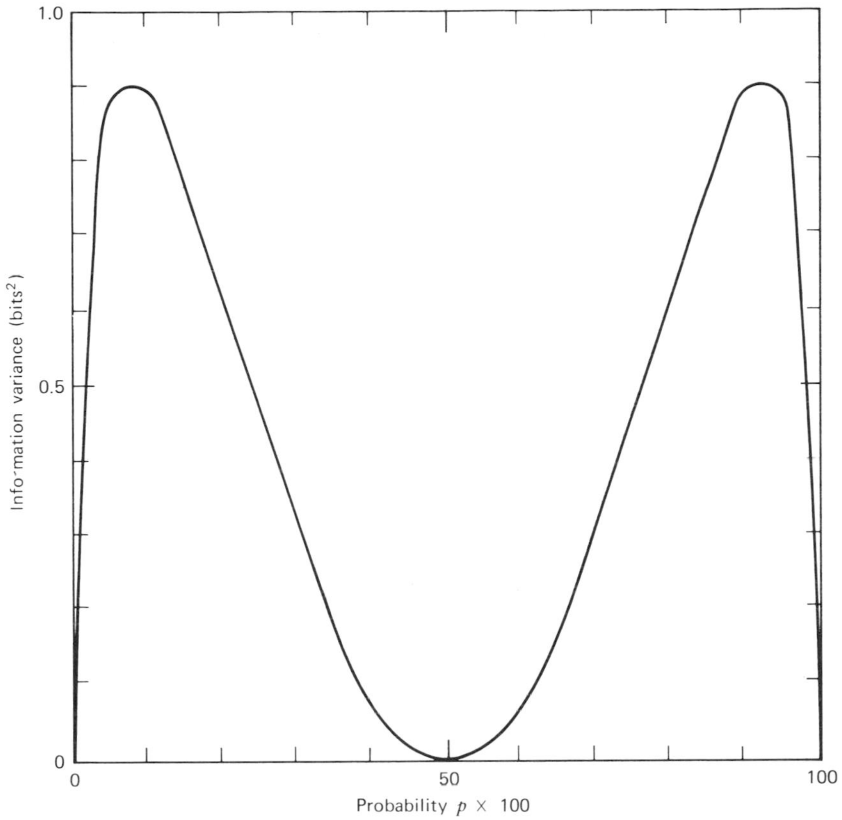

Figure 2-2. The information variance curve, giving the information variance for a two-event set as a function of the probability of one of the events.

formation theory suggests that this may be the case. If we were dealing with continuous probability distributions in social measurement, the entropy variable would be restricted to interval-scale measurement. For finite event sets, however, entropy is on a ratio scale, and we have the additional possibility that absolute entropy levels, as well as entropy differences, may be significant.

From the derivation of entropy it is clear that entropy is independent of the population size of the system. The entropy for a set of events does not have any necessary relation to the number of people who may be causing the events to happen or to how often the events actually occur. In fact, it is not necessary that any event occur for entropy to be calculated if the probabilities are known. Entropy is therefore an intensive variable. So far, there has been no apparent need for an extensive acrossvariable, but the possibility cannot be excluded *a priori*. The extensive acrossvariable is also missing in the thermodynamic and economic system measurement patterns (Figure 1-1); so the extensive acrossvariable is not absolutely necessary to theory construction. The existence of both extensive variables in physical systems is associated with oscillatory system phenomena based on energy transfer. Thus cyclic or oscillatory patterns in social systems might also suggest the need for an extensive acrossvariable.

The tentative pattern of social measurement variables is shown in Figure 2-3. A comparison of this pattern with other patterns indicates that entropy is analogous to temperature, price, or voltage in other systems.[10] The analogy with temperature is particularly interesting for measurement scales. Temperature can be measured on interval scales, as Fahrenheit or Celsius, or on the absolute Kelvin scale, which has an absolute zero. In analyzing heat flow across or between systems we ordinarily use the interval scale, taking differences in temperatures. But many physical phenomena are directly related to specific absolute temperatures; freezing or boiling points of materials are familiar examples. In general terms, one usually finds that the essential nature of the system may change in relation to absolute levels, but within narrow ranges on the absolute scale one can use interval-scale differences to explain system dynamics and the interaction between systems. In the analysis of social systems we also find that certain system properties depend on absolute entropy values, while interval-scale values are sufficient for the conventional analysis of system change.

A very interesting and significant problem (which we will just mention) is whether the energy concept of physical systems can be extended by analogy to social systems. Interaction is certainly possible between the various

	Extensive/state	Intensive/rate
Throughvariable	Event quantity N	Event flow dN/dt
Acrossvariable		Entropy or average information H

Figure 2-3. The tentative social measurement pattern.

kinds of physical systems, as from mechanical to thermodynamic. And energy allows a quantitative accounting of such interaction. Energy is "conserved" as it passes from one type of system to another. Where people are the system elements, instead of atoms or molecules, we have both economic measurement variables and the social measurement variables introduced here. The question is whether an energy concept can be devised for the quantitative measurement of the direct interaction between economic systems and social systems, as defined here. We will see that economic change is often associated with social entropy change, but whether the analogy can be completed will not be resolved in this study.

In a formal systems analysis we are primarily interested in values of the measurement variables and algebraic relationships between them and less concerned with the details of measurement procedure. There is a degree of separation between the analysis of systems and the actual measurement operations. In the case of entropy we have a formal definition of a measurement in terms of event sets, but this definition is well removed from its interpretation in a social system. However, what constitutes making an entropy measurement of a social system is itself highly important. (Entropy measurement is explored in detail in Chapters 3 and 4.) An interpretation of social entropy measurement must take into account two salient features of the measurement process: the origins of the event sets in a social system; and the independence of the entropy measurement from the meanings or content of the events. Before showing how these two aspects of entropy measurement apply in specific measurements, we first discuss them from a more general perspective.

As an aid to the understanding of social entropy we can briefly consider social contexts that lend themselves to entropy measurement. Suppose that a set of choices is given to a group of people: each person has to make a choice of one of the alternatives but can choose no more than one. The act of choosing could be considered as an event. For a group of people we could estimate the probability that each choice would be taken. Using past information on relative frequency of occurrence, we could estimate the percentage of people likely to take each choice. The ratio of people taking each choice to the total population size would give the corresponding probabilities of each event. And knowing the probability associated with each event we could calculate the entropy of the choice situation. (If the population is large the ratios could take on virtually a continuous range of values between zero and one, and the possible range of entropy values would thus be approximately continuous over this range.) The entropy is a measure of how much uncertainty we have about a random individual's expected choice, or equivalently, of how the group will apportion its choices among the alternatives. For a set of choices, entropy can also be interpreted as a measure of the freedom of choice available to those making the decision.[11] If virtually everyone made the same choice, we might infer in one context that people were not completely free to choose more equally among the alternatives.

In other social contexts entropy might be thought of as a measure of heterogeneity, nonconformity, or lack of consensus in a group of people. The greater the heterogeneity or nonconformity in the group with respect to a set of possible actions, the greater will be the uncertainty about any one person's behavior, and thus the greater the entropy.

One of the most striking features of the entropy measurement is that it is "content free." In a communication system the entropy or average information of a message is independent of whatever the meaning or content of the message is for the people who send or receive it. The information of a message or symbol depends only on its probability of occurrence. Of course, this contrasts with the more prevalent usage of the term "information." It is perhaps less confusing to think of entropy as the amount of information that would have to be known to remove all the uncertainty about what will happen in a given situation.[12] In a social system entropy for a set of events, actions, or choices must also be independent of whatever the content of these events is. It does not matter, for the purpose of entropy measurement, what people are doing or choosing; only the nature of the situation, its *structure,* is taken into account. (The events must be identifiable and distinguishable from one another, of course.) The content-free aspect of social events might be thought of in the same way that one distinguishes linguistic structure, such as grammar, from the meaning of individual sentences. Structure implies pattern and organization, or, in other words, predictability in a society. Entropy is thus an inverse measure of the degree of structuralization. The idea of social structure is well exemplified by the sociological concept of "role." A role is a socially prescribed pattern of behavior. Applied to a role, an entropy measurement could describe the ambiguity in the role or the degree of nonconformity a person in that role showed toward the expected behavior pattern.

It may seem astonishing that we would set out to analyze social phenomena and entire social systems without specific regard for the semantics of the phenomena, the meanings of the actions for the people who are doing and observing them. Nonetheless, there is a significant class of social phenomena that can be explained in a purely structural way. The reason this can be done is simply the truism that without a great deal of structure and predictability in social affairs, societies just would not be possible. But remarkably, people can organize their collective social affairs into entropy-measurable event sets with a high degree of quantitative accuracy. They can establish event sets by probabilistically categorizing and constraining behavior, activity, choices, and so forth. In other words, we will see that people are able to handle social events quantitatively by means of perceived entropy values and event information much as they are able to operate in an economic system by means of quantitative price information. (Strictly speaking, the quantitative aspect of social entropy applies only to us as observers; it is the prior qualitative judgment of social uncertainty levels that applies to members of the society.)

If we can measure entropy, we can also measure information variance. Thus many of the preceding remarks on social entropy also pertain to social information variance measurement. For a given numerical entropy value, many different event sets and combinations of event probabilities will result in the same value. These combinations will differ in the value of the information variance. An entropy value does not completely determine the value of the information variance, nor an information variance value the entropy. Thus there is the possibility that a society may also use information variance to organize social events independently to some degree of entropy. (Of course, one cannot have the variance without having the entropy). If such variance related phenomena are observed, we can construct an additional two-variable pattern for social systems by using the information variance as an intensive acrossvariable along with the throughvariables of the entropy pattern (see Figure 2-3).[13] When the number of events in the event set is held fixed, however, the entropy and information variance are more nearly equivalent measures; there is much less freedom for the information variance. In the two-event case, as shown in Figures 2-1 and 2-2, a given entropy value always determines the value of the information variance, although the reverse is not true. For sets with more than two events a greater degree of flexibility in information variance is possible.

CHAPTER THREE

System Measurement

3-1. Measurement in the Unitary Social System

Conceivably, we could apply the proposed social measures to a wide variety of social systems, ranging from kinship groups to business organizations, mass movements, national populations, or even international systems. We would have to devise an appropriate system model for each specific application. For the rest of this study we shall concentrate on a single system model, the unitary model, as applied to the populations of national political systems or their subsystems. A detailed examination of a single type of model has the dual advantage of testing the validity and practicality of the proposed measurement variables while at the same time providing significant new explanations for certain kinds of social phenomena. Once we are able to analyze unitary social systems, we can begin to extend the methods of analysis to more complex systems, following the analogies of the physical sciences. If we can analyze entire national populations successfully, we shall be encouraged to apply similar methods to smaller, subnational, social organizations.

To think of a nation as a unitary system implies that we must view people within the system as indistinguishable (or interchangeable). They cannot be identified according to their membership in particular social groups or social classes. For such a system we postulate that the macroscopic measurement variables adequately describe the state of the system as a whole, provided that equilibrium conditions are satisfied. In measurement applications here we focus almost exclusively on the entropy variable. We do not measure throughvariables directly, except to indicate relative population sizes of the systems, which are proportional to the extensive throughvariable. To investigate the validity of the entropy variable and its interpretation as a social measurement, we can consider relatively isolated and static systems of arbitrary sizes: cases where there is little concern about the actual values of the throughvariables and where flow or interaction between systems can be ignored. Furthermore, because of the direct proportionality law for intensive variables, we will be able to determine a throughvariable flow rate up to a constant multiplier from the intensive acrossvariable (entropy) values alone. Thus we do not need direct measurements of all variables, even in the analysis of dynamic systems. The specification of throughvariables is discussed in greater detail in Chapter 6 when we consider interaction between systems.

An entropy value for a unitary social system is analogous to a temperature reading for a thermodynamic system, such as a volume of a gas. In a state of temperature equilibrium one temperature measurement describes the whole volume or any part of it. If a social system is in an entropy equilibrium, a single entropy measurement describes the state of the system or any subsystem. For a system in partial equilibrium, the entropy values of its subsystems must be known. *The entropy measurement gives the average social uncertainty about what will happen for events in event sets in the social system.* The entropy measurement is independent of whatever the content of the events is. Therefore, we must assume that we would find approximately the same entropy value in different event sets within the system. This would imply a uniformity in how people construct their collective event sets; that is, people would act the same way toward different event sets, regardless of the specific nature of the events. These assumptions about social entropy measurement lead to an important hypothesis that can be tested in a real social system, giving a good assessment of the validity of our initial assumptions about social uncertainty and its measurement.

Recall what is necessary for an entropy measurement to be defined. There must be a set of mutually exclusive events so that for a person in the system one and only one of the events is possible at a given time. And we must be able to estimate the probabilities of occurrence of each event for some collection of people, or for people considered at random. Naturally, the set of events must exist within the system. The set of events cannot be a purely arbitrary designation; it must be a property of the system itself, not a function of an observer or remote social scientist. Fortunately, there is a social situation which fits these criteria remarkably well: an *election*.

An election offers eligible voters two kinds of choices, two sets of possible actions. A voter must choose whether to vote or abstain; and if he decides to vote, he must choose between the alternative political parties or candidates (for a single office). Both of these situations fulfill the requirements for an entropy measurement. Although we may not know the probabilities for the choices beforehand, the actual election results can be used retrospectively to compute the probabilities. Or one can imagine that if a second election took place immediately after the first election, the probabilities calculated for the first election would accurately foretell the second. As an example we can calculate the entropy $H(T)$ in an election where 60% of the eligible voters voted and 40% did not, that is, where the turnout was 60%. The probability of an eligible voter voting was thus .60 and of not voting .40. We have

$$
\begin{aligned}
H(T) &= -.60 \log .60 - .40 \log .40 \\
&= .44 + .53 = 0.97 \text{ bits}
\end{aligned}
$$

If the people who did vote divided their ballots among three political parties in the proportion 50, 30, and 20%, we could make a second entropy calculation $H(P)$ as follows

$$
\begin{aligned}
H(P) &= -.50 \log .50 - .30 \log .30 - .20 \log .20 \\
&= .50 + .52 + .46 \\
&= 1.48 \text{ bits}
\end{aligned}
$$

To have an entropy measurement for a national political system we need to have a national election so that we can capture the complete set of interrelationships among people throughout the system. A national election is usually of such prominence in a society that it can be assumed that the great majority of the voting age population is aware of the election and thus confronted with the alternative choices. Elections have additional advantages as measurements: they have precise points in time; reasonably accurate election data is readily available for most nations; historical data can be used; and elections involve large numbers of people, which should serve to bring out any macroscopic system properties. The fact that we can interpret elections as entropy measurements is an unexpected benefit which immediately puts electoral phenomena within the range of explanation of the general theory being constructed.

In many large national political systems electoral activity varies widely from one region to another. In these instances subsystems must be the unit of analysis since the system is clearly not homogeneous. But we still require that a national election, not a local election, be the entropy measurement. A national election would presumably be necessary to include interaction between the subsystems. Ordinarily we would expect that the subsystems were not completely isolated from one another and some amount of interaction would likely exist; we could say that the subsystems were only quasi closed.

It is important to see how the entropy or uncertainty arises in considering an election as a macroscopic measurement of social entropy. Certainly an individual voter knows, at least after some point, whether he is going to vote or not, and if so, for whom. Or at least he knows after he has voted. There is no uncertainty about an individual's own choices. Even from one election to another we would usually expect a high degree of consistency in a person's voting choices. Yet as soon as a fairly large number of people is voting it is no longer possible for a less than omniscient observer to follow the voting intentions and habits of each individual. Therefore, when the number of people in the system is large, they must be viewed as indistinguishable, and the observer must rely on statistical information about their collective voting behavior. (By "observer" we mean either the remote social scientist or a member of the system observing or knowing in a statistical way the behavior of innumerable other people in the system with whom he may be in some way interrelated.)

The uncertainty arises because of the statistical or probabilistic nature of our knowledge about the system as a whole, and is therefore a macroscopic system property. If we knew the voter turnout was 60%, we could say nothing more about exactly which members of the population constituted that 60%. Even saying that the probability of a specific individual's voting was 60% is not the same as specifying his behavior; he either voted or did not. The analogy to macroscopic measurement in thermodynamic systems is that every molecule "knows", by virtue of its position and velocity, exactly where it is going. But to describe this system, an observer is forced to rely exclusively on statistical knowledge about the whole collection of molecules as they are observed simultaneously. For the individual molecule the laws of classical mechanics are assumed to hold; for the system and its observer, the macroscopic laws of statistical physics and thermodynamics apply.

With respect to the measurement of uncertainty or entropy we can also see how the idea of equilibrium enters into the picture. If a system remains in an equilibrium, we would expect the turnout in successive elections to remain about the same, say at 60%. But we do not know which of the electorate constituted that 60% in any election. And, in general, we would not expect that exactly the same people voted in each election. From one election to the next some voters will become abstainers, and some abstainers will become voters. What we do assert for an equilibrium is that on the average there is no net change in the turnout over time. This same logic applies to the choice of political parties. Although the entropy calculated from the percentages of votes for each party would remain constant over time, we can expect that the people voting for the respective parties (or the parties themselves) will not be the same in every election. This reasoning extends to other social choices or event sets as well.

It is not clear whether the information variance should also be constant in a system at a given equilibrium level of entropy. An entropy equilibrium without a fixed information variance would imply that the underlying probabilities in the event set might change but the average information remain about the same. Thus increased uncertainty or lessened probability for one event could be offset by decreased uncertainty and increased probability about another in the event set. In general terms, this could mean that if some people acted more unpredictably, others would compensate for this and act more predictably to keep the average information the same. It might also be the case that a flexible variance would mean less awareness of the variance among the population, and hence more random fluctuation in its value. Empirical studies in this book show that the information variance need not be uniformly fixed for a given entropy level.

For an equilibrium we also require a high degree of homogeneity across the system. Turnout should not be greatly different in one part of a system than in another part. Entropy calculated from political party voting should also be uniform across the system. If these conditions are not satisfied, the system must be analyzed as a composite or heterogeneous unitary system, and a trend toward increasing system homogeneity can be anticipated.

The Entropy Hypothesis. With no additional assumptions than we have made already, we are now in a position to generate a very interesting hypothesis. There are two possible entropy calculations we can make from a single election. One measurement is based on the voting-abstention choice and denoted by $H(T)$; the other measurement $H(P)$ is made from the distribution of votes among the political parties or candidates. Note, however, two major differences between the two measurements. They involve different event sets, and the number of people making the party choice, that is, the number of actual voters, is only a fraction of the number of eligible voters if the turnout is less than 100%. Thus $H(P)$ is a measurement for a subset of the people who are measured by $H(T)$. The relationships between these sets and the respective measures are shown schematically in Figure 3-1.[1] We have assumed that entropy is an intensive measurement and not dependent on the number of people being measured. Therefore the set of voters should have the same entropy level as the set of eligible voters, or the entire population, although each set is only a partial subset of the next. We have also assumed that the entropy measurement is independent of the content of the events. Thus a reasonable conclusion would be that the two separate entropy measurements $H(T)$ and $H(P)$ should be equal. But this is only partially true. The range of entropy values for an event set also depends on the number of events in the set. So there are two possible hypotheses we could test. Either (1) $H(T) = H(P)$ or (2) $H(T)$ is equivalent to $H(P)$ if the number of choices in each set is taken into account. Empirical evidence will show the second of these hypotheses to be correct.

In order to put the measures $H(T)$ and $H(P)$ on an equivalent basis, we need only to divide each by the maximum value possible in each set. In this way the ranges of the two variables will become identically 0 to 1. The maximum entropy for n events is $\log n$. In the $H(T)$ set there are only two

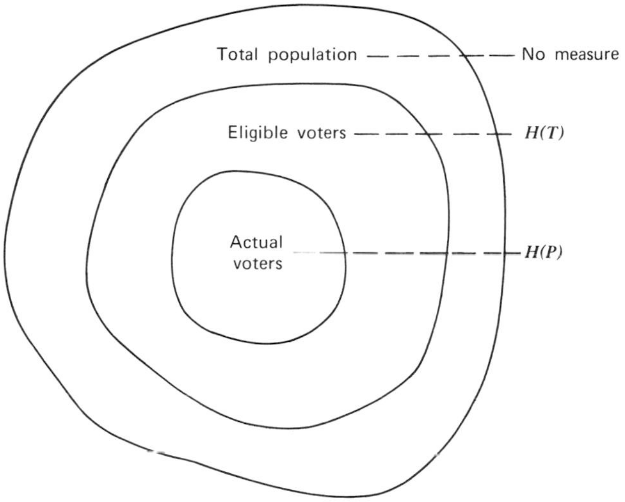

Figure 3-1. Election entropy measurements, showing the intensive character of the entropy measure.

possible events, and log 2 equals 1. Thus we have for n events in the $H(P)$ set

$$\frac{H(T)}{1} = \frac{H(P)}{\log n}$$

or

$$H(P) = \log n \, H(T) \tag{3-1}$$

We can say that $H(P)$ is ratio-scale equivalent to $H(T)$ or that $H(P)$ and $H(T)$ give measurements of equal redundancy for a fixed value of n; changes in the two measures taken as percentages of their values are equal.[2] The hypothesis that this equivalence relation (3-1) holds in an actual social system will be called the *entropy hypothesis*. Its verification implies the existence of a fundamental regularity in social behavior, a social "law", for which (ratio-scale) entropy is the appropriate measure.

For each of the measures $H(T)$ and $H(P)$ we require a high degree of homogeneity across a system in an equilibrium. The degree of homogeneity of the two measures may certainly differ in a system if equilibrium conditions are not satisfied. A given level of voter turnout does not inherently imply that there must always be a certain distribution of votes among the parties. The microscopic processes that result in a given level of voter turnout are to some extent independent of the processes involved in party voting. So, possibly, homogeneity might be attained in a system for one of the two measures but not the other; the relaxation rates of the two processes might differ. If a high degree of homogeneity is attained for entropy values for one event set, but not for others, this is also called a partial equilibrium. In this partial equilibrium we can also expect a trend toward a greater homogeneity and equivalence of measurement.

To avoid confusion between the two varieties of partial equilibria, we can refer to partial equilibrium for subsystems as acrossvariable equilibrium and to partial equilibrium for separate event sets as intensive equilibrium. These terms indicate which aspect of the entropy measurement is most relevant. Of course, both types of partial equilibria can occur simultaneously. And in a rapidly changing society it would be difficult for people to maintain consistent and uniform behavior patterns, so we would expect to find measurement differences from one part of the system to another as well as between event sets.

The entropy hypothesis (equation 3-1) establishes the relationship between $H(P)$ and $H(T)$. We can conveniently discuss this relationship using turnout levels instead of $H(T)$ values. For a two-event set the entropy is completely determined by the probability of either of the two events. Thus we could plot $H(T)$ as a function of voter turnout. This graph would be exactly the same as the entropy curve of Figure 2-1, except that turnout values would be on the horizontal axis instead of p values. Since $H(P)$ is a function of $H(T)$ we can also plot $H(P)$ values against turnout. For each value of n (in equation 3-1) and each value of turnout there is a possible $H(P)$ value. The $H(P)$ values for all values of n and turnout form a series of expanding curves, similar to the entropy curve for two choices (Figure 2-1) but multiplied or "stretched" by a factor of log n. Each point on one of the curves represents an $H(P)$ value and a turnout value that a system or subsystem could have in an equilibrium. A series of entropy curves is illustrated in Figure 3-2. Note especially that all the curves are symmetrical about the 50% turnout line; this implies again the content-free equivalence of the two events in the $H(T)$ set (voting and abstention) for a given pair of event probabilities.

To describe change in a macroscopic unitary model, we must find the state of the system at successive equilibria. (This is the method of comparative statics.) The entropy values of a system changing its state over time, over successive equilibrium states, must lie on the series of entropy curves for $H(P)$ and turnout values (Figure 3-2). A system must "move" or change along these curves or from one curve to another. By analogy to orbital motion in mechanical systems, we shall refer to these curves as *orbits*; they are paths along which a changing system can have a sequence of equilibrium

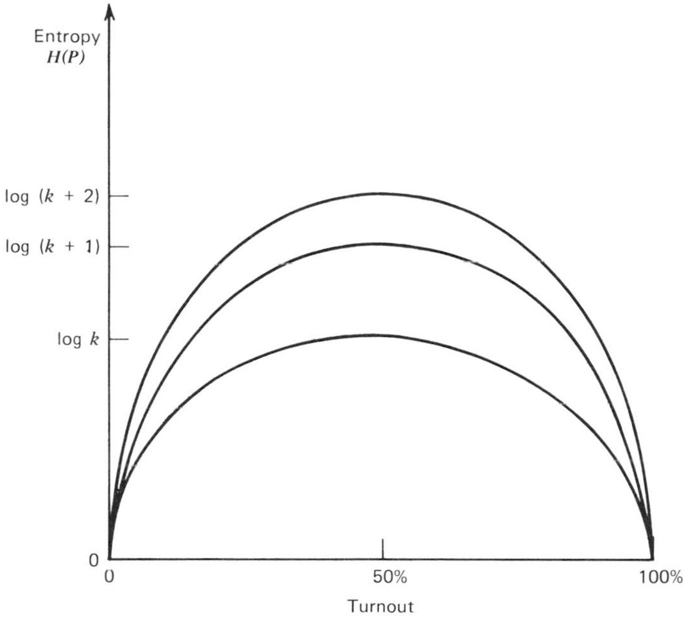

Figure 3-2. Entropy curve orbits: equilibrium points satisfying the entropy hypothesis.

states. The kth orbit will mean that the number of events in the $H(P)$ or political party event set is k. If a composite system is in a partial or intensive equilibrium, the subsystems will be located at various points on the curves. If we find this to be true for actual political systems, we will have confirmed the entropy hypothesis.

The orbital representation of equilibrium values brings out an important difference between the two entropy measurements $H(T)$ and $H(P)$. $H(T)$ is necessarily limited in value to the range 0 to 1. But $H(P)$ can increase to any value if the number of events in the event set increases. In other words, the number of choices in the $H(T)$ set is always fixed; there is no third alternative to voting or abstention. But the number of choices in the $H(P)$ set will increase or decrease as the number of political parties changes from one election to another. From the derivation of the entropy measure, we have no reason to assume that the entropy values should be limited to the range 0 to 1. Therefore we must conclude that $H(T)$ is not sufficient to measure system entropy; only $H(P)$ can give the entire range of possible entropy values. $H(T)$ would only be an adequate measure of social entropy if the number of choices in the $H(P)$ event set were also known. The $H(P)$ measurement will consequently be the primary measurement of social entropy. The $H(P)$ and

$H(T)$ measures will be used together to gauge the extent of disequilibrium in a system according to how well the respective values fit the predicted equation 3-1 and the orbital curves.

The possibility of change in the number of events in an event set complicates the analysis of social systems. Social systems can change their states semicontinuously along entropy or orbital curves when the number of events is constant, or they can change in discrete units when the system moves from one orbit to another. The analysis of social systems must account for both types of change, the discrete and the continuous. And specifically, we must be able to explain the relationship between change in $H(P)$ and $H(T)$. We use the orbital representation of possible system states again in Chapter 5 to analyze these alternative forms of system change, once the entropy hypothesis itself has been confirmed. In testing the entropy hypothesis, we discover that the hypothesis must be modified to account fully for the patterns of change when systems move from one orbit to another.

3-2. *Hypothesis Testing*

The entropy hypothesis is the primary test of whether there are observable macroscopic social phenomena that can be quantitatively described by entropy or social uncertainty measurements, being therefore intensive and content free. The hypothesis states that $H(P)$ is a function of $H(T)$ in an equilibrium system. Since $H(T)$ is completely determined by the voter turnout, we can equivalently find the relationship between $H(P)$ values and turnout values; the assumed relationship is given by the orbital representation of equilibrium states (Figure 3-2). Thus a homogeneous system should have turnout and $H(P)$ values that put it on an orbital curve, or a collection of subsystems which are themselves in equilibria should be distributed along the orbital curves.

Since we have no way of determining whether a system is in an equilibrium before measurement, we must begin the analysis of a system by partitioning the system into a collection of subsystems. The smaller the subsystems are, the more likely they are to be homogeneous, provided that they are not too small to exhibit macroscopic properties. But we must also choose subsystems for which election data is available. Each subsystem, being a system itself, is a case for testing the hypothesis. By partitioning a system into a large number of subsystems, the number of potential test cases for the hypothesis greatly expands over what it would be if national political systems were taken alone.

The advantage of having more test cases is partially offset, however, because subsystems are not completely independent of each other. If the system is not in equilibrium, there will presumably be a trend toward greater homogeneity among the subsystems. Hence, we must assume that subsystems would seldom be completely in equilibrium states, and this will appear as a source of error in testing the entropy hypothesis. There may also be random fluctuations or variations in subsystem entropy levels due to local conditions. We have no way to control these sources of error, as we might in an analogous experiment in a physics laboratory; social systems must be analyzed in their natural condition. This is an acceptable problem, however, since we are not only interested in testing a hypothesis under ideal conditions, but also in examining how well it does apply to actual social systems where some degree of disequilibrium can be expected.

To test the hypothesis we will examine a number of empirical cases and employ a variety of analytic methods. The use of alternative methods permits a closer study of different aspects of the data and helps to uncover any bias a particular method might introduce into the interpretation of research findings. The three principal analytic techniques we will use are curve fitting, tests for symmetry, and the examination of extreme values or boundaries of data distributions. In each of these techniques mathematical analysis can be combined with visual or graphical interpretation of data.[3]

Curve fitting is an averaging technique that permits us to determine whether a collection of subsystems is distributed along particular curves, as the entropy curves of the orbital representation. It also measures how close the data is to the curve. We will use curve fitting to see how well subsystem distributions fit the expected entropy curves, as well as to describe patterns of error or deviation away from the expected curves. First, we will fit a curve of the general form $aH(T)$ to the data. (The curve $aH(T)$ will be expressed as a function of turnout.) The coefficient a of $aH(T)$ is a constant multiplier of the $H(T)$ values; thus $aH(T)$ is an arbitrary multiple of the two-event set entropy curve (Figure 2-1). The constant a is estimated in the process of curve fitting. Since $aH(T)$ is the hypothesized shape of the data, this should be a reasonably good fit, with a close to $\log n$ for a fit to subsystems in the nth orbit. As a standard of comparison for the $aH(T)$ fit, we will also try a fit of the second degree polynomial curve (a parabola), which has the general form

$$f(t) = a_0 + a_1 t + a_2 t^2$$

where t is the turnout (expressed as a percentage) and a_0, a_1, a_2 are the arbitrary coefficients to be estimated. The coefficients are estimated according to the conventional "least squares" criterion. That is, the coefficients are determined so that the sum of the squares of the vertical distances from the data points to the curve is a minimum for all curves of that general form.[4] Estimates of how well the curve fits the data include the estimates of the standard error of the coefficients and the standard error of the distance from data to curve (the residual error).[5] About 70% of the data points will lie within a distance of one standard error from the fitted curve.

Although the $aH(T)$ curve is the expected shape of data for any orbit, there are several advantages in fitting the parabolic curve as well. In the first place, the parabolic curve can give a convenient description of the data distribution if the data does not fit an entropy curve closely. If the data fits an entropy curve it will also fit a parabolic curve fairly well, because an entropy curve or orbit is roughly parabolic in shape. But if the data begins to disperse away from the entropy curve, that is, if the subsystems are not close to equilibria, the pattern of this dispersion should show up in the parabolic curve fitting. The parabolic curve could become more or less sharply curved than the entropy curve. If the experimental data were actually closer to linear than curvilinear, a rather flat part of the parabolic curve would be fit to the data by the curve fitting algorithm. In other words, the class of parabolic curves has more freedom than the $aH(T)$ curves; the latter are more constrained in their possible size, curvature, and location, as a function of turnout. Disequilibrium will show up in the $aH(T)$ fit as well as the parabolic, of course; the coefficient a may be higher or lower than an expected value of log n, or the error estimates may be large. But the $aH(T)$ fit alone does not give a very complete description of the nature and distribution of errors.

A second use of the parabolic fit is to allow some consideration of alternative hypotheses, in addition to the "null" hypothesis of no relation at all between $H(T)$ and $H(P)$. Ideally, we would like both to confirm the entropy hypothesis and simultaneously to reject any possible alternatives. This would be especially crucial if it were necessary to choose between several alternative theories that predicted data distributions similar to the entropy curves. As it is, we have no close alternatives to the entropy hypothesis at present, and we have no way to determine whether there may be alternative theories that would also predict the same results. Nevertheless, it is still desirable to see whether the data might have a consistent pattern substantially different from the entropy curve. This would imply that our basic assumptions about social measurement were faulty and that we should seek an alternative theory. The parabolic curve can represent a fairly general class of alternatives ranging from linear distributions to single-curved distributions of varying position and curvature, while still being able to approximate the entropy curve well enough for error description.

Perhaps the most specific alternative to the entropy hypothesis is that of linearity between turnout and $H(P)$. Such hypotheses have been made in political science under a different terminology. Recall that $H(P)$ is a maximum for an event set when the underlying probabilities are equal. In an election, probabilities will be equal when the political parties are most competitive, each receiving the same share of the popular vote. Thus $H(P)$ can be interpreted as a measure of "party competitiveness." As the parties become more competitive, in terms of more equal shares of the vote, $H(P)$ increases. It has often been said that party competitiveness increases with voter turnout; and a linear relationship is usually implied. Some political theorists, however, have suggested that party competitiveness should decrease with increasing turnout. The entropy hypothesis states that neither of these two contradictory alternatives is correct if the whole range of turnout is considered: competitiveness should increase with turnout less than 50%, but decrease with turnout over 50%. (Compare Figure 3-2.) Parabolic curve fitting alone or compared with linear curve fitting provides a means for determining whether experimental data is closer to linear than parabolic in form, and so allows a rejection of the incorrect hypotheses. Note also that in the case of the entropy hypothesis at least, we imply no causality in the turnout-competitiveness relation; the relation is instead one of equivalence based on macroscopic measurement properties. The fact that it is an *equivalence* relation has important consequences for political theory—a point that we discuss later.

If we find that a heterogeneous system has subsystems on several orbits, another opportunity for parabolic curve fitting arises. We expect that subsystems at different entropy levels will show signs of disequilibrium because of the interaction between them. If the subsystems with different entropy levels are also in different orbits, we must anticipate some kind of interaction or "attraction" between orbits, from subsystems in one orbit to those in another. By the use of parabolic curve fitting to data aggregated for several orbits we may be able to describe the resulting disequilibrium patterns. The curve can indicate across-orbit patterns as well as within-orbit patterns, something the $aH(T)$ fit does poorly. This same analytic problem also results when changes are occurring in a system in such a way that subsystems are moving from one orbit to another as people increase or decrease the number of political parties from one election to another. In Chapter 5 we explain from theoretical considerations the disequilibrium patterns most likely to occur during system change. In testing the entropy hypothesis, however, we are concerned only with describing patterns. In other words, we show how the errors found in testing the hypothesis are still consistent with our initial assumptions about system measurement when system change is taken into account.

It is not necessary for the $aH(T)$ curve to fit the data better than the polynomial curve. For systems in disequilibrium, the polynomial curve will quite likely give a better fit. Thus the testing of the entropy hypothesis is instructive in showing that "goodness of fit" should not be the sole criterion for establishing a theoretical model.[6] Our purpose is not merely to describe data distributions, but to *explain* why they are even approximately the way they are. The polynomial curves by themselves do not give us an understanding of the origin and meaning of the entropy-turnout distributions of subsystems.

Testing for Symmetry. One of the most interesting aspects of the entropy hypothesis is the expected symmetry about the 50% turnout line.[7] In fact, the orbital representation was designed to bring out this symmetry. (Symmetry does not imply that subsystems would be distributed on either side of the 50% line as mirror images, but that the shape of their distribution is symmetrical.) The $aH(T)$ fit by itself does not give an especially good test of how symmetrical the data is. The $aH(T)$ curve cannot shift with respect to turnout regardless of how the coefficient a is selected; its maximum is always at 50% turnout. And error estimates for this fit would not specifically describe shifts of symmetry or loss of symmetry. The parabolic curve, however, is symmetrical about its maximum or minimum, and we can calculate where the maximum is located if it has one. The maximum should be near 50% turnout if the hypothesis holds and the subsystems are near equilibria. If the system is in disequilibrium, we can still estimate how well the symmetry is preserved. The parabolic fitting also permits us to consider alternative hypotheses that would predict shifts in the line of symmetry. The maximum or minimum of the parabola is located at a turnout of M, where

$$M = \frac{-a_1}{2a_2}$$

and a_1 and a_2 are the coefficients estimated in the curve fitting procedure. Whether the curve has a maximum or minimum at M is given by the sign of the coefficient a_2. A negative coefficient implies a maximum; a positive coefficient implies a minimum. The curve fitting algorithm does not necessarily restrict the maximum or minimum of the parabola to be within the data range or even the 0 to 100% interval of turnout, nor does it test only for parabolas curved in one direction (up or down).

Because each orbit is symmetrical about the 50% turnout line, any collection of orbits is also symmetrical. We can therefore combine data for subsystems regardless of their orbit and still test for the symmetry of the overall distribution. Judging from the symmetry implied by the entropy hypothesis, we might also guess that if the hypothesis is true there may be a high degree of symmetry in possible errors or disequilibrium patterns. If a system is changing from one symmetrical pattern to another, as between orbits, it may preserve the symmetry even during the period of change. So it is also important to observe the degree of symmetry when a system is clearly in disequilibrium. If there is change between orbits, combined orbit data can be evaluated for symmetry.

A third major analytic procedure involves the study of extreme or boundary values of a distribution of data points.[8] Unfortunately, analytic methods for studying contours or shapes of data distributions are poorly developed, and one must use *ad hoc* procedures. Curve fitting gives average locations of distributions but does not specifically relate to contours of distributions. There are cases where entropy and information variance data present striking boundary patterns, apparent even from visual inspection of the data. These patterns are often the result of constraints on the absolute values of the measurement variables due to inherent characteristics of social systems. A knowledge of such constraints is very important to the understanding of dynamic system phenomena since they are exceptions to the general laws that govern conventional system dynamics within the constraints.

Along with the problem of confirming the entropy hypothesis there is the question of what degree of accuracy should be required in the prediction of $H(P)$ and turnout values. No fixed rules are available to tell us how accurate a scientific explanation must be. In the physical sciences, errors in theoretical predictions vary greatly from one branch of theory to another. A fairly large error may be tolerated if there are no better ways to predict values than the theory in question, or if experimental handicaps inhibit the control of extraneous effects. Thus we can accept some error in entropy prediction, but exactly how much we cannot resolve in advance.

Estimation Errors. If we were trying to estimate system entropy levels from small samples of voters, there would be an additional source of error. An advantage of the large numbers of people involved in elections is the resulting accuracy of the entropy measurement (assuming that the election statistics are reliable). The relation between sample size and the accuracy of entropy estimation has been derived by Basharin.[9] If $\hat{H}$ is the estimate of entropy calculated from observed relative frequencies of occurrence of events (that is, the event set probabilities are estimated from the observed frequencies), the expectation or mean of $\hat{H}$ is

$$E(\hat{H}) = H - \frac{n-1}{2N} \log e + \mathcal{O}\left(\frac{1}{N^2}\right) \qquad (3\text{-}2)$$

with

$$Var(\hat{H}) = \left(\frac{1}{N}\right)\left(\sum_{i=1}^{n} p_i \log^2 p_i - H^2\right) + \mathcal{O}\left(\frac{1}{N^2}\right)$$

for a sample of size N and an event set of size n. The term $\mathcal{O}(1/N^a)$ designates a quantity of order N^{-a} with a greater than zero. $\hat{H}$ is a biased, consistent, asymptotically normal estimate of the entropy H. Thus the estimates of H will tend to be too low on the average. The amount of bias will increase as the sample size decreases or as the size of the event set increases. For large N, as we have in election data, the error is negligible. But there may be applications where entropy must be calculated from relatively small samples, and in these instances sample errors must be anticipated.

A more important source of error in entropy estimation is at the microscopic level of social processes. The equilibrium state of a social system will be a result of the actions people take, whether consciously or subconsciously. If the people in a society are to achieve or maintain an equilibrium level of entropy, they must have some knowledge of the social uncertainty level on which to base their choice of action. They can acquire such knowledge through the perception of relative frequencies of occurrence of events in social event sets. But observed frequencies are only estimates of the actual probabilities of events, and a person in a society usually has only small samples of other people's behavior. Under social conditions where communication or interaction among members of a society is exceptionally limited or reduced, many would very likely underestimate the social uncertainty level. Poor estimation of the uncertainty level would cause many people to act as if the entropy level were other than what our macroscopic, objective entropy measure would indicate. Such microscopic errors might then appear as "errors" in macroscopic measurements or as perturbations in system dynamics.

Without a greater knowledge of micro-level communication patterns in actual societies, we cannot predict whether micro estimation errors will noticeably increase errors in testing the entropy hypothesis. The presence of this effect in our macroscopic observations would give us somewhat higher entropy values than predicted, and the magnitude of error would tend to increase as the number of political parties increases. If the number of events in the $H(P)$ set is larger than the two of the $H(T)$ set, there would also be a differential error between the two entropy measures.

Since we have only macroscopic data available, we approach the testing of the entropy hypothesis from a strictly macroscopic viewpoint and evaluate its explanatory power as a macroscopic law. However, we do keep in mind that a higher degree of explanatory power, or lower errors, would be possible if we had a greater understanding of the microscopic processes. (Further discussion of micro entropy estimation continues in Appendix II.) For now, we can best proceed by testing the validity and accuracy of the entropy hypothesis in actual political systems.

3-3. *Case Studies on the Entropy Hypothesis*

We have selected a number of cases to test the entropy hypothesis. These cases include one or more elections in each of several countries: the United States, India, and Japan. Data from Germany is analyzed in a later section. These cases were chosen because of the availability of suitable electoral data and because the countries themselves provide a good test of the hypothesis. The United States, India, and Japan all have frequent elections but are quite dissimilar in other respects. It is a stronger test of the universality of the hypothesis to select countries that appear fundamentally different from one another than to examine only those most alike, as the United States and Canada or Western Europe alone. The culture, economic development, political history, and social composition of the United States, India, and Japan are extraordinarily varied. Even within these countries great diversity exists. The three countries also have contrasting political systems and electoral procedures.

To make a national entropy measurement, we use a national election in each case. In the United States a presidential election, that is, the popular vote for the president, fits this specification best as a single national choice situation. In Japan and India the election most like a national election is the parliamentary election (for the lower house of parliament); there is no popularly elected executive comparable to an American president. In American presidential elections the method of election is based on pluralities in the respective states. India has a similar method for its parliamentary representatives; a single representative is elected by plurality of votes from each electoral constituency. Japan has a form of proportional representation on a constituency basis, and several candidates from different political parties may be elected from each constituency. These variations in electoral procedures let us discount the possibility that the form of the election is crucial in confirming the hypothesis.

The subunits chosen for analysis as subsystems were states in the United States, electoral constituencies in India, and both electoral constituencies and prefectures in Japan. In the analysis, we compute $H(P)$ and turnout values for each subsystem separately. Electoral constituencies are apportioned so as to be of approximately equal population, but states and prefectures are not equal in size. This provides another check on the independence of the (intensive) entropy measurement from population size. We have no fixed rule to guide the selection of subunits, but we must select units for which election data is available.

The fact that the substantive content or meaning of elections differs from one country to another, from one subsystem to another, and from one election to another (and perhaps from one person to another) is a further test of the content-free nature of the entropy measurement. There is a wide range of political parties, election issues, candidate personalities, ideologies, and so forth. The significance of an election itself may differ among the countries. But for entropy measurement these are irrelevant factors and should not affect the appearance of the predicted relationship between $H(P)$ and $H(T)$ or turnout.

For India and the United States the elections we use are all in periods of universal suffrage. We compute voter turnout as the fraction of people who by virtue of their age were potentially eligible to vote and did. This is somewhat arbitrary since minor changes in voter eligibility requirements would probably not be detectable in testing the hypothesis. But the view taken here is that voter registration laws which may have the appearance of reducing turnout (or sometimes increasing it) are merely reflections of the general social conditions that entropy is designed to measure.[10] There may, of course, be time lags between the changing of social conditions and the changing of electoral laws. A more difficult question is how turnout should be computed when large segments of a population are uniformly disenfranchised, as, for example, women. A valid social entropy measurement may be possible if the measurement is the same but based on fewer people, owing to the intensive nature of the entropy variable. We examine this problem in greater detail in the case of Japan. India and the United States present good tests of the symmetry implied by the entropy hypothesis because the range of turnout in subsystems of each country is large and includes turnout values below 50%. In most other countries turnout values below 50% in national elections are rare.

The various subsystems observed at different elections in the several countries are all cases for testing the entropy hypothesis. These cases are to varying degrees statistically independent of one another. Although a particular empirical result might be found purely by chance in any given case, the chance of finding the same result or the same regularity of behavior in a number of independent and semi-independent cases is very much less. Once the entropy hypothesis is found to hold in a number of cases, the possibility of this happening by accident can be completely disregarded. This does not mean, however, that the hypothesis should be accepted uncritically. The merits of the hypothesis and the underlying theory must be judged on more comprehensive grounds. We must evaluate how well the theory predicts and explains what we find experimentally. To this end, the values and error estimates provided by the curve fitting are useful in assessing the accuracy of our explanations and in predicting under what conditions a gain or loss in accuracy may occur.

The United States. The United States has been characterized by remarkable stability in its number of political parties over its entire history; only infrequently has a third-party presidential candidate garnered a noticeable percentage of the vote. Voter turnout levels have perhaps been less consistent, but ordinarily they show a high degree of uniformity over consecutive elections in individual states. Thus we see indications that the United States has been near partial equilibrium over most of its history. In order to simplify the analysis we will consider elections that have high or low entropy levels in the period from 1920 to 1968. This is the period of universal suffrage, and election data is more reliable than for earlier periods. By picking out high and low entropy elections for this period we will be able to test the hypothesis over a wide range of entropy levels and determine whether the system has ever attained a three-party equilibrium. First, we will test the third-party elections of 1920, 1924, 1948, and 1968. These were the only significant third-party elections during the entire period and should have the highest entropy values. In these elections all votes not going to the two major party candidates will be classified as "third-party" votes and taken as a single choice. Election data is available on this tripartite basis. Usually there are parties in all elections receiving fractions of 1% of the vote. The inclusion of these parties as separate choices is immaterial because the corresponding $-p \log p$ term of the entropy sum is small; for 1%, $-p \log p = 0.066$ bits, and for $p = 0.1\%$, $-p \log p = 0.010$ bits. It is doubtful that these very minor parties would be considered as recognized national choices by the majority of people in the system.

The data set consists of a point for each state for each election; each data point represents a pair of values, the entropy $H(P)$ and the voter turnout in that state and election. Only the contiguous 48 states are considered; Alaska, Hawaii, and the District of Columbia are excluded from the sample. If there was less than 0.1% of the vote for third-party candidates in a state, we classified it as a two-choice situation. (Computational procedure also requires a somewhat arbitrary nonzero lower limit to party size.) Only states with three choices are included in the final sample for the four third-party elections, which are then analyzed separately. These four elections are also combined, and the hypothesis is tested for the total sample.

It is interesting to note that different third parties were involved in each election. In the 1920 election the Socialists with Debs as candidate were the strongest of several minor parties. In 1924 the Progressives with LaFollette gained a substantial share of the vote, while the other minor parties lost strength compared with 1920. The 1948 election had several minor parties including the Southern based States' Rights party with Thurmond and a new Progressive party with Henry Wallace. (Because of the regional bias of these two parties there was never a significant four-party contest in any state.) George Wallace was the principal third-party choice in 1968.

The opposite case of a low third-party vote and low entropy is well represented by the 1940 presidential election, one of the least competitive in American history. In testing the entropy hypothesis we shall analyze this election as both a three-choice and a two-choice event set. First, we include in the sample only those states having more than a 0.1% third-party vote in 1940. Second, we compute the entropy for the two major parties alone. These five elections: 1920, 1924, 1940, 1948, and 1968 should together comprise the highest as well as some of the lowest entropy levels in American states over this period.

The results of the curve fitting are given in tabular and, for some elections, graphical form. (See Table 3-1 and Figures 3-3 to 3-4.) We can make several observations immediately. First, the entropy curves and polynomial curves have about the right size and location for all elections, as predicted

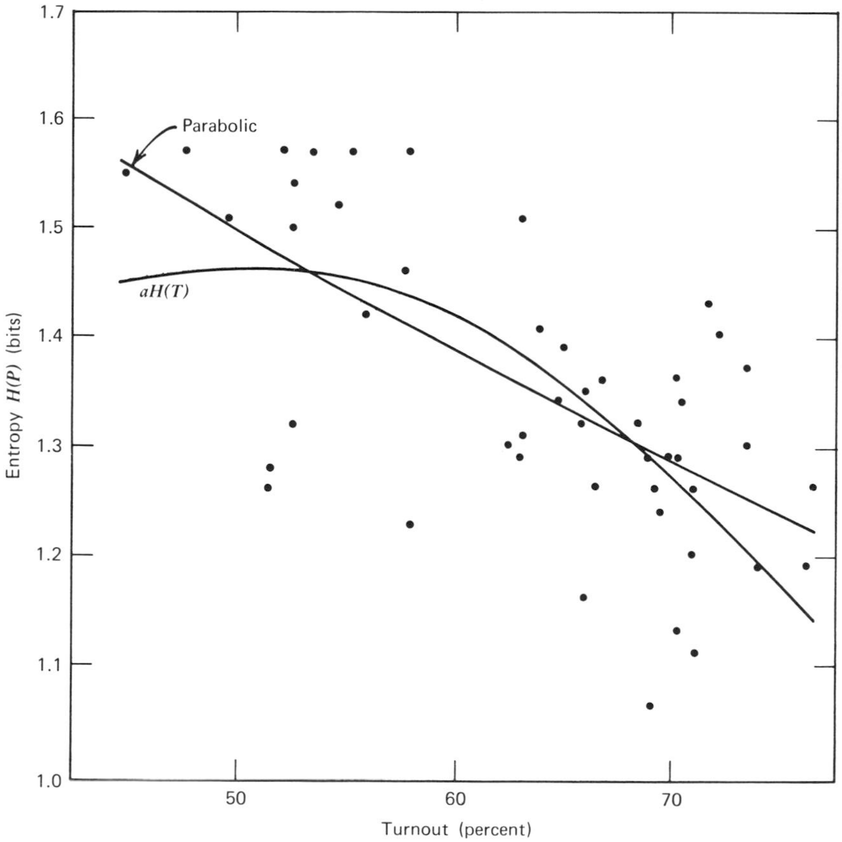

Figure 3-3. Entropy hypothesis test: United States, 1968, parabolic and $aH(T)$ curve fittings.

Table 3-1. United States: Entropy Hypothesis Test; Results of Fitting the Parabolic Curve $f(t) = a_0 + a_1 t + a_2 t^2$ (with t% Turnout) and the Curve $aH(T)$ to $H(P)$-Turnout Distributions for States

Election	Number of Choices	Number of States	Polynomial Fit a_0, a_1, a_2/ Errors	Maximum at Percent Turnout	Standard Error (bits)
1920	3	45	.77, .016, −.00016 .10, .005, .00006	49.9	.12
1924	3	48	.63, .025, −.00022 .12, .007, .00008	56.6	.18
1948	3	45	1.02, .012, −.00015 .16, .008, .00009	37.7	.14
1968	3	48	2.27, −.019, .00007 .90, .030, .00024	[a]	.10
Above 4	3	186	.72, .022, −.00021 .08, .004, .00004	51.4	.17
1940	3	35	.46, −.016, −.00012 .06, .003, .00003	70.5	.05
1940	2	48	.18, .024, −.00017 .06, .003, .00003	68.8	.08
			$aH(T)$ fit a/error[b]	Maximum at 50% turnout	
1920	3	45	1.21/.02		.15
1924	3	48	1.41/.03		.19
1948	3	45	1.26/.03		.18
1968	3	48	1.46/.02		.11
1940	2	48	1.12/.03		.16

[a] Minimum is outside range of data; data closer to linear.
[b] Predicted equilibrium values for a: 1.58 for three choices; 1.00 for two choices.

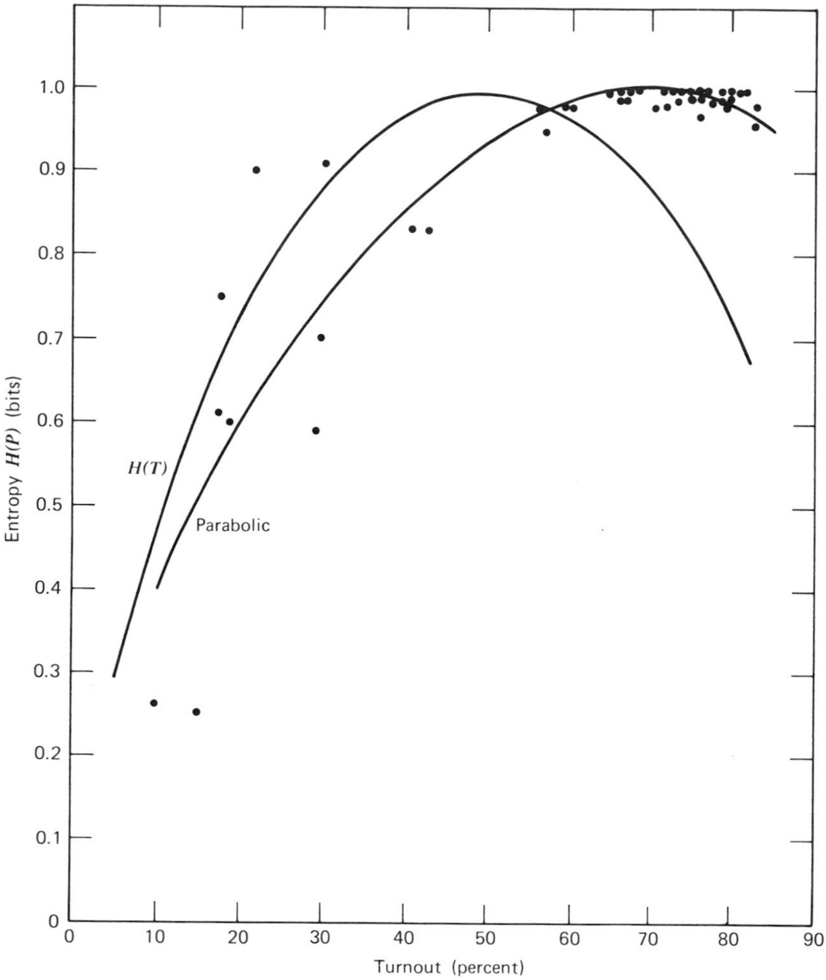

Figure 3-4. Entropy hypothesis test: United States, 1940, parabolic and $H(T)$ curve fittings.

by the entropy hypothesis. No case presents a dramatically unexpected pattern. For 1920 and 1924 and the aggregate four elections the maximum values of the parabolic curves are at 49.9, 56.6, and 51.4% turnout. These maxima are strikingly close to the expected 50% mark. In the 1968 election only a few states had turnout rates less than 50%, and none less than 44%. As a result, in 1968 $H(P)$ is strictly decreasing with increasing turnout for most subsystems. Thus the slightly curved decreasing line fit to the 1968 data in the parabolic curve fitting is quite acceptable, and it gives a fit whose standard error is only slightly better than for the $aH(T)$ fit (Table 3-1).

In the third-party elections the estimated coefficients of $aH(T)$ are all somewhat less than the equilibrium orbit value of log 3 = 1.585 bits. This indicates that as a whole the United States never had sufficiently high entropy values during the period 1920 to 1968 to attain a partial equilibrium with most states in the third or three-party orbit. The conditions causing increased entropy levels in these elections were transient, and relaxation processes subsequently returned the system to its normal two-party state. The United States is thus an example of a system remaining near a partial equilibrium over an extended time.

The elections with the highest values for the coefficient a—1.41 in 1924 and 1.46 in 1968—also show the closest correspondence between the polynomial fit and the $aH(T)$ fit, as measured by the standard error. (The explained variance is also highest and closest together for both of these fittings: 45–40% of total variation for the parabolic, and for the $aH(T)$ 40–35%.) In all cases the polynomial fit is slightly better than the $aH(T)$ fit, but this difference diminishes as the subsystems approach partial equilibrium in the third orbit. In other words, the polynomial curve gives a better description of the location of the subsystems when there are strong signs of disequilibrium; but the two curve fittings become more nearly alike when the system approaches partial equilibrium, as indicated by the value of the coefficient a. As the 1920 election shows, even when there is a fair amount of disequilibrium, the symmetry about 50% turnout may be preserved quite well, and the data distribution may show a strong, nonrandom, pattern similar to the expected result in shape if not location. (Explained variance for the 1920 election in the parabolic fitting is still at about 30%, although it is not significant for the $aH(T)$ fit.)

The 1940 election gives nearly the same result as a two-party or three-party election. Thus the inclusion of the small percentage of votes to third-party candidates is of little consequence. In the 1940 election a scatter plot of the data shows many states having entropy values close to 1.0 bits and lying in the turnout interval of about 55 to 80% (Figure 3-4). This concentration of data shifts the parabolic maximum to near 70% turnout (and leads to an explained variance of nearly 80% for the parabolic fit). The data for states with turnout below 50% (primarily in the South) fits the expected pattern better. The 1940 election indicates that when only two major parties are competing, there may be a fairly wide range of party vote percentages and turnout values that still allow a system to be near an equilibrium. For a two-choice event set, either $H(T)$ or $H(P)$, the entropy for a 50 to 50% split is 1.0 bits; for 60 to 40% it is 0.97 bits; for 70 to 30% it is 0.88 bits; and for 80 to 20% it is 0.72 bits. Thus the entropy value drops off very slowly at first as the probabilities change from equality. A group of subsystems having a turnout range of about 50 to 75% and a similar range of party percentages would all be within 10% of the average group entropy value. Such conditions typify two-party elections in the United States, at least outside the South. This means that even small changes or deviations in subsystem entropy levels can lead to apparently large changes in electoral outcomes if only turnout and party percentages are considered.

Inspection of the data distributions, the fit curves, and the standard error estimates reveals that the large majority of data points are within 10 to 15% of the entropy value nearest on the curve. In comparison with the entropy curves, the parabolic curves for all elections are flatter. The residual errors tend to increase, the actual values being higher than predicted, as the turnout becomes greater than or less than 50%. As other cases also show, this is a typical pattern of errors. It becomes pronounced when there is a great deal of ongoing change in a system, especially when there is change between orbits.

The error estimates for the coefficients (Table 3-1) give some additional information about the curve fitting. The error in the third coefficient a_2 is of particular interest. When this coefficient has a negative value, the parabola has a maximum, not a minimum. Therefore, if the coefficient error is large compared with the coefficient—say, greater than half its value—it would not be possible to say with confidence that the data confirmed the hypothesis of curvature in that particular direction. As a rule of thumb, coefficient errors should be less than half the coefficient magnitude before the curve is accepted as a good fit.[11] The 1968 election illustrates this. The errors in the coefficients are large, implying that the parabolic curve defined by the coefficients is not a very precise or unique description of the data distribution. The coefficient values could be changed quite a bit, even to the changing of their signs, and there would be little increase in error in the overall fit (the standard error). This explains why the $aH(T)$ fit is nearly as good as the polynomial fit in 1968, judging by the standard error estimates, despite the fact that the $aH(T)$ curve is markedly different in shape outside the range of the data and has a maximum at 50% turnout.

We can also examine the distribution of extreme values in the data distributions. Inspection of the combined data for the four third-party elections (1920, 1924, 1948, 1968) shows that the largest values of $H(P)$ also tend to lie on an entropy curve. The combined data distribution could be described as semicircular, having a "rising sun" appearance. In Table 3-2 the states are ranked by turnout level, and the largest entropy values for any state in successive intervals of voter turnout for the combined four elections are given. Without exception these values are either strictly increasing or then strictly decreasing from one interval to the next. For example, no state with

Table 3-2. United States: Maximum Entropy Value by Turnout Interval for Combined Elections 1920, 1924, 1948, and 1968

Interval of Turnout (%)	Number of States in Interval	Maximum Observed Entropy (bits)	Predicted Maximum for Three Choices (bits)
0–10	2	0.72	0.74
11–20	12	1.39	1.14
21–30	11	1.47	1.40
31–40	5	1.48	1.54
41–50	18	1.57	1.58
51–60	50	1.57	1.58
61–70	62	1.52	1.54
71–80	26	1.44	1.40
81–90	0	—	—
91–100	0	—	—

a turnout value between 20 and 30% has an entropy value higher than the largest value for states in the 30 to 40% interval, and so forth. The maximum predicted value for each interval for the three-choice event set is also given in Table 3-2. The observed maxima are close to the predicted values. (Explained variance is about 85%.) This pattern holds even though the number of states in each interval varies. One might expect that intervals with more states would have higher maxima, but the observed pattern appears to be relatively independent of numbers of states in the intervals. The minimum values, however, do not exhibit a strong pattern over the turnout range. Nor do we find the same strong pattern in the 1940 election, since many values are close to the absolute maximum of 1 bit for two choices. As we see in other cases, this pattern for three-party elections arises in systems where the number of choices increases with entropy levels. This is in contrast to the 1940 election where many entropy values are high for a two-choice equilibrium at the respective turnout levels, but the number of available choices had still not increased.

We have repeated the above procedures for the analysis of information variance levels in the same elections. Instead of entropy values, information variance values were plotted against turnout for the states. The general test is whether the data for the information variance has a distribution similar to that of the information variance curve for two-event sets (Figure 2-2). The results of parabolic curve fitting are given in Table 3-3 for the four third-

Table 3-3. United States: Information Variance Test

Election	Number of Choices	Number of States	Polynomial Fit a_0, a_1, a_2/Errors	Minimum at Percent Turnout	Standard Error (bits²)
1920	3	45	.54, .008, −.00010 .21, .010, .00012	(maximum at 40.9)	.25
1924	3	48	1.22, −.020, .00014 .19, .011, .00013	73.0	.27
1948	3	45	1.31, −.033, .0003 .17, .009, .0001	56.8	.16
1968	3	48	−.91, .030, −.00014 1.53, .050, .00041	[a]	.18
above 4	3	186	1.10, −.020, .00016 .11, .005, .00006	60.7	.25

[a] Maximum outside range of data; data closer to linear.

party elections and the combined set of elections. Since the turnout values lie within a range of about 10 to 80%, the predicted pattern for the information variance is an inverted parabola having a minimum near the 50% turnout point. As the results show, the parabolic curve does have about the right shape in each election, except for the one in 1920, but the minimum values are not as close to 50% as the entropy maxima in the same elections, except for 1948. The errors are greater for the information variance curve fitting than for the corresponding entropy data. This indicates that the information variance is a less valid measure of macroscopic phenomena than entropy, which in turn may mean that people are less aware of or more flexible about information variance levels in their society. The general shape of the information variance data, however, is additional corroboration of our basic measurement hypotheses.

In summarizing the American election data, we see that the curve fitting reveals distinct and strong patterns in the data for all the elections analyzed. Although differences occur from one election to another, these are differences of quantitative level more than of the basic pattern, which is consistently near that of the entropy curve—parabolic, concave downward, and symmetrical about the 50% turnout line. This holds for data having a distribution of $H(P)$ values from 0.2 to 1.6 bits and turnout values between 10 and 80%. Despite the strength of these findings, they have not been anticipated in any of the extensive literature on American elections or voting behavior.

The most accurate quantitative predictions are for the upper contours of the combined three-party election data; within 10% intervals of turnout, observed $H(P)$ values are, on the average, within 0.1 bits of the predicted values. Errors nearly this small are also found in the 1968 election for the entire data set, as shown by the curve fitting, which represents average tendencies in the data. In this case, the error of 0.1 bits corresponds to an error of less than 10% in the prediction of $H(P)$ values from turnout. Such error magnitudes are certainly respectable for a scientific theory.

In the other elections we have to consider errors of somewhat greater magnitude, especially for the $aH(T)$ curve fitting. But the greater error in these elections does not lead us to reject the basic hypothesis; instead, it suggests that we must allow for changes in the shape of the distribution in periods of system change or relaxation. In such instances a parabolic curve better describes the distribution than a multiple of the entropy curve. This is true, for example, in the 1920 and 1948 elections. System entropy levels were clearly increasing from 1920 to 1924, and the increase in 1948 was only temporary and primarily restricted to the South. And in fact, the entropy hypothesis was not intended to handle patterns of system change or relaxation. These factors could be explicitly incorporated, however, in a more refined and complex version of the entropy hypothesis. In other words, variation in errors of prediction does not imply that large numbers of people are suddenly acting according to different rules that are unrelated to social uncertainty. On the contrary, the persistence of the same basic patterns over the entire period 1920 to 1968, despite the vast changes one ordinarily supposes have taken place in the United States, calls attention to the fundamental role of uncertainty in social processes. One might also expect that the long history of democratic elections in the United States, and possibly the high level of socioeconomic development, would be important factors in giving rise to macroscopic entropy patterns. But the next case study, of India, contradicts the possibility of these factors as either favoring, or disposing against, the applicability of the entropy hypothesis.

India. In testing the entropy hypothesis for India, we use a single election, the 1962 parliamentary (*Lok Sabha*) election.[12] Data was available for electoral constituencies in most Indian states, but Kashmir and Assam were excluded. There are nearly 500 constituencies in all, and the population of a constituency is about one million. According to Indian election law, one legislator is elected from each constituency, but the number of political parties competing may vary from one constituency to another.

Some constituencies had as few as two national parties competing, others as many as six. In addition, there were sometimes independent or local party candidates; we consider these to be a single alternative choice in any constituency, although there were instances of more than one independent candidate. Thus, the total number of possible choices in any constituency was seven. In a few instances we found irregularities in the data, and these constituencies were dropped from the analysis; several uncontested constituencies were also excluded. The methods used to analyze the Indian data are the same as for the United States. The only difference is that we analyze each orbit separately, since the distribution of subsystems (constituencies) ranges over several orbits. The constituencies are grouped according to the number of party choices in each and analyzed as groups. We can also analyze the set of constituencies as a whole, by combining orbits, which gives us an opportunity to compare entropy-turnout patterns for individual orbits with the pattern for the entire system. The results of the curve fitting are in Table 3-4 and Figures 3-5 to 3-6.

The $aH(T)$ curve fitting gives values of the coefficient a that are only 8 to 16% lower than the expected value of log n for each orbit, except the first (Table 3-4). And the coefficients strictly increase from one orbit to the next, as expected. The $aH(T)$ fit is nearly as good as the polynomial fit in most orbits; the polynomial standard errors are only about 10% lower. The magnitude of errors is about the same as that found in the American case, although this magnitude indicates a lower percentage error in the higher Indian orbits because the entropy values are higher there. The parabolic curves are again flatter than the corresponding entropy curves, a pattern observed in the United States to a lesser extent.

The maximum values of the parabolic curves for the third orbit and for the combined orbits 2 to 4 and 2 to 7 are very close to the predicted 50% turnout: at 44% in the third orbit, and at 50 and 47% in the combined orbit cases. The combined orbits display the symmetry in the data particularly well. (See Figure 3-5.) This is much less evident in the parabolic curves for the individual orbits; except for the third orbit, their extrema fall outside the range of the data; the fit curves are closer to linear. In these instances, however, the large error estimates of the coefficients indicate that parabolic curves more like the entropy curve and having maxima nearer 50% turnout would give curve fittings not substantially poorer.

When the data for all subsystems is combined, the pattern of the data becomes visually perceptible and very distinctive. (See Figure 3-6.) The pattern of the data overall is much more apparent than for the individual orbits. The data has a semicircular contour even more pronounced here than in the United States for the combined third party elections. The upper boundary of the Indian data is approximately parabolic or entropy curved in shape, and the Indian constituencies are almost entirely below the upper

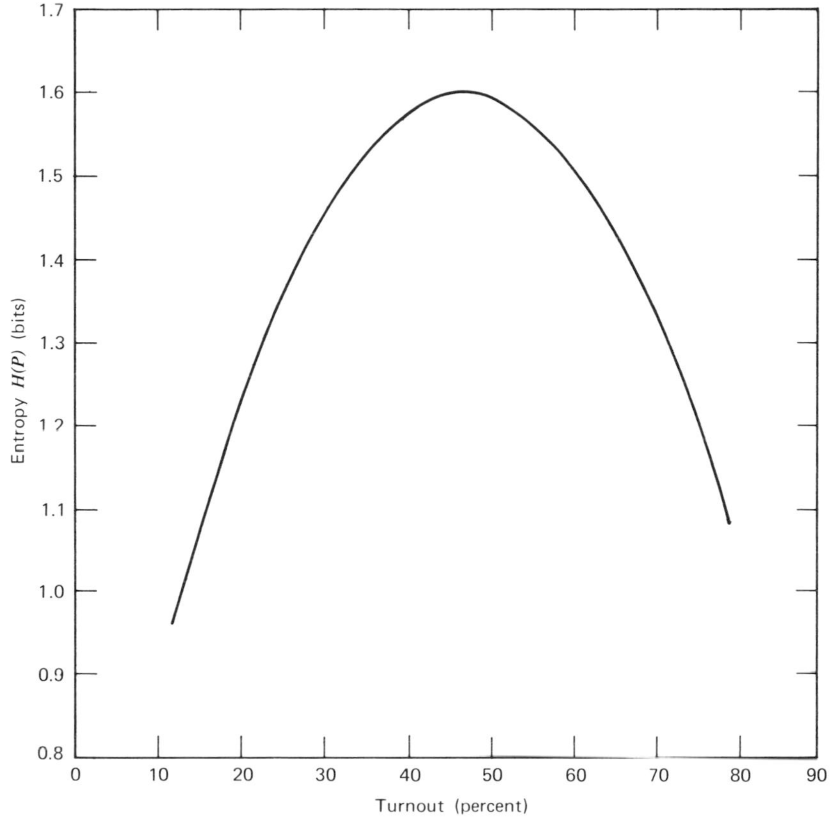

Figure 3-5. Entropy hypothesis test: India, 1962, parabolic curve fitting to the data for combined orbits.

contour of the distribution. In contrast, the lower boundary of the distribution is much flatter.

We can examine the upper contour of the data distribution in two ways. First, we can examine the maximum entropy values in consecutive turnout intervals and compare them with the maximum interval values predicted by the entropy hypothesis; this is done for the combined orbits 2, 3, and 4. The results of this analysis, given in Table 3-5, are as strong for India as for the combined three-party elections in the American case as shown in Table 3-2. (Explained variance is about 80%.) We can also find the maximum values for the entire set of constituencies by selecting the largest (and next largest) entropy values in consecutive groups of 40 constituencies. The constitu-

Table 3-4. India (1962): Entropy Hypothesis Test

Orbit Number (Number of Choices) (n)	Number of Constituencies	Polynomial Fit a_0, a_1, a_2/Errors	Maximum at Percent Turnout	Standard Error (bits)
2	85	.85, .0018, .0000022 .08, .0035, .00037	[a]	.10
3	156	1.20, .010, −.00011 .12, .005, .00005	44.2	.13
4	115	1.81, −.0019, −.000028 .34, .013, .00012	[a]	.18
5	69	2.12, −.0013, −.000058 .50, .020, .00021	[a]	.18
6	22	3.42, −.038, .00026 1.65, .060, .00055	[a]	.30
7	9	sample too small for fit		
2–7	456	.473, .048, −.00051 .197, .008, .00008	47.0	.37
2–4	356	.765, .026, −.00026 .158, .006, .00006	49.7	.29

		log n	$aH(T)$ Fit a/Error	Maximum at 50% turnout	
2	85	1.00	1.01/.02		.14
3	156	1.58	1.46/.01		.15
4	115	2.00	1.69/.02		.20
5	69	2.32	1.94/.02		.20
6	22	2.58	2.20/.07		.31
7	9	2.81	2.42/.03		.10

[a] Maximum or minimum outside range of data; data closer to linear.

encies are rank ordered according to their turnout value and grouped into consecutive units of 40, with the extras at high turnout added to the final group. The results, in Table 3-6, show that with only one exception (the second maximum), the group maxima are either strictly increasing or then strictly decreasing from one group to the next as turnout increases. The absolute maximum falls at 54% turnout, again close to the predicted

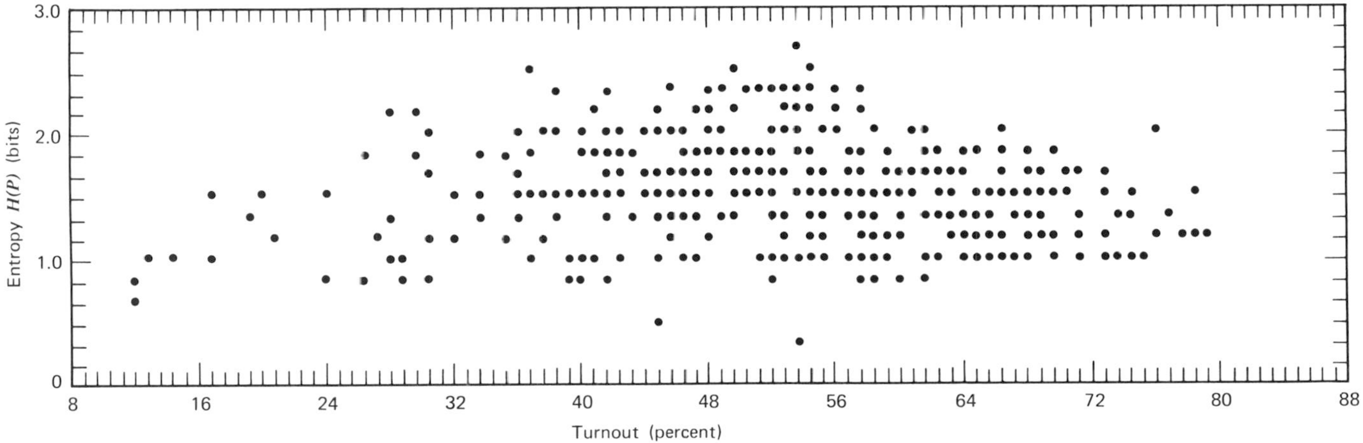

Figure 3-6. Entropy hypothesis test: India, 1962, for combined orbits.

Table 3-5. India: Maximum Entropy for Combined Orbits 2 to 4 by Intervals of Turnout Percent

Turnout Interval	Number of Constituencies	Maximum Observed Entropy $H(P)$ (bits)	Predicted Maximum for Four Choices[a] (bits)
0–10	0	—	—
11–20	8	1.50	1.45
21–30	12	1.78	1.76
31–40	34	1.96	1.94
41–50	76	1.93	2.00
51–60	100	1.87	2.00
61–70	92	1.85	1.94
71–75	27	1.74	1.76
76–80	7	1.55	1.59
81–100	0	—	—

[a] Explained variance is about 80% when the observed values are compared with either the predicted interval maxima or the predicted values of entropy at the turnout values where the observed maxima occur.

entropy curve maximum. Similar results are obtained if other methods of selecting boundary values and smoothing out minor variations are used.

The pattern of contour values and the very strong across-orbit curve fitting results are not directly explained by the entropy hypothesis. What we find is that in a system where there are subsystems distributed over several orbits, the overall across-orbital distributions fit the entropy hypothesis better than the distributions for individual orbits. And in the case of India at least, the predictive accuracy for the across-orbit distributions is nearly as good as it is for the United States in single-orbit elections. The fact that there are subsystems in several orbits over a wide range of entropy and turnout values in India, indicates a great deal of disequilibrium in the system. As we see in Chapter 4, one can infer that there has been a great deal of change in entropy levels in the system owing to factors associated with its economic development. The resulting distribution of subsystems can only bc accounted for when change between orbits is also considered. We return to this problem in the analysis of system dynamics in Chapter 5. We can conclude by saying that the evidence for the existence of entropy-measurable social phenomena is just as strong in India as in the United

States, and that social uncertainty is just as big a factor in electoral outcomes. But we must accept the fact that the entropy hypothesis does not completely describe systems where there are across-orbital distributions of subsystems, as in cases of rapid system change.

Japan. In the case of Japan, as with India, we again test the entropy hypothesis for a political system with a relatively short history as a democratic nation. It has often been said that the democratic institutions of Japan, including a multiparty system and free elections, were simply imposed on or grafted onto older forms of social and political activity. But Japan is a marked contrast to India in its high level of industrialization and socioeconomic development; it is the only instance of a highly developed, non-Western nation. Nevertheless, we see again that length of democratic tradition and level of development have no substantial impact on the existence of entropy-measurable phenomena seen in elections. As with India, however, we must allow for the distribution of subsystems across multiple orbits; Japan presents a case of considerable change in entropy levels and numbers of political parties over successive elections.

Let us analyze two periods of parliamentary elections: from 1920 to 1937, and from 1949 to 1967. There were 15 elections altogether over these years. The principal difference between the elections of the prewar period and the postwar is that suffrage was much restricted in the earlier elections. Prior to

Table 3-6. India: Maximum Entropy in Intervals of 40 Constituencies Ranked by Turnout (Orbits 2–7)

Interval Number	Maximum Entropy (and Next Largest) (bits)	Value of Turnout at Maximum
1	2.20 (2.10)	28%
2	2.43 (2.39)	37%
3	2.32 (2.20)	46%
4	2.36 (2.33)	49%
5	2.44 (2.38)	49%
6	2.61 (2.37)	54%
7	2.47 (2.38)	54%
8	2.15 (2.02)	58%
9	2.06 (2.02)	62%
10	2.04 (1.88)	66%
11	2.01 (1.81)	76%

1943 the suffrage was limited to males 25 years or older, and prior to 1925 there were other more severe restrictions on eligibility. As eligibility expanded from 1920 to 1949 the number of potential voters increased from 3 million in 1920 to over 40 million in the postwar elections. Of course, part of this growth was due to increasing population. The Japanese case presents an opportunity to test the entropy hypothesis under conditions of changing suffrage and voter turnout definition.

Japan is divided into 46 prefectures which are in turn divided into electoral constituencies of about equal population size. The number of electoral districts or constituencies was reduced in the elections after 1927 to about 120, a reduction from about 240 in the several preceding elections.[13] For the prewar elections, political party voting statistics are available for each constituency, but turnout data exists only at the prefectural level. In the postwar elections all data is for prefectures only.[14] Thus in the prewar elections we must use mixed constituency-prefecture data.

Japan is similar to India in that the subsystems are distributed across multiple orbits in most elections. The record of elections over the period of 1920 to 1967 shows that there has been a great deal of change in the political party system, with subsystems continually changing from one orbit to another. These political changes have been associated with fundamental social and economic changes in Japan during this period. (These are discussed in Chapter 4.) As a result, the distribution of subsystems predicted by the entropy hypothesis is best illustrated by across-orbit or combined-orbit data. The dispersion of subsystems is not as severe in Japan as it was in India during 1962, however; Japan shows a greater homogeneity across the system in most elections.

Since several orbits are involved in each election—up to nine in some—we can expect a larger error in the curve fitting than for the single-orbit American cases. There would also be greater error in Japan because of the rapid changes in entropy levels. The high entropy levels in many elections may also lead to greater error through the effects of microscopic estimation errors, which will increase with the number of political parties competing.

The Japanese elections all show the expected entropy-turnout pattern reasonably well, although in the prewar elections the effects of reduced suffrage must be taken into account. For the postwar elections, entropy decreases with increasing turnout; turnout values for the prefectures are consistently above 50%. The results of parabolic curve fitting for elections in 1949 to 1967 are given in Table 3-7 and Figure 3-7. The polynomial curves fit to the data are decreasing, slightly curved lines over the range of the data, and their near linearity again accounts for the high coefficient errors. For the $aH(T)$ fit to the same data, the standard error estimates are the

Table 3-7. Japan: Entropy Hypothesis Test (Combined Orbits)[a]

Election	Polynomial Fit a_0, a_1, a_2/Errors	Standard Error (bits)	$aH(T)$ Fit a/Error	Standard Error (bits)
1949	4.20, −.047, .00027 3.34, .090, .00060	.21	2.80/.06	.32
1952	4.76, −.061, .00032 4.45, .117, .00077	.26	2.68/.07	.33
1953	7.97, −.148, .00093 3.62, .098, .00066	.25	2.76/.07	.35
1955	3.47, −.033, .00019 5.16, .135, .00088	.21	2.69/.06	.32
1958	4.84, −.084, .00050 5.14, .133, .00086	.21	1.76/.05	.25
1960	5.83, −.108, .00066 4.54, .122, .00082	.22	1.87/.05	.25
1963	3.03, −.020, −.000011 3.06, .085, .00058	.21	1.85/.04	.21
1967	20.52, −.460, .0028 6.45, .170, .0011	.28	2.13/.06	.30

[a] There are 46 prefectures for each election.

same or nearly as small as the parabolic errors in the most recent several elections. The poorest $aH(T)$ fittings occur in the early postwar elections, when there was a transient period of disequilibrium due to the effects of the war and occupation. The magnitude of the postwar disequilibrium can be seen in the high entropy levels of the early postwar elections and the subsequent relaxation to lower entropy levels. The coefficient a decreases from 2.80 in 1949 to 1.76 in 1958. In the later elections the subsystems were more successful at maintaining equilibrium levels, as exemplified by the smaller changes in the coefficient a and the smaller errors. (And explained variance increases in the last elections to the 30–45% range.)

The prewar elections of the 1920's and 1930's present an interesting contrast to the postwar elections. Turnout for the prewar elections is computed as the percentage of eligible voters who voted. But the suffrage was greatly restricted during this period. When parabolic curves are fit to the entropy-turnout data for the separate elections, an unexpected result ap-

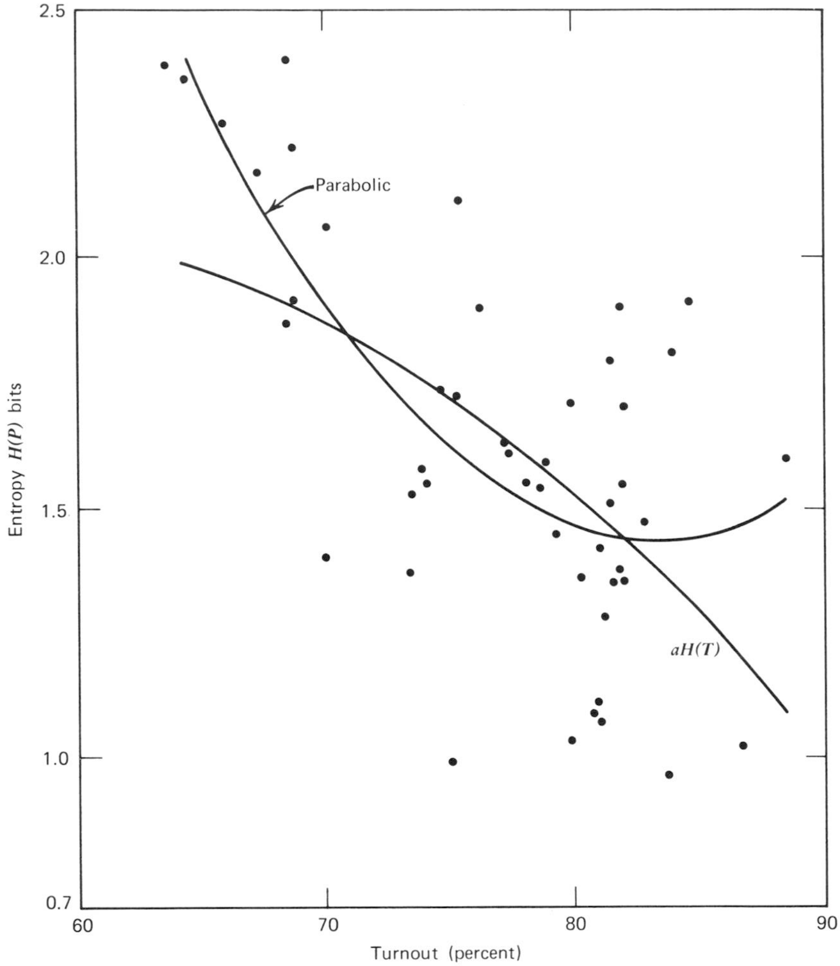

Figure 3-7. Entropy hypothesis test: Japan, 1967, parabolic and $aH(T)$ curve fitting to the data for combined orbits.

pears. Even though most prefectures had turnout values over 50% during the prewar elections, definite parabolic maxima occur in the distributions for several elections. These maxima are located at turnout values greater than 50%, and they progress from high turnout values toward the 50% mark over successive elections. Parabolic curve fitting locates a maximum at 90% turnout in 1924, at 80% in 1928, and at 67% in 1930. The 1920 election is similar to the 1924 election; and the last elections of this period, in 1936 and 1937, begin to resemble the postwar elections more closely. As the error estimates show, in Table 3-8, the parabolic fit is fairly good in both 1924 and 1930. The trend and consistency of these results is well illustrated by parabolic curve fitting to the last five elections of the period aggregated together. They have a maximum at 60% turnout (Table 3-8).

The shift of the entropy data distribution toward symmetry at 50% turnout corresponds to the increase in the number of eligible voters over this period. Suffrage after 1925 was restricted to males over 25 years old, and before 1925 there had been additional restrictions on voter eligibility. If we had computed turnout using the number of males over 21 years instead of the number of eligible voters, the entropy-turnout distributions would be closer to the predicted locations; the maxima would not be shifted so far to the right. It is difficult to estimate the difference in shift that would arise from the two possible turnout calculations, but it seems that if we had used the other method the entropy distributions would be centered more nearly at 50% turnout. Thus it appears that the eligible voters, in arriving at their collective choice of voting or abstention, were already affected by, or taking into account in some way, the fact that a significant number of adult males were being disenfranchised. This latter group apparently was perceived in the society as being equivalent to eligible nonvoters, perhaps because of a general indistinguishability of people in the two groups at the micro level. These remarks do not apply to the effect of women's suffrage, however. We have no evidence that women's suffrage, which came into force after the Second World War, had a significant bearing on electoral distributions. Women's voting has been slightly different from men's in the postwar elec-

Table 3-8. Japan: Shift of Symmetry in the Entropy Hypothesis Test because of Expanding Suffrage (Combined Orbits)

Election	Number of Constituencies	Polynomial Fit a_0, a_1, a_2/Errors	Maximum at Percent Turnout
1924	258	−50.1, 1.12, −.0062 18.5, .41, .0023	91.3
1928	116	3.46, .120, −.00076 5.09, .129, .00082	79.3
1930	118	−1.67, .093, −.00070 2.64, .068, .00044	67.0
combined: 1928, '30, '32, '36, '37	564	.012, .050, −.00042 .751, .021, .00014	60.0

tions, but not enough to alter noticeably the distributions of entropy-turnout values.[15] The introduction of women's suffrage in other political systems has shown a similar lack of effect on popular voting patterns. Thus we see that under certain conditions we can have a valid entropy measurement from a smaller set of potential voters than there are under universal suffrage; this shows again the intensive nature of the entropy measure.

The case of a low entropy system. We can add a fourth case study to emphasize the universality of the measurement principles.[16] Elections are also held in the Soviet Union, and we can use Soviet elections as entropy measurements, just as any other elections.[17] In Soviet elections the turnout rate is always about 99%. The percentage of voters who vote for the official party candidates is about the same; it is essentially a one-party election. Nevertheless, there are people who choose not to vote and voters who do not vote for the party candidate. The entropy measure $H(P)$ can be calculated for the two-choice situation (party candidate or not) and compared with the turnout-abstention entropy $H(T)$. If the probability of one of two choices is 99%, the entropy is less than 0.1 bits. Social entropy in the Soviet Union is close to the absolute zero point. Since the entropy is nearly the same in all regions of the country, the entire system is in an equilibrium; and the entropy has changed very little over successive elections.

Entropy measurement in the Soviet case is a simple exercise, but significant all the same. First, it lends some understanding to the meaning of zero entropy. One would expect to find highly predictable, conformist behavior in virtually all social choice situations. This description apparently fits Soviet society, although it is hard to be precise about it. We can find many comparable examples of low entropy systems. States in the American South following Reconstruction also were essentially one-party systems, and had very low turnout rates. And there are other familiar examples in the catalogue of authoritarian political systems.[18] But just as low entropy systems fall within the scope of our theory, we cannot dichotomize between "free" and "controlled" elections. As for the measurement and analysis of social phenomena here, any difference between democratic and authoritarian systems is one of quantitative degree. This also implies that the dynamics of change between the two kinds of systems, democratic and authoritarian, can be analyzed on a single continuum.

Some question can be raised in the measurement of very low entropy systems as to whether the unitary model still applies. In every political system, people are also members of smaller, local, business and social organizations, which are also social systems. In the cases previously analyzed, we have not distinguished people on the basis of their attachments to local social systems. And the macroscopic patterns of the aggregate national voting behavior indicate that people were interrelated to one another on the broader scale of the subsystem or system, reaching beyond membership in local organizations. It is this extended set of interrelationships that the unitary system model is intended to describe. In a very low entropy system this model may no longer hold, however; people may be interrelated only through membership in local systems that are relatively isolated from one another. We may still be able to make a valid unitary system measurement, but this may be of limited use in understanding social dynamics. Change may have to be studied primarily in terms of group behavior within local systems. These systems may not be well suited to application of the unitary model, which would be the case if the local systems were hierarchical organizations. As discussed in Chapter 4, hierarchical organizations are characterized by the maintenance of entropy differences across strata of the hierarchy, which prevents the trend toward homogeneity necessary for a unitary model.

3.4 Conclusions on System Measurement

The three case studies of the United States, India, and Japan demonstrate the existence of a class of collective, macroscopic, social behavior that is based on at least some aspects of the level of uncertainty in a society. The entropy measure is a valid and unique measure for this class of behavior, although both validity and accuracy depend on how close a system or subsystem is to an equilibrium state. The testing of the entropy hypothesis brings out the intensive nature of the entropy variable as well as the independence of the measurement from the specific content of the events in the event sets. Of the two possible electoral entropy measurements, the political party system related measure $H(P)$ will be the primary measure of entropy for national political systems. $H(T)$ has a subsidiary value when used in conjunction with $H(P)$ to assess the extent of system disequilibrium. The number of events in the $H(P)$ event set is also an important system property, setting the range of possible entropy values for the set. Whether the entropy measure also plays the role of an acrossvariable in social systems analysis remains to be confirmed, and a demonstration of this property is made later when system dynamics and the interaction between systems are studied (Chapter 6). We have not yet resolved two other questions. First, are political event sets, such as elections, equivalent to nonpolitical social event sets for the purpose of entropy measurement? Second, how capable are social systems of maintaining an equilibrium at a given entropy level? These questions will be taken up in the next chapter.

The finding that *elections* are entropy measurements is significant in itself. Elections are the foundation of the democratic political process. They are meant to offer the individual voter a set of alternative choices from which he can select the one most suited to his ends and values. This presumes an individualistic rationality in the voting process, a personal calculus of preferences among alternatives. As the sum of individual voting decisions, the outcome of an election serves to legitimize the winning candidate, party, or policy; it is the collective decision and the will of the people. Voter participation in elections is highly valued and often interpreted as a measure of popular support for the democratic process itself.

All of these basic tenets of democratic theory must be reexamined when elections are seen as entropy measurements. Some voters may indeed operate with individualistic rationales and decide between issues and parties on the merits of their substantive contents. But the outcomes of elections are determined primarily by the collective macroscopic voting patterns seen in the case studies, and this points to a different interpretation of the democratic process.

In the first place, the entropy measure prompts us to view the set of election alternatives as a whole. Although an individual voter has only one choice in the event set, the empirical evidence shows that voters are allocating their votes on the basis of how other voters are likely to vote in order to maintain event probabilities commensurate with the equilibrium entropy level. One might say that voters are voting for the set of events and not for any particular event in the set. In order to achieve the necessary distribution of votes among alternatives, voters are making choices that they would not make in an isolated or noncollective choice situation; that is, they are not making "rational" choices from the perspective of an individualistic logic or personal preference ranking of the alternatives. This interpretation is supported by the equivalence of the $H(P)$ and $H(T)$ measures. Since the entropy $H(P)$ is already determined up to a scale factor ($\log n$) by the turnout and is symmetrical with respect to the voting-abstention probabilities, one would have to say that nonvoters are as much a part of the decision between candidates or parties as are the actual voters. But this would be nonsensical to an individualistic voting logic. Similarly, one can argue that if nonvoters are a part of the election decision making without voting, then the turnout level cannot be used as an indicator of active participation and support for the democratic process. And finally, we must also accommodate the content-free nature of the entropy measurements. The same macroscopic voting patterns hold regardless of the specific electoral issues, parties, candidates, and so forth. We find, for example, that three- and four-party constituencies in India show essentially the same collective voting patterns as do American states in third-party elections. Yet what similarity in election issues could explain the observed correspondence, and what form of individualistic voting rationale would have caused Indian voters to make the same kinds of collective electoral decisions as American voters? We must also conclude that if the voters are not making decisions on the basis of a preference ranking of alternatives and are not discriminating among choices on the basis of content, the results of the election—the winning party or issue—simply cannot be regarded as the popular preference.

The conclusion that many, if not most, voters do not make "rational" decisions in terms of a content-oriented preference ranking of electoral alternatives has also been reached in numerous previous investigations of voting behavior. The most extensive studies of voting behavior have been based on the results of survey interviews.[19] The usual procedure is to draw inferences from aggregated survey responses and known background factors of those interviewed. Typically, these studies relate voting behavior to such factors or "causes" as social class, education, group affiliation, parental attitudes, and so forth. These studies are essentially negative in their explanations of voting behavior; that is, they offer much evidence to contradict traditional theories of rational voting behavior but do not construct a positive, general theory of voting, or indicate that a different rationality may be involved. Even when election outcomes can be correlated, after the fact, to particular attitudes about the candidates or issues, these methods cannot make good quantitative predictions about other elections or about elections in other political systems. Since attitudes and election issues may easily change from one election or system to another, a theory that depends on such considerations will have a very limited applicability and generality. Of course, people will have attitudes about elections, but the question remains whether attitudes cause behavior or whether attitudes are adjusted to rationalize behavior already likely or determined. Furthermore, any survey of the voting motivations of people must presume a theoretical bias that will be reflected in the type of questions people are asked. For example, if a researcher believes that attitudes about candidates will determine electoral outcomes, he will ask potential voters the appropriate questions; and voters will, in turn, give answers about their attitudes that may very well be correlated with election results. In contrast, if one assumes that social uncertainty is a key factor in explaining voting behavior, then different questions will be asked in a survey. One would try then to determine how successful people were in predicting election results, how they thought other people would vote, or how much knowledge they had of others' probable voting behavior, and how it would influence their decision.

Many election studies arrive at conclusions similar to those of the survey-based voting studies but use aggregate election statistics. For instance, some studies show changes in aggregate voting patterns that are correlated with relative sizes of social classes in the population, or with fluctuations in economic conditions, among many other possibilities. Such findings are not necessarily incompatible with the results presented here, and may support these findings if suitably reinterpreted. The problem in aggregate voting studies is that we still do not know how factors such as economic conditions or social class come to affect voting behavior. If we observe that changes in economic conditions cause a change in voting for the political parties, does it mean that people are voting because of immediate economic motives? Or is it that a change in the economy will affect the level of uncertainty in a society through the effects of changed probabilities of unemployment or of changes in income. Our conclusion is that although some people may directly associate their voting act with economic benefit, for most people economic change will only affect their voting behavior if it first affects the perceived social uncertainty. (This problem is considered again in the next chapter when we discuss changes in entropy levels.)

Since many factors in social affairs are related to predictability of behavior, including parental expectations, social class membership, and so forth, we can expect that in any given election or social system some of these factors would be highly correlated with variation in voting behavior. Because these factors would undoubtedly vary from one society to another, or over time in a given society, they cannot be used to give general, universal explanations of voting behavior.

Despite the large literature on empirical voting studies, of both the survey and aggregate statistical variety, these studies are of little use in either confirming or rejecting the entropy hypothesis. They make no specific, quantitative, numerical predictions about electoral behavior, as we have made here with the entropy hypothesis. They seldom try to relate voter turnout to political party voting, and they are often concerned with the fate of particular political parties, not with the system of parties taken together. Furthermore, they are usually restricted to single nations, with national level data only, over short periods of time, during which the total variation in turnout or entropy may be quite small. What can be concluded from this body of literature is that the varying theoretical assumptions (often only implicit) produce noncomparable results.

There is a group of theoretical studies on rationality in decision making that has lead to results more directly comparable with ours than those of the survey or aggregate data varieties. These studies have originated in economic theory, where questions of rationality in social choice are also relevant. Although the economic-based studies make little use of empirical data, they arrive at some conclusions of interest to us here. These studies consider what is implied when one assumes that alternative social choices, such as voting choices, can be ordered in terms of relative preference by members of a population. This ability of people to order alternative choices by preference is, of course, a basic tenet of traditional "rational" voting theory. Under the basic assumption of a preference ordering there are two principal directions in which theoretical arguments have proceeded.

The first branch of theory, originated by Arrow, has to do with the possibility of aggregating individual preference rankings into a single order which would "represent" the society as a whole, as a social choice.[20] Without giving proper credit to the skill of the mathematical reasoning involved, the main conclusion of these studies is that an aggregate or social choice function which would always represent the ranking of individual choices is impossible (Arrow's paradox); this is proven under very general and reasonable conditions of how people in a society could order alternatives. In an electoral context, one would assert that the relative electoral outcomes of a set of multiple alternatives cannot, in general, be "representative" of individual preference rankings. This conclusion interests us here because it is a negative, contradictory conclusion about the possibility of elections being aggregate social choices in the traditional sense.

Another branch of election studies derived from economic theory assumes both a preference ranking of alternatives and a set of probabilities associated with the chance of each alternative's occurrence. A utility function or measure is then constructed to assign an expected gain to an individual's choice according to how much he prefers one alternative to another and what the respective probabilities of occurrence are. That is, each alternative has a numerical utility value, or the set of alternatives has an average value. This function, which was invented by von Neumann and Morgenstern, is a fundamental measure on an interval scale.[21] The utility measure is a content-oriented measure, with respect to the alternatives, since one must be able to rank one alternative over another. One must also make some assumption about how a person acts once he has determined the utility of the alternatives; a frequent assumption is that people act to maximize expected utility. The utility measure offers a rather general way of dealing with alternatives and thus avoids some of the problems cited above when explanations of voting choice rely too heavily on specific attitudes or values pertaining only to a limited social context. But the utility measure has not, in the author's view, fulfilled the prospect of leading to general, context-free explanations of voting behavior.

Some of the difficulties in constructing a scientific theory with the utility measure are again related to the problem of aggregating individual utilities into a group function. Different people may very well have different utility scales and order alternatives in different sequences. The preference ranking does not explicitly incorporate any factor related to social interaction or to the effect of others in assigning the expected gains for an individual's choices. Furthermore, the utility measure does not suggest any necessary correspondence between different sets of alternatives, nor does it help us to understand why there may be a change in the number of alternatives in an event set. We can handle these problems much better with the entropy measure. Because the utility measure is an interval-scale measure, it cannot account for the ratio-scale properties of macroscopic phenomena seen here and subsequently in the text. Still, this does not necessarily mean that a utility theory of voting could not produce interesting results compatible with our assumptions and findings; and there are utility voting studies that have led to "statistically significant" findings. This is possible because a utility measure can be associated with the same event set for which the entropy is defined. We can construct an expected or average utility measure for an event set that is a negative linear transformation of the entropy for the same set.[22] The utility $U = -aH + b$ where H is the entropy and a and b are undetermined constants. (The constant b implies the change from ratio to interval scale.) Thus we might indeed find utility-related voting behavior if we look for it; but this would lead to a superficial and misleading explanation of the underlying (entropy-related) social phenomena and a loss of information about the phenomena due to the interval-scale restriction.

Past studies of elections, whether based on empirical or mathematical research, have had the effect of greatly modifying or rejecting traditional ideas about social choice and elections. But these studies have done this in a negative way, by contradiction and failure, and have not produced an alternative theory of electoral behavior that is general, nomic, predictive, or even quantitative to the extent of an exact science. Only the utility approach goes so far as to generate a fundamental measure on an interval scale. Since all of these studies incorporate the principle that alternative social choices can be ordered according to personal preferences, one is led to conclude that this assumption is of little relevance to actual behavior in a social choice context. Once we abandon this idea, it becomes very natural to look for a measure such as entropy that does not rely upon the specific content of events or their relative preference. The research findings presented here certainly support this conclusion.

The rationalistic voting theorists have raised the argument that people do not have sufficient knowledge, education, and so forth, to make rational choices. There may be the added presumption that voters *should* behave rationally, or would, if they had adequate knowledge upon which to make their decisions. From an entropy interpretation of elections, this argument must also be rejected. Taking elections as entropy measurements and viewing the accuracy of results of the entropy hypothesis test, one must conclude that voters "know" what they are doing, in some sense, and are indeed making rational decisions informed by the level of uncertainty in their societies. Rationality here should be expressed as a collective rationality, not an individualistic rationality, and should be judged in terms of fixing the entropy level of an equilibrium state. Whether voters should disregard their collective rationality and vote on the basis of a personal logic is another question. But this would require large numbers of people to act in ways apparently contradictory to their natural social tendencies, an unlikely prospect in any case—if not a presumptious expectation.

These remarks should not be construed to mean that electoral outcomes or election winners are completely predetermined by the entropy level of the equilibrium state. If more than two choices are possible, the event probabilities can vary somewhat and yield the same entropy level. Or the number of events in the event set may change, causing a redistribution of votes. There will also be fluctuations and regional variations in entropy and turnout levels due to random or local conditions, so that in equilibrium states where event probabilities are nearly equal, the chances for different electoral outcomes are especially great. Where contesting political parties have nearly the same shares of the vote, it is also possible that relatively small numbers of voters acting out of individualistic rationales, economic motives, or other idiosyncratic factors, might swing the election from one party to another. If the variation in entropy is small, however, it would be extremely difficult to prove convincingly what had affected the balance of the parties at the election. The actions a government takes (or fails to take) may also affect future electoral outcomes by fundamentally altering the social structure so that the system moves to a new entropy level. Yet in all these possibilities there does not seem to be any way in which we can put individualistic rationality back into voting theory where it would explain voting behavior to an observably significant extent (of greater magnitude than "errors" in this theory), so long as elections arise from the same underlying social processes.

At first glance it seems conceivable that political parties could switch event probabilities from one election to the next, resulting in a different electoral outcome but leaving the system entropy level unchanged. This would imply a limited chance for an individual or social preference ranking of political parties based on content or election issues. This would not be possible if the system population maintains the event probabilities continuously over time, between elections. Instantaneous yet synchronized party switching by large numbers of people seems most unlikely. But any gradual shift of the probabilities of events would change the system entropy level, and so a switching of event probabilities would not be possible in an equilibrium state. For the links between probabilities and events to be broken, it would be necessary that the event-probability pairings be temporarily "forgotten" by a large part of the population. If elections are held fairly often in a country, this would be unlikely to happen. Except for political systems where event probabilities are close to being equal (as in the United States), reorderings of party voting percentages are infrequent in political history. In Japan and India, for example, the same political parties have dominated virtually every election, and little change has taken place in the ordering of parties by their relative shares of the vote.

It may seem strange that the measure of a social system would be an election, since an election is itself a social event and intimately a part of the ongoing social and political processes in the system. In a physical system we usually think of a measuring instrument as separate or separable from the system it would be measuring. And at least in classical physics one does not think of the measurement as affecting the fundamental nature of the system. Yet a national election certainly is a major factor in the definition and constitution of a national political system. One may even doubt whether a national political system would be able to continue its existence without national elections. An election may serve to establish interrelationships among people across a system that would not otherwise exist; in effect, the election may be establishing the system it would be a measurement of. Other nonpolitical social choice situations can also be seen as system defining. We could say that if it were not for social choices or event sets, people would not know exactly what the structure of their society was; or in the extreme, there would be no structure.

At the micro level the occurrence of an event set such as an election forces people to identify with or to be identified with specific alternatives of the event set. Each arrangement of the identifications of specific people with specific events could be called a micro state. Before an event set actually occurs, no determinate specification of the micro state of a system is possible; there exist only probabilities associated with the identification of people to events. Thus the occurrence of the event set, which is to say the measurement of the system, puts the system into a specific micro state. The measurement of the system forces to occur a particular one of the many possible, macroscopically equivalent, arrangements of people and events.

This picture of social entropy measurement as an interaction between the system and the measurement process is not at all peculiar to social systems. A very similar measurement problem arises in quantum physics when micro-level phenomena, such as atomic phenomena, are studied by means of macroscopic measuring devices. (All of our physical measuring devices are macroscopic.) We cannot make measurements of physical systems at the atomic level without affecting the state of the system. The effect of the measurement on the system is to force the system into a particular micro state, which may then continue to exist for some brief duration. Until an observation or measurement is made of the system, micro states can only be described by probability distributions. In the subjectivist interpretation of quantum theory one says that specific micro states do not even exist until an observation is made.[23] Our purpose here is not to discuss quantum physics but to point out the immense subtleties of the measurement process when a statistical system is involved, and when we try to know or predict the state or nature of the system at the micro level with our macroscopic observables. It is no longer possible to think of the system as separate from the means we use to observe it, and the system is no longer comprehensible in itself as an entity separate from the measurement process.

CHAPTER FOUR

Measurement Equivalence and Range

4-1. Equivalence of Social and Political Entropy

Until now we have relied exclusively on elections as entropy measurements. The use of elections was fortuitous, however. Nothing in the derivation of the entropy measure suggests that only elections could serve as entropy measurements. The content-free nature of the entropy measure implies that entropy measurement should not be dependent on political events. Therefore we must conclude from our theoretical assumptions that if other means for measuring social entropy levels in national political systems had been available, they would have yielded the same results. We would expect to find the same quantitative degree of conformity or consensus in other areas of social choice as we found for electoral choices. But there are practical difficulties in confirming this hypothesis. Methods of measuring a social entropy level other than elections are not easy to apply; no data exists on social choices in general that approaches elections in quantity or convenience. Furthermore, the electoral choices are themselves part of the system-defining process in a social system, and it is questionable whether any other social choice situation would encompass the complete set of system interrelationships induced by the occurrence of elections in national political systems. We would expect nonelectoral social choice situations to be more localized in scope within the system and primarily restricted to subsystems. Despite these experimental and theoretical handicaps, it is still possible to find substantial evidence that political entropy measurements are highly representative of other social choice situations.

Another method that we could use, in principle, to measure social entropy is to measure how successful members of the system are at predicting future social events.[1] This method is not as feasible as the use of elections, but it is a heuristic aid in judging the relative entropy levels of different social situations or social systems.

Among social settings that might have contrasting entropy levels are those one might classify as rural or urban. The rural or urban distinction is commonplace in both popular and scientific usage. In virtually all parts of the world, notice is given to the contrary styles of life in rural and urban areas. City life is characterized as offering greater diversity, greater occupational variety, heterogeneous social groups, and so forth. Rural life, on the other hand, we often regard as conservative, uneventful, and unvarying. Rural society is depicted as static and traditional, or in other words, is highly predictable. The effect of urbanization in modernizing countries is often (but not always) to break down traditional behavior patterns. If we were to try to predict the behavior of a randomly chosen rural person in comparison with that of an urban resident, it would seem easier to predict behavior in the rural case. The rural to urban dimension should be a progression of increasing entropy in many phases of social life. We can formulate this hypothesis as an empirical test and examine whether political entropy levels increase with the degree of urbanization within systems. This allows an indirect test of the equivalence of political and nonpolitical entropy measurements.

To test the hypothesis that entropy increases with urbanization we can use again the Japanese elections of the postwar period, which were included in the entropy hypothesis test (Section 3-3). Census data on urbanization in Japan is available and gives the percentage of each prefecture's population residing in urban areas. This measure of urbanization characterizes the prefecture as a whole, in accord with a unitary model of the system. Census data is available only at five-year intervals, however, so that election data must be matched with the corresponding time of the census data. We can rank order the 46 prefectures according to the urban population in each, from the least urban to the most urban and calculate the entropy $H(P)$ and turnout values for elections close in time to the census data. We have done this for elections from 1949 to 1967 and for the 1955 and 1965 censuses. Entropy and turnout values are plotted separately against urbanization values by prefecture and election; a second degree ploynomial curve (a parabola) is then fitted to the data. (Since turnout is always over 50% in these elections, we can plot turnout instead of $H(T)$; there is no problem with double values.) The polynomial curve gives entropy or turnout as a function of prefecture urbanization percentage.

The results of the curve fitting are summarized in Tables 4-1 and 4-2. Note also Figures 4-1 and 4-2. Both polynomial curves have the expected shape and direction over most of the range of the data in all elections: turnout strongly decreasing, and $H(P)$ strongly increasing, with increasing urbanization. The increase in entropy from low urbanization to high urbanization is as much as 1 bit in the later elections. Essentially the same pattern is found for all eight elections, regardless of the census year of the

Table 4-1. Japan: Entropy $H(P)$ as a Parabolic Function of Prefecture Urbanization (Percentage)

Election	Census Year	Polynomial Fit a_0, a_1, a_2/Errors	Standard Error (bits)	Minimum at Percent Urbanization
1949	1955	2.21, .00069, .000017 .16, .01003, .000126	.21	−20.6
1952	1955	1.93, −.0016, .00010 .20, .0121, .00015	.26	8.3
1953	1955	2.15, −.0052, .00015 .19, .0115, .00014	.24	17.3
1955	1955	2.16, −.0100, .00018 .16, .0097, .00012	.20	28.2
1958	1955	1.35, −.0070, .00014 .16, .0095, .00012	.20	24.4
1960	1965	2.01, −.022, .00021 .63, .019, .00014	.21	52.8
1963	1965	1.83, −.020, .00022 .64, .020, .00014	.21	44.4
1967	1965	1.73, −.020, .00029 .80, .024, .00018	.27	34.7

urbanization data. Although the polynomial curves are close to linear over most of the data, they do show slight bends and have extrema at the low urbanization end of the scale.

The appearance of minima for all the $H(P)$ curves and maxima for all the turnout curves (Tables 4-1, 4-2) is an interesting finding. It means that among prefectures having very low urbanization the initial effect of increasing urbanization is to decrease the local entropy level; this happens at urbanization percentages of 40 to 50% for the 1965 census. Apparently, the first stages in the urbanization-modernization process temporarily increase the homogeneity and consensus at the local level, perhaps by overriding traditional particularisms such as kinship-based power structures. But in the long trend, the effects of urbanization and the closely allied forces of industrialization and economic development greatly increase the entropy levels.

The distribution of prefectures along the polynomial curves shifts over time so that they "move" along the curve toward increasing urbanization. this is particularly well shown by the *H*(*P*) curves in the last three elections, 1960, 1963, and 1967. The minima shift toward decreasing urbanization over this period (Table 4-1). We can assume that urbanization had continued to increase over this period also, but we must use the same urbanization value for each prefecture in each election over this period. Thus the distribution of the prefectures does not shift toward increasing urbanization, as it would have if we had used the actual but unknown urbanization values. Instead, the fit curve shifts the opposite direction, to the left; the minima shift from 53 to 44 to 35% urbanization. In effect, the election data alone has already taken into account the changing urbanization level over this time. This effect is less evident in the earlier elections owing to the much greater disequilibrium in the system as a whole. The turnout data (Table 4-2) shows a similar shifting of maxima. Overall, the turnout-urbanization curve fitting seems more accurate than the entropy-urbanization, indicating perhaps that turnout values and *H*(*T*) are more nearly equivalent to

Table 4-2. Japan: Turnout as a Parabolic Function of Prefecture Urbanization

Election	Census Year	Polynomial Fit a_0, a_1, a_2/Errors	Standard Error (Turnout %)	Maximum at Percent Urbanization
1949	1955	72.5, .30, −.0056 4.6, .28, .0036	5.95	26.6
1952	1955	77.7, .31, −.0075 3.0, .19, .0023	3.92	20.9
1953	1955	79.0, .11, −.0055 3.4, .21, .0026	4.36	10.3
1955	1955	80.7, .0079, −.0032 3.3, .2036, .0026	4.28	1.25
1958	1955	79.6, .15, −.0048 3.4, .21, .0026	4.38	15.7
1960	1965	55.2, .90, −.0088 13.4, .41, .0030	4.49	51.4
1963	1965	58.8, .81, −.0086 14.4, .44, .0032	4.82	46.8
1967	1965	64.4, .64, −.0068 13.5, .41, .0030	4.50	47.2

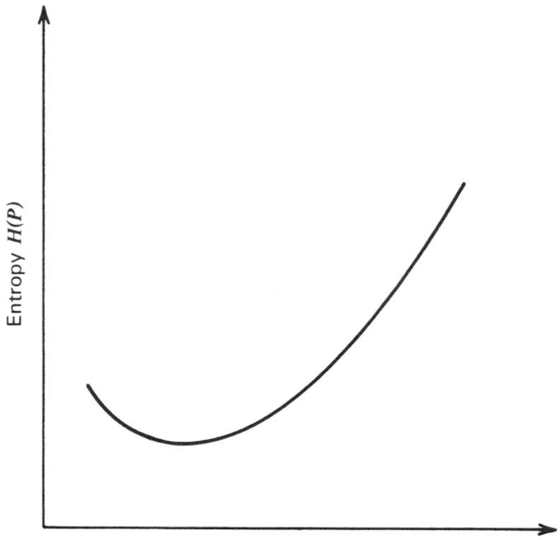

Figure 4-1. Typical entropy-urbanization curve.

local entropy levels and less affected by across-system interaction than $H(P)$ values. Especially in the last elections of this period, the entropy and turnout curves are very nearly the inverse of one another, having maxima and minima at almost the same urbanization levels. This correspondence simply reaffirms the strength of the entropy hypothesis.[2]

It is important to note that the entropy-urbanization pattern holds for all eight elections. That is, it persists despite the great fluctuations in system entropy levels in the early postwar elections. (Compare Table 3-7.) Thus one pattern of change is superimposed upon another: the transient effects of the war and occupation on top of the rural to urban trend. The war-related disequilibrium was system wide, increasing the entropy levels in all prefectures regardless of their degree of urbanization. These two sources of change together have been the most important factors affecting system entropy levels and change in the number of political parties.

We can contrast the entropy-urbanization pattern in Japan with that of India. If we analyze entropy-urbanization data for India, using the 1962 election and the 1960 census, we find that only the most urbanized Indian constituencies (about 10-20% of the total) share the Japanese pattern.[3] In highly urban Indian contituencies there is decreasing turnout (over 50%), an increasing number of political parties, and increasing entropy as the urbanization level increases. For less urban constituencies no consistent pattern emerges. However, in comparing the range and level of urbanization in Japan with India one finds that only the most urban Indian constituencies are as urbanized as any Japanese prefecture in 1965. Virtually all of India would fall in the rural category by Japanese standards, or by almost any standard. And in Japan, urbanization is strongly associated with industrialization and other aspects of economic modernization; this is much less true of urbanization in India. Thus the development of urban centers without accompanying economic development may not be sufficient to alter traditional, rural-oriented, social behavior patterns.

Despite its low level of urbanization and economic development, India demonstrates that a substantial change in entropy can result from other causes of social change. We have found that voter turnout in Indian constituencies in the 1962 election increases rapidly and consistently with the level of literacy in the constituencies.[4] This is true at least up to the point where turnout begins to decline with high urbanization. As the voter turnout increases from below 50% to above 50%, entropy $H(P)$ first increases with turnout and literacy, then it decreases. The average net change in $H(P)$ is almost 60%, with entropy ranging from less than 1.0 bits to nearly 1.6 bits and then decreasing as much again. Entropy reaches a maximum at an intermediate level of constituency literacy, about 20 to 25%. The highest entropy levels attained by constituencies are over 2.0 bits. (Since turnout increases with literacy, the resulting change in $H(P)$ is approximately that found in testing the entropy hypothesis for combined orbit data; one can

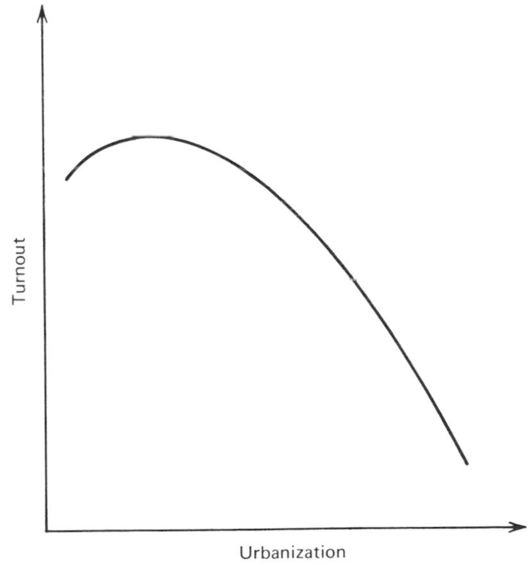

Figure 4-2. Typical turnout-urbanization curve.

think of literacy as being on the horizontal axis instead of turnout. See Table 3-4 and Figures 3-5 and 3-6.)

This effect can be simply explained. The change in a traditional society from a predominantly illiterate population to a predominantly literate one is profound.[5] A change in literacy also implies changes in education, communication, and occupational possibilities, among other consequences. As the location of the entropy maximum indicates, a peak of social uncertainty is reached somewhere between low and high literacy, apparently when the society is most evenly divided between its traditional preliterate customs and semimodern activities. This is the point where there would be the greatest uncertainty about individual life styles and the greatest mixture, or perhaps confusion, of old and new ways. Whatever the exact nature of the changes induced by literacy and related factors, the entropy measure does capture this fundamental social change and describe it quantitatively. (Japan is uniformly and highly literate and cannot be compared with India in this regard.)

The studies of India and Japan show that entropy levels in a system can change as a result of one or more causes. In contrast, the United States and the Soviet Union are examples of systems that have maintained reasonably constant entropy levels over long periods of time. Only the American South has shown a large change in entropy levels, increasing from the near zero levels of the post-Reconstruction period. According to our proposed social theory, the state of a system is an equilibrium condition that does not change except as the result of environmental influences on the system. Thus in the cases of Japan and India we must determine whether the observed changes can reasonably be ascribed to exogenous forces. We can adopt a fairly general interpretation of the environment of a social system: it includes whatever is physically beyond the spatial boundaries of the system besides whatever phenomena are in principle beyond the range of the measurement variables, even if for the same set of people. Subnational social systems, such as organizations, should probably be considered as environmental for now, although the relation between these systems and a national system is unknown. The importance of measurement range is illustrated by physical systems. One can, for example, analyze a mechanical system separately from a thermodynamic system although both may be in reference to the same set of physical objects. Many of the changes that occur in social systems stem from economic conditions and from decisions people make using economic system variables; these are exogenous forces, as we have defined them. Changes in urbanization and industrialization, and even literacy, ultimately originate largely in the economic systems of the nations. Thus there is good reason to regard the origins of entropy change in Japan and India as externally induced; they are not "spontaneous" changes in entropy-measurable phenomena.

A general criterion that might be used in determining whether a force causing an entropy change was exogenous would be to estimate whether a change in entropy levels or in the categorization of social events into event sets could alter or remove the source of change. In the case of urbanization one might ask whether an increase or decrease in the level of conformity or consensus in the society would substantially alter the rate or reasons of people moving to cities, or change the patterns of industrial employment in cities. This is unlikely, since the reasons would usually be economic. The example of the Soviet Union shows that a considerable amount of urbanization can take place without a change in entropy levels; and a low entropy level will not inhibit urbanization. Similarly, the effects of economic depression, war, famine, or any of the many accidental happenings in life are usually beyond the control of any collective categorization or perception of social events that a population might accomplish. On the other hand, social events that can be modified by the pressures of social conformity, such as "neurotic" or criminal behavior in certain instances, are endogenous social phenomena. There may also be complex interactions between various separate social, economic, and perhaps technological or physical systems. These systems could be coupled to one another, reciprocally affecting one another in ways extremely difficult to analyze.

This discussion of social equilibrium maintenance is to some degree unsatisfactory, however, because we have no independent quantitative measure of the capacity of a social system to resist change in its equilibrium state. We can observe that a system has changed for some definite reason, but there is no way to determine experimentally whether one system would have been less affected than another by a certain "quantity" of exogenous force. If a direct quantitative correspondence between economic and entropy social systems can be found, that is, an energy concept, it will be possible to predict entropy changes with greater accuracy. The rate at which a force is applied to a system also appears to be crucial. The fact that entropy has attained much higher levels in Japan than in the United States seems to be particularly the result of the much more rapid economic modernization in Japan.

A possible factor in the ability of a system to maintain an equilibrium at a given entropy level may be the number of different event sets existing in the society. To change the entropy level permanently, event probabilities in each set would have to be changed. But if the social processes associated with different event sets are semi-independent of each other, as for the $H(P)$ and $H(T)$ sets, it would seem more difficult for a population to change a greater number of event sets. A temporary change in one event set could be observed and acted against by people's using unaffected event sets as standards of comparison for the equilibrium level. Although the correct explanation of equilibrium maintenance remains a problem in the development of a social theory, in practice one can usually find good explanations for system entropy change. Even fairly small changes in system entropy usually involve (macroscopically) observable social processes having a profound effect on many aspects of social and economic affairs. But determining what are the micro-level effects of the processes is a much more difficult task.

We can find additional examples of the equivalence between social and political entropy levels. Soares and deNoronha have made an extensive analysis of urbanization in Brazil using an entropy-like measure calculated from the vote for political parties.[6] The authors base their analysis on urban municipal elections (for the *Camera dos Vereadores*) in 14 Brazilian states during 1954 and 1955. They have classified urban areas into three categories, depending on whether the population is (1) less than 10,000; (2) 10,000 to 50,000; or (3) over 50,000. The authors report that in almost every instance entropy increases with urbanization in each state. (This happens in 26 of the 28 possible cases.) They also show that the number of parties increases as urbanization increases over time. (This is also true of Japan and India for the most part.) The authors emphasize that the rise in entropy, in our terms, is the result of increasing *social* differentiation (as among classes) associated with urbanization and industrialization, which proceeded rapidly in Brazil during the 1950's. It can be added that voter turnout computed from the number of persons old enough to vote also increased over this period from a very low initial level (less than 50%). Suffrage was restricted to literate adults and the literacy rate grew rapidly with the improving economic conditions, much as it did in India.

Another example of the strong effect of community consensus and homogeneity on entropy levels is given indirectly by Butler and Stokes in their analysis of British parliamentary elections.[7] They show that whether a person votes for the Labor or Conservative parties is conditional on the composition of his local constituency population. Although a working-class voter might be expected to vote for the Labor party (out of class interests or tradition) and a middle-class voter more likely to vote for the Conservatives, these probabilities are actually a function of the proportional mixture of the two classes in a constituency. The more that one class is in the majority, the more likely are residents of the *other* class to vote as the majority class votes.

A very interesting research study of community consensus at the micro level has been done by Milgram.[8] He demonstrates the strong tendency of an individual to agree with a majority view even when he knows it is wrong. Milgram finds that Norwegian test subjects were consistently more conformist than French subjects when faced with this conflicting choice situation, regardless of the content of the choice or its supposed importance. When a person thought that his decision would be known or become known to the majority, he was even more likely to conform with the majority view. The author also compares the differences in conformity between Norwegian and French subjects with similar differences in the conformity levels of the two nations, as manifested in diverse aspects of social activity. Milgram's study reinforces the conclusions reached here from macroscopic observations only. It also indicates that elections may serve to standardize entropy as a measure of group conformity, since under a secret ballot system what is known about the voting choices of people is the same for all systems. But the equivalence of $H(T)$ and $H(P)$ shows that this may not be a particularly significant factor since the likelihood of public knowledge is different in each case. Milgram's finding that conformity *differences* hold up in a variety of experiments, even if the levels of conformity change for the two groups of test subjects, points to the possibility of using entropy differences for analyzing the interaction between groups of people or social subsystems.

Without directly measuring social entropy in nonelectoral choice or event situations, we have substantial evidence that political or electoral entropy levels are equivalent to the nonpolitical social entropy levels for the same system. Thus we have no firm basis in measurement for distinguishing nonpolitical social systems from political systems. We could view political events that are directly related to voting participation or political party voting as epiphenomenal, derivative of the underlying social structure. But "equivalence" seems a better description of the connection than "epiphenomenon."

The general analytic problem in social analysis and measurement is to determine what event sets exist in a society and whether they are equivalent to one another. Possibly, a social system may have classes of event sets that are completely independent of each other. Then we would still apply the same methods of analysis, but each class of event sets would have to be measured separately. In determining the event sets that exist in a system and the degree of partial equilibrium with respect to other sets, one always must be careful to determine exactly which group of people is involved in each event set, or what size subsystem matches the range of collective decision making for a given event set.

4-2. *Social Uncertainty*

The discussion of measurement equivalence gives a clearer picture of the range of entropy measurement and of the social phenomena that can properly be analyzed by the ensuing social theory. In this section we continue the theme, summarizing the properties of entropy-measurable social phenomena and further investigating the range of explanation implied by the measurement variables.

It is a far reach from having a mathematical formula for the entropy measure, borrowed as it was from information theory, to understanding how and why this particular mathematical form should be used to interpret social phenomena. The electoral phenomena observed in testing the entropy hypothesis demonstrate a class of social behavior that can be analyzed with the entropy measure. But knowing that such a class exists does not end the problem. We must still determine how much of the activity in a society we can ultimately explain through entropy measurement. As nearly as we can judge from available evidence, entropy measurement can be applied to a much broader class of social activity than just elections or electoral choices. We find a close correspondence or equivalence between the degree of social uncertainty in electoral and nonelectoral situations. Even if people in a society were able to dichotomize between two separate choice situations and operate in each independently of the other, it appears that entropy measurement would still apply to each set of choices. In a variety of social contexts where conformity, consensus, heterogeneity, or predictability of events are concerned, entropy is the right measure to quantify the situation. To understand why this is so requires a better appreciation of how event sets come into being and how social events are perceived at the micro level, that is, by persons in the society.

Let us try to infer what must happen at the micro level for the observed macroscopic patterns to appear. When we compute the macroscopic entropy level of a system, we are duplicating the same kind of knowledge about the system that is available to its members at the micro level. By observing the relative frequencies of alternative events or the percentages of people who can be identified with alternative social categories, anyone will have the necessary knowledge of the system to make an entropy calculation. The entropy calculation would be more localized in the system than a system-wide measurement, of course; and it would be subject to possible sampling errors. We can also assume that in a social system with a large number of people it would be impossible for anyone to have a detailed knowledge of the behavior of many specific individuals. But a person could know the probabilities of events, or the percentages of people in categories or groups, without having to keep track of which individual was associated with which event or group or how many people were involved altogether.

This amount of knowledge would also be potentially available to someone moving about in the society and coming into contact with unfamiliar persons outside his immediate circle of acquaintances. If a person does not specifically know the people he is dealing with, the most information he can easily acquire about them is an estimation of the probabilities of their observable actions. Thus the most information generally or always available to people in a society is a knowledge of probabilities or frequencies of occurrence of alternative events. People can estimate these probabilities merely by observing the actions of other people. But then if people are acting or making choices on the basis of this probabilistic or statistical knowledge of their society, it will be possible to analyze their behavior with the entropy measure. As we have seen in the derivation of the entropy measure, it is uniquely suited to statistically perceived phenomena (assuming that the intuitive entropy axioms also hold). No other quantification of average uncertainty for event sets is possible that is not equivalent to the entropy measure.

We can conclude that entropy-measurable phenomena are those resulting from the actions individuals take on the basis of their own (nonnumerical) estimates of the social uncertainty or entropy of their society. It is not clear what the underlying psychological processes are, but we can expect to find these phenomena in large, complex societies simply because of natural limitations on human capability to know what is going on and what other people are doing.

If people are restricted to estimating probabilities of alternative events, it is still not quite apparent why there should be categories of social events or event sets. In other words, why are there socially agreed upon categories such as "Republican" and "Democrat"? The reason seems to be that a collective categorization of events is necessary to keep social uncertainty levels within reasonable bounds. Consider, for example, a hypothetical society where any individual could publicly introduce a new category of behavior as an alternative to existing categories. If this were to happen frequently, the total number of categories a person would have to keep in mind in observing the behavior of others would multiply enormously, and the probability of occurrence of any event would correspondingly decrease. As the entropy function shows, an increasing number of low probability events would lead to an increase in entropy levels, even if any one person only had to deal with a limited number of other people and their alternatives.

Psychologists have found that the limit on entropy capacity for an individual is only about 3 bits.[9] This corresponds to the ability of a person to discriminate equally well among at most eight categories for a single observable quantity or dimension at one time. Other experiments have shown that if group agreement is required in classifying an observation by category, the group entropy is similarly limited and perhaps somewhat lower than for individuals.[10] (In comparison with these psychological limits of about 3 bits, the highest entropy level attained by any subsystem in the previous case studies was about 2.6 bits, observed in India and Japan (1949).

(See Figure 3-6.) Thus if a population does not strongly control the categorization of social events, the social entropy level will quickly increase and exceed individual capacity. Such an uncertainty filled society would become incomprehensible to its members and, in effect, would no longer be a society as we would recognize one. The events of a social event set must therefore be few in number, and some events must have fairly high probabilities to keep the entropy level low. This means that individuals must perceive events according to definite, widely agreed upon social categories and must act in ways that others will be able to identify as recognized and expected types of events. Note also that probabilities are not inherent in actions themselves but arise in their perceptual categorization. Efforts by a population to maintain the predictability necessary for a society will appear as social consensus or the pressures of conformity. In using terms such as conformity, however, one must also keep in mind whether a fixed two-event set is referred to, or whether there is the possibility for change in the number of events in the set; a different amount of "conformity" may exist on each scale, as seen by the relation of $H(T)$ to $H(P)$.

As long as randomness and uncertainty about human behavior exist in societies, people will have a social-psychological need to construct low-entropy event sets. Thus it is important to realize that social structure, the catergorical constraints on social behavior, the recognized patterns of interaction between people across a society, ultimately derive from human variability and human limitations on perceiving and knowing.

As imperfect as our understanding of microscopic social processes may be, we have good reason to believe that there is a correspondence between macroscopic entropy measurement and the perceptual and cognitive processes of individuals. This is quite a remarkable correspondence. It is by no means common to other scientific theories that the mathematical forms used in describing and predicting system events reveal any deeper understanding of the essential nature of the phenomena. In classical mechanics, for example, no more complete explanation of physical phenomena is possible than that given by the differential equations of motion in a system. But the equations themselves give no hint why they may be inevitably the result of deeper properties of the physical world and our perception of them. Only in more recently developed theories of physics, such as statistical mechanics or relativity theory, do we reach an understanding of phenomena where the physical laws are themselves seen to be necessary outcomes of intrinsic system properties (such as randomness) and our observation or measurement of the system.[11] Yet such completeness in explanation should be a goal of any scientific theory. As Eddington writes in his classic text on relativity theory, "The building process of the mathematical theory must keep step with that process by which the mind of the percipient endows with vivid qualities certain selected structural properties of the world."[12] The social theory we can construct through entropy measurement is uniquely appropriate to, and offers very complete explanations for, a definite class of social phenomena. This is true not just because we can mathematically quantify and predict social behavior, but because people themselves act and perceive events in a certain way that makes a specific mathematical form necessary to an explanation of their collective behavior.

Social Uncertainty in Organizations. The study of social uncertainty can be extended to organizations, which include business organizations, government bureaucracies, special interest associations, and so on. The additional factor we must look at in organizations is hierarchy. We can conceive of an organization as a number of strata of people arranged in a hierarchical structure. Within any single stratum we can view the people as indistinguishable or interchangeable, and their set of interrelationships will probably be uniform enough to let us use a unitary system model to explain within stratum behavior. But from one level of an organization to another people must be distinguished by their relative positions in the hierarchy. A directional component in the hierarchical structure causes asymmetrical relationships across the strata. Organizations are usually constructed so that people in higher levels have the ability or power to modify the behavior of people in lower levels; the reverse is not usually possible, although it may happen.

We can represent the behavior of people at each level of organization in probabilistic terms. There is a set of actions each person can take according to his role in the organization and place in the hierarchy. Although a person's activities may be highly predictable in an organization, everyone usually has some discretion. Because of the hierarchical, usually downward, flow of communications in an organization, we will be able to predict what is normally going to happen at a lower level if we know what order or instruction has been promulgated at a higher level. In probabilistic terms this means that probabilities at lower strata are conditional upon probabilities of events at higher strata. Of course, people often have some leeway in how they carry out management directives, which implies that lower level behavior cannot be completely determined from observation of upper level behavior. The amount of independence, or conversely the amount of control, between layers of the hierarchy is an important structural characteristic of any organization. The total amount of freedom of action, at any level of the organization, regardless of its control, is also an important structural property. These two structural properties can be analyzed with the entropy measure or the related functions which make use of conditional probabilities. (See Section 2-2.) Other organizational properties fitting into the same information theory framework are the amount and rate of communication between organizational strata; we can measure communication flow with the throughvariables of the two-variable measurement pattern proposed for social systems. All these organizational properties are macroscopic if organizational strata are taken as wholes.

Regardless of what the function of an organization is intended to be, a substantial part of the internal activity of an organization results from its structural properties. The overall dynamics of an organization—and especially the relationships between hierarchical levels—are greatly determined by the actions people take in response to the amount of uncertainty or freedom (entropy) in their roles and its dependence on other people. The efforts people make to increase or maintain their freedom of action, often in response to the efforts of others to attain a greater control over it, lead to patterns of conflict and change in the organization. As often happens, concern with issues of uncertainty and its control may take precedence over the functional purpose of the organization. (A labor strike is an extreme example of this). Dysfunctional patterns may arise and inhibit the intended functioning or make purposeful change and improvement in organizational efficiency impossible; organizational goals may be thwarted by structural behavior patterns. The satisfaction that people take in their organizational roles may also depend to a large extent on structural properties such as freedom of action.

Perhaps the only thorough analysis of the effects of uncertainty on organizational activity is by Crozier.[13] His analysis is quite extensive, and we will only summarize a few of his observations here. Although Crozier does not use the entropy measure or quantitative analysis, his line of argument fits well in the framework of analysis sketched immediately above. He finds that in organizations power relationships and bargaining develop around sources of uncertainty, places in the organization where behavior is unpredictable. Discretion in organizational roles arises from uncertainty in the tasks themselves and from flexibility in interpretation of work rules, which are intended to make role behavior predictable. There is also a natural variability due to human spontaneity and originality. The ultimate origin of task uncertainty may be the organization's external social environment or random physical occurrences, such as the breakdown of machines. Conflict develops in an organization when management tries to increase the predictability of workers and workers try to increase or maintain their degree of independence and unpredictability in role situations. But, in general, any conflict over the control of uncertainty can lead to dysfunctional patterns. Even if hierarchical pressures are reduced, within-strata pressures of group conformity will become salient components of organizational dynamics. Since there will always be some uncertainty in an organization, the potential for conflict and dysfunctional patterns will always exist; overly routinized, bureaucratic patterns (in the pejorative sense) are inevitable. (Not all social conflict can be traced to hierarchical structure, however, as we shall see later.)

Modern organizations have been able to reduce the amount of predictability required of their members or employees, since greater understanding of human behavior has reduced the conformity required to achieve specific tasks. Greater understanding has reduced the anticipated uncertainty while educational training has regularized behavior patterns. As Crozier further describes, workers do not value participation in decision making in itself and will resist it if they fear that their participation will only reduce their independence. (This restraint may compare with the decision to abstain from voting in elections.) In studying the bureaucratic patterns of various nations, Crozier points out that many countries, such as France and Japan, have shown a great flexibility in the content of bureaucratic roles and situations over time, while maintaining a rigid equilibrium in the structural aspects of organization. Flexibility in content, made possible by the content-free nature of entropy-measurable phenomena, has allowed rapid social change in content while maintaining traditional social structures to a remarkable extent. The rapid modernization of Japan has been an outstanding example of this.

Usually it is hard to study actual organizations and make quantitative measurements of behavior patterns. One method that may be applied in certain cases is the analysis of entropy levels of organizational communication. Individual words in messages or policy statements are the events of the event set, which is all possible organizational words. The probabilities of word occurrence can then be estimated from samples of written or transcribed communications. Such methods have been used in linguistic analysis and in the literary analysis of texts. We can view an organization's communication as a "dialect" of the natural language of the society. Every organization has a specialized vocabulary, a limited number of terms and concepts that it uses in its internal communication and *vis-a-vis* the public.[14] Since the nature of communication is usually carefully controlled in organizations, it can provide a good indicator of the entropy state of the organization.

There is little direct evidence to show that one level of entropy in an organization may be better than another level for achieving some organizational goal. The absolute entropy level, however, may be important in determining an organization's capacity for dealing with environmental problems. We can think of entropy as a measure of the complexity of a problem. For example, the number of "yes" or "no" questions one would have to ask to solve a problem would indicate the number of entropy bits required for solution; that is, it gives the uncertainty about what the solution is.[15] Since individual and group capacity for processing uncertainty at any time is quite limited, an organization has to break down a problem to a number of successive stages or partial solutions each within the capacity of persons in the organization. To cope with or adapt to an environmental problem it may be necessary for behavior patterns within an organization to be altered to a commensurate degree, but in an overly routinized bureaucracy such adaptation may be impossible. Or the nature of the problem may not be perceived by the organization if information from the environment is overly constrained or filtered down to fit the lower capacity of the organization.[16]

Although questions of social engineering are beyond the scope of this book, we must certainly take into account the nature of entropy-measurable social phenomena and the structual properties of social systems in any purposeful attempt to change patterns of social behavior or to achieve specific social goals. Any significant social reform involves changes in the relationships between people across a social system as well as change in the frequencies of occurrence of social events or the number of alternatives. In other words, social change will affect structural properties of a social system in addition to whatever content changes are intended.

It seems doubtful that a program of social reform or a social goal could be attained efficiently, if at all, without considering such factors as: (1) the separate effects of the program on social structure and social content; (2) the natural tendency of a system to maintain a structural or entropy equilibrium, perhaps counteracting any intended change, producing unintended results, or offsetting reduced uncertainty in one area of social activity by increasing it in another; (3) whether a human tolerance for uncertainty may be exceeded; (4) what psychological costs or benefits are involved for persons in a structual change; and (5) what the effects will be on other systems, social, economic, or whatever.[17] Problems of implementing social change are further complicated by the natural tendencies in the dynamic processes of systems, which are analyzed in the next chapters.

CHAPTER FIVE

Intensive Dynamics

5-1. Change in the Orbital Model

In this chapter and the next we analyze those changes that are most likely to occur during periods of system relaxation, as when a system is forced to a new equilibrium entropy level. The analysis is restricted to unitary system models applied to national political systems or their subsystems. The main attention is on the nature of change in entropy measurements. Entropy-related change can be conveniently divided into two categories: intensive and acrossvariable. These terms reflect which aspect of the entropy variable, as an intensive acrossvariable, is most pertinent. Since we can base entropy measurement on more than one event set for the same system, we must analyze how change in one event set's measurement of entropy may be related to change in another event set's. This is referred to as the analysis of intensive dynamics. Specifically, we are interested in the relation between change in $H(P)$ and $H(T)$, the two electoral measurements of entropy. We want to determine the likely paths of system change in the orbital representation of entropy equilibrium states. Analysis of change in $H(P)$ also includes explanation of change from one orbit to another, which is to say, change in the number of events in the event set or change in the number of political parties from one election to the next.

The other major type of system change during relaxation periods is the tendency of a spatially heterogeneous system to become increasingly homogeneous across the system for any single measure of entropy, that is, for any single event set. This category of social change, called acrossvariable change, is taken up in Chapter 6. Of course, we may find both kinds of change, intensive and acrossvariable, occurring simultaneously in a system.

System change, as represented in the orbital model (Figure 3-2), can take place either within an orbit or from one orbit to another. The primary analytic questions are what disequilibrium patterns will tend to arise during relaxation periods, and what the final equilibrium state will be, as given by

$H(P)$ and $H(T)$ or turnout values. Another question of interest is when change between orbits is likely to happen, or, conversely, when within-orbit change is more likely.

Consider a system that is forced to change to a new equilibrium at a different entropy level. There may be various paths the system could take within and between orbits that would lead to the same net change in entropy yet allow a new equilibrium to be attained. For any equilibrium value of $H(P)$ innumerable points at different turnout values have the same $H(P)$ value. For a given entropy value $H(P)$ in one orbit we can always find two points in each higher orbit with the same $H(P)$ value, and possibly in lower orbits as well. (This is easily seen by drawing a horizontal line through an $H(P)$ value in Figure 3-2 and observing where the line intersects the curves.) If a change to a specific $H(P)$ value is required, it is not clear to which of the points the system would move. The only distinguishing feature of the equal $H(P)$ points is that they fall at different turnout values. Since we must take into account change in $H(T)$ as well as in $H(P)$, the following hypothesis seems reasonable: a system passing to a new equilibrium tends to change in such a way that the net change in $H(T)$ is a minimum for the required change in $H(P)$. That is, the system takes the shortest path; the shortest path is the one requiring the least change in $H(T)$. This hypothesis is also reasonable from another standpoint. It seems natural that a change in $H(T)$ would be continuous over time; the system would not jump past one equilibrium point to another farther away, as measured by change in $H(T)$.

The hypothesis of minimum $H(T)$ change may need some additional qualification, however, as this example illustrates. Suppose that a system is at 70% turnout and the entropy is increasing, but the system should attain its final and nearest equilibrium where $H(P)$ would have to be in the next higher orbit. That is, the increase in entropy will exceed the capacity of log n for the initial orbit. And suppose, too, that the anticipated final equilibrium state would fall at 80% turnout in the next higher orbit. Then, to establish a new equilibrium the system would have to *decrease* $H(T)$ (increase turnout over 50%) while at the same time *increasing* $H(P)$. Intuitively this seems to be a contradictory and unlikely path. It does not seem that people would change their behavior simultaneously in opposite directions, becoming more conformist about one event set and less about another. We find it much more plausible that as the entropy level begins to increase, both $H(P)$ and $H(T)$ will begin to increase. In effect, the system does not "know" where its final state should be when the entropy level first begins to increase and so may not take the optimal path to a new equilibrium. If the entropy level of the system increased to the point where it exceeded the orbital capacity, it could jump to the next higher orbit, but the path of change would be away from the equilibrium point in the higher orbit. The result of such a change would find the system in a prolonged period of disequilibrium, at least while the entropy continued to increase and perhaps for some time after. A similar case arises when a system must decrease its entropy level. Very likely, both $H(P)$ and $H(T)$ will begin decreasing together even if this is not the shortest path to the new equilibrium point. One would not expect $H(T)$ to increase while $H(P)$ was decreasing.

Relaxation paths are shown in Figure 5-1 for the cases of increasing and decreasing entropy. The predicted relaxation paths are labeled AB and the unlikely paths AC; the parenthetical letter indicates the orbit at point B. In the case of decreasing entropy we would expect a system to fall to a lower orbit rather than decrease in the same orbit to achieve any fairly large entropy reduction; otherwise the hypothesis of minimum change in $H(T)$ would be contradicted. These hypothetical relaxation paths are the disequilibrium patterns observed in testing the entropy hypothesis. They lead to a flattening of the distribution of subsystem entropy values within an orbit as entropy levels are increased or decreased fairly rapidly or by fairly large amounts. The effect is symmetrical for the cases of increasing and decreasing entropy.

To complete the preceding argument we would have to know the relative rates of change of the two measures $H(P)$ and $H(T)$, that is, the derivative $dH(P)/dH(T)$. The slope of the relaxation path will be determined by this ratio of change. For the kth orbit we have at equilibrium

$$H(P) = \log k\, H(T)$$

and thus the ratio of change near an equilibrium is

$$dH(P) = \log k\, dH(T)$$

or

$$\frac{dH(P)}{dH(T)} = \log k$$

We have no way to determine how a change in the economic system of a nation, for example, would affect the rate of change of $H(P)$ or $H(T)$. But we must assume that the greater or more rapid the change in the environmental forces on a system, the more rapidly it will have to adjust its entropy level. If the induced change in a system were small and gradual, it could possibly move through a sequence of equilibrium states lying close together along an orbital curve; in this case $dH(P)/dH(T)$ would be close to log k for the kth orbit. But if the system must increase its entropy level by a large amount or very rapidly, we would anticipate that the ratio of change

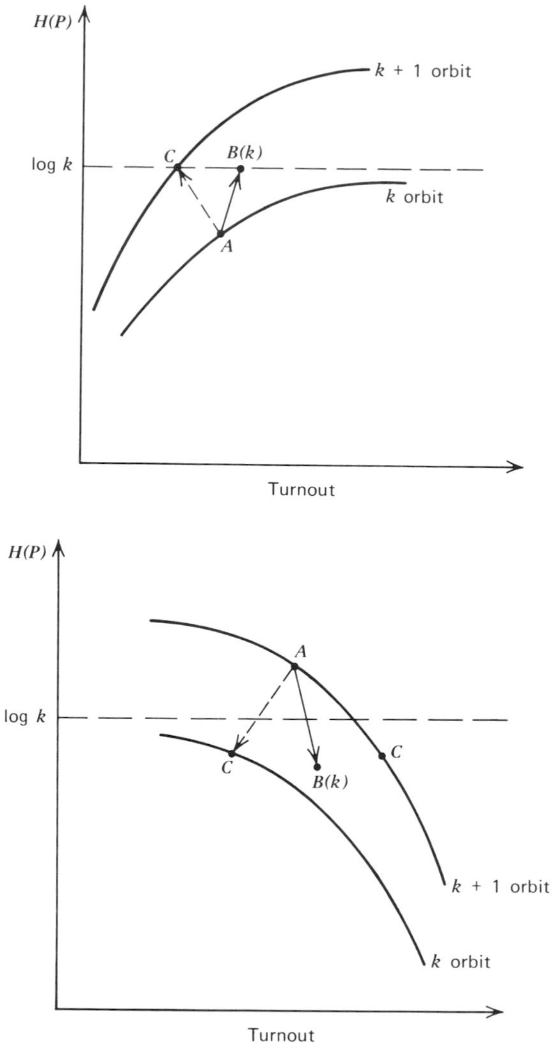

Figure 5-1. Hypothetical relaxation paths.

$dH(P)/dH(T)$ would also increase rapidly; the system would move toward a higher orbit, changing its $H(T)$ value as little as necessary. The result would be paths of change similar to those predicted in Figure 5-1.

There is no fixed rate at which the entropy of a system must change as a function of its orbital location. The derivative $dH(P)/dH(T)$ is not necessarily fixed at log k for the kth orbit. On the contrary, unless all the probabilities in the event set are nearly the same there is considerable flexibility in how the entropy can change. For example, if 10% of those voting for a dominant political party with 50% of the vote were to shift to a party having only 5% of the total vote, the net increase in system entropy would be greater than if the same 10% shift had gone to a party with 20% of the vote. The relative weight of a party with a given percentage of the vote in the total entropy can be assessed from Figure 5-2, the graph of $-p \log p$ as a function of event probability p. The entropy is a summation of terms of the form $-p \log p$ (bits); there is one term for each event or political party. The graph and the accompanying table of values indicate that $-p \log p$ increases very rapidly with small values of p but then reaches a maximum when a party's percentage of the vote is 37%; as p increases beyond 37%, $-p \log p$ decreases to zero. Thus we can conclude that if a system must increase its $H(P)$ level rapidly or to a large extent, the smaller parties will increase at the expense of the largest, or new parties will emerge, drawing their strength from the largest parties. If a political party has about 30% of the vote already, a further increase in its share will not appreciably increase the overall system entropy. On the other hand, if a system must rapidly decrease its entropy level, it seems likely that the reverse shifts in probabilites will occur; the larger parties will gain at the expense of the smallest. The shifting of percentages between political parties during periods of

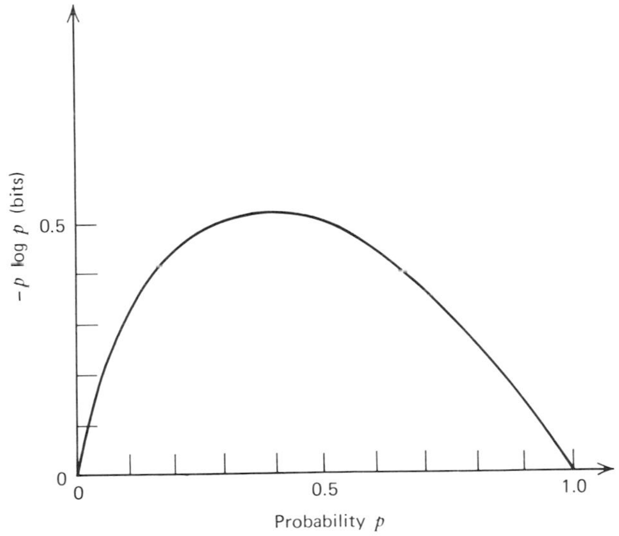

Figure 5-2. The $-p \log p$ curve. Where p = .10, .20, .30, .40, .50, .60, .70, .80, .90, 1.0; and $-p \log p$ = .33, .46, .52, .53, .50, .44, .36, .26, .14, 0.0.

entropy change may appear as coalition formation or dissolution among the various political parties. If the exact amount of system change were predictable, we might be able to give a better estimate of the amount of change likely to occur in each party's percentage of the vote, using the information provided by the $-p \log p$ curve.

The movement of systems or subsystems between orbits can be analyzed from a simpler perspective if the rate of change in $H(P)$ is much greater than for $H(T)$, or in other words, if the systems are moving at high slopes or nearly vertically up or down between orbits. In this case the chance of a system moving to another orbit, for a given amount of added or subtracted entropy, is primarily a function of the distance between orbits. For any turnout level the distance between adjacent orbits decreases as the orbit number increases. At a voter turnout of t the absolute separation of the k and $k+1$ orbits can be calculated from the equation $H(P) = \log k\ H(T)$. If $H(T; t)$ is the value of $H(T)$ at a turnout of t, or equivalently, the value of $H(P)$ in orbit two at that turnout, then the distance between orbits is

$$\begin{aligned} D(k, k+1; t) &= \log(k+1) H(T; t) - \log k\ H(T; t) \\ &= [\log(k+1) - \log k] H(T; t) \\ &= \log\left(1 + \frac{1}{k}\right) H(T; t) \end{aligned}$$

The interorbital distance $D(k, k+1; t)$ is greatest when $t = 50\%$ and declines to zero as t goes to either 0 or 100% turnout. For all values of t the distance approaches zero as k becomes very large.

We will predict that as a change in system entropy exceeds the interorbital separation at a given turnout value, a change between orbits will become increasingly likely—even if the amount of change would not cause the system to exceed its orbital maximum. The appearance of a new political party or the disappearance of an existing party will become increasingly likely, depending on the direction of change. Thus for a given or random amount of entropy change, movement between orbits should be more likely for systems or subsystems having turnout values closer to 0% or 100%, or for systems in higher orbits than lower at a given turnout value. If a system is in an equilibrium near 50% turnout, the system is already near its orbital maximum, and we would predict that an increase in entropy would tend to push the system to a higher orbit. If the turnout of a system is closer to 25 or 75%, change between orbits is less likely for a given rate or amount of entropy change, and one would expect a greater degree of within-orbit change before a system might jump to another orbit.

Possibly, a threshold effect may exist in the origination of new political parties. We might expect that if the entropy maximum of an orbit were only temporarily exceeded by a small amount, there might not be sufficient impetus to cause the formation of a new party. In a large national political system the threshold may have to be exceeded over a large portion of the system before a new national party arises; and some minimum time may be required for a system to generate a new party, depending on system size or other factors. In general, the rates at which systems change in time or the time lags in various processes are important system characteristics and may provide insight into the microscopic processes of the system.

5-2. Case Studies in System Relaxation

We can review the three cases analyzed in testing the entropy hypothesis, the United States, India, and Japan, to determine how their relaxation patterns conform to the hypothetical model.

The most distinguishing feature of the American case, in contrast to other countries, is the infrequence of third-party elections and the transience of third parties. India and Japan have several political parties, have variations in the number of parties across subsystems, and have frequent changes in the number of parties. Political theorists have questioned many times whether a two-party system is inherently more stable than a multiparty system, if stability is taken to mean less subject to fluctuations in the number of parties. If we compare the differences in entropy levels between successive orbits, it does appear possible that a two-party system is more stable than a multiparty system. For a given level of voter turnout or $H(T)$, it takes more entropy to raise a system or subsystem from the second to third orbit than to go between any other consecutive orbits. Furthermore, since the higher orbits become increasingly closer to one another, jumps between orbits would become increasingly likely. However, the distance between orbits also varies with the turnout, so that to compare the stability of two systems we would have to consider their turnout levels as well. A two-party system at very high or very low turnout would not be particularly stable. Although a two-party system may be more stable, in general, than a multiparty system, the greater capacity for within-orbit change may also allow prolonged periods of disequilibrium of the sort pictured in Figure 5-1 and observed in American elections.

The case of India offers a good example of the effects of extensive subsystem change. Although our data is for only a single election, we are able to infer the direction of change from the correlation of turnout and literacy, which we presume to have been increasing over time. The main trend of change in India is thus in the direction of increasing turnout, and the subsystems tend to move clockwise around the entropy curve. Some subsystems at fairly high turnout levels have moved in the reverse direction, however, due to the effects of urbanization and related economic development. We can reconstruct the movement of the subsystems as follows. Initially at low turnout and low entropy, the subsystems begin to increase their entropy levels fairly rapidly. As the subsystems approach the maxima for the lower orbits, many subsystems will shift to higher orbits. As $H(P)$ increases, $H(T)$ will also be increasing, but at a slower rate. Thus as the turnout approaches 50%, the number of subsystems in higher orbits continues to increase. As the turnout exceeds 50% and $H(T)$ decreases, the subsystems fall rapidly to lower orbits, but in such a way that $H(T)$ does not increase.

If the subsystems are consecutively aggregated by orbit, the symmetry in the rising and falling entropy patterns becomes apparent. If the second and third orbits; the second, third, and fourth; and the second through fifth orbits are aggregated and compared we find that each aggregation of subsystems has the appearance of a truncated (topped) entropy-curve bounded region. Parabolic curve fitting shows that the maximum of the parabola is near 50% turnout in each successive case.

Since systems tend to increase their entropy levels within orbits, approaching the maximum before jumping to the next higher orbit, the distribution of subsystems of a rapidly changing system will tend to lie across two or more orbits with the subsystems closer to 50% turnout in the higher orbits. The distribution of subsystems remaining in lower orbits will tend to be flattened out against the log k lines for those orbits. We have observed this as a stationary result in elections in both India and Japan. It explains why across-orbit or aggregate-orbit curve fitting supports the entropy hypothesis better than within-orbit curve fitting in these cases. We can examine this effect directly with over-time data in the case of Japan. We have predicted that change between orbits should be more frequent at very low or very high turnout levels and also near 50% turnout, for random changes in entropy. In the intermediate turnout ranges, say around 25% and 75%, there is greater likelihood of within-orbit change. We can test this hypothesis for the eight Japanese elections between 1949 and 1967 by assessing the number of subsystems switching orbits from one election to the next, relative to the number of subsystems not changing orbit.

We assign an integer score to each prefecture or subsystem depending upon how many orbits it moves, up or down, from one election to the next. That is, we assign a value 0, 1, 2,. . . . There are 46 prefectures and 8 elections, which gives $46 \times 7 = 322$ interelection data points. The change or index value for each prefecture was plotted against the turnout level where the change did or did not occur, that is, for the first election of each election pair. We fitted a second degree polynomial curve to the aggregated data and

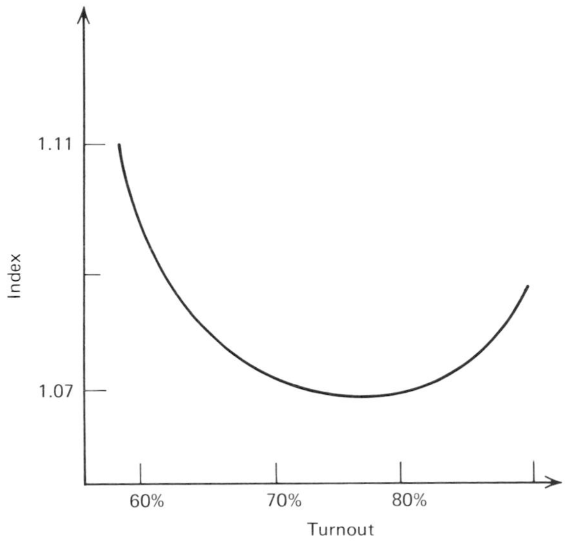

Figure 5-3. Frequency of orbit changes.

the result is illustrated in Figure 5-3. Although the trend is not strong, it has the expected shape. The curve increases as turnout approaches 50% and 100% and is lowest in between, having a minimum at about 75% turnout. Error estimates are not very meaningful for the curve, however, since the dependent variable takes on only integer values and the error distance to a continuous curve is necessarily large. Other factors, such as possible biases in the magnitude of entropy change in relation to turnout, are not considered in this test. The results of the test reconfirm our explanation of the stationary patterns observed in individual elections. It is interesting to note the great amount of orbit switching which occurred during this time period in Japan. Of the 322 possible cases there were 226 (70%) with an interorbital change. In those cases where subsystems remained in the same orbit over two elections, we found that the absolute ratio of change in $H(P)$ to change in turnout increased with turnout values (which were always over 50% in this period); this is, again, the predicted relaxation pattern.

CHAPTER SIX

Acrossvariable Dynamics

6-1. Social Entropy as an Acrossvariable

This chapter is concerned with a range of analytic and substantive problems different from those encountered in testing the entropy hypothesis and in interpreting its social significance. On the technical side, we have the very important question of determining whether a political system exhibits the necessary equilibrium-restoring property, namely, that a spatially heterogeneous system will tend to become increasingly homogeneous over its area. This is an empirical question we can investigate independently of our earlier assumptions and conclusions regarding the entropy hypothesis; it is a separate line of inquiry. Once this property is verified, it becomes possible to develop a mathematical model of entropy change across large geographic areas and generate in turn a number of conclusions about how the spatial distributions of entropy in national political systems should appear. The mathematical model is necessarily complex, although completely conventional; but in practice, the conclusions are easy to apply to the analysis of political systems.

While our first concern is with technical problems and verification of the necessary empirical facts, a number of social and political issues relate directly to the study of spatiotemporal entropy patterns. The tendency of a heterogeneous system to become increasingly homogeneous implies an interaction between subsystems, or in other terms, a diffusion of change across the whole system. If the entropy level of one subsystem is changed by an exogenous influence, this will subsequently have an effect on other subsystems. The rate at which this diffusion occurs, the relaxation rate, will depend on many underlying factors affecting the extent of communication or association of people in and between the subsystems. Obviously, if there were little or no intersubsystem communication, there would be no diffusion of change. These are very elementary principles, but when applied to the analysis of national political systems they give an overall view of communication patterns in the system. In particular, we can observe the degree of regionalism in a system, or alternatively, the lack of integration of geographic regions into a cohesive, uniform, national political system. A relative lack of interaction between one or more regions will give rise to certain identifiable patterns in the distribution of entropy levels.

Problems of national integration have had a great affect on the political life of many nations. In the most serious instances, secessions have occurred or civil wars have erupted. Thus, the techniques developed here have a diagnostic or predictive value in assessing the likelihood of political problems as they may arise from a failure in national integration. We can also show that "regionalism" is a concept that requires more careful application than is usually the case. One must distinguish regionalism due to differences in entropy levels in separate regions from the regionalism caused by the relative isolation of one region from another. For example, the American South presents contrasting kinds of regionalism before the Civil War and in more recent years. But first, we must return to our investigation of entropy as a measurement variable.

In our tentative categorization of social measurement variables we classified entropy as an intensive acrossvariable. The intensive nature of the entropy variable has been shown in testing the entropy hypothesis. In this chapter we demonstrate that the entropy variable also has the properties of an acrossvariable.

Let us review the meaning of an acrossvariable and its importance in analyzing the dynamic behavior of a system. If a system is spatially heterogeneous, such that the intensive acrossvariable has different values in two or more regions of an isolated system, the system will tend to change and will become increasingly homogeneous with respect to the intensive acrossvariable. The final homogeneity is actually achieved by the diffusion or flow of some quantity throughout the system until homogeneity is attained. It is differences in the amount or density of this quantity across the system that cause intensive acrossvariable differences. The flow from one region to another is measured by the intensive throughvariable. To an approximation, this rate of flow is linearly proportional to the difference of the intensive acrossvariable values across the two regions; the greater the difference, the faster the flow. Ordinarily, the direction of the throughvariable flow is from the region of the higher value of the intensive acrossvariable to the lower, although in some kinds of systems analysis the reverse is true. The use of intensive acrossvariable differences implies again the interval-scale requirement for this variable; when only differences in values of the variable are used, the location of the zero point on the scale is immaterial. For convenience, the zero point is often assigned to the lower value of a pair of intensive acrossvariable measurements.

Examples of these dynamic properties in various systems are: (1) the flow of heat energy between regions of unequal temperature in a thermodynamic system; (2) the flow of electric current between regions of unequal voltage in an electrical system; and (3) the flow of a commodity in an economic system between markets where the prices for the commodity are unequal, the goods moving from the lower price market to the higher. The trend toward increasing homogeneity can be called an "irreversible" process, since the system cannot restore itself to its initial or earlier unequal values.

We can measure intensive acrossvariable differences without knowing the rate of throughvariable flow in the system. And since the rate of flow is approximately proportional to the difference, we can explain the dynamics of the system with the differences alone, provided that the constant of proportionality is known. Even if the constant is not known but a proportional flow is assumed to exist, change in the differences over time can still be predicted up to a constant multiple of their actual values. Thus if we seek only to predict change in the values of the intensive acrossvariable in a system, we have no need to make throughvariable measurements at all. Regardless of what the rate of flow is, the intensive acrossvariable differences will change in a predictable manner. This property of dynamic systems enables us to decide whether social entropy behaves as an acrossvariable in a dynamic social system without actually measuring the social throughvariables, such as event flow, in our previous terminology. In fact, we do not even need to know exactly what a social event flow is or how it could be measured.

In the historical development of the science of thermodynamics measurement of the intensive acrossvariable, temperature, became possible at a much earlier time than measurement of the throughvariables. As a result, the dynamic properties of thermodynamic systems could be analyzed by physicists using temperature measurement alone even before they understood the true nature of the throughvariable flow. They had only to infer the existence of some kind of thermal flow or interaction, proportional to temperature differences, for a workable analytic theory of system dynamics to be possible. We are in a similar position when we seek to develop a social theory, for we have a much clearer idea of how to measure social entropy than social event flow. By necessity, the development of an analytic theory of social dynamics must retrace the steps of thermodynamics. We can turn this to an advantage, however, by taking over the methods used in thermodynamics and applying them to the analogous analytic problems in social dynamics.

Consider a thermodynamic system consisting of two subsystems at unequal temperatures. Let the difference in the two temperatures be $U(0)$ at the time of our first observation of the system, that is, when time $t = 0$. We want to know what the difference in temperature $U(t)$ will be after an elapsed time period of length t. Let us also assume that the two subsystems remain approximately uniform with regard to the internal temperature of each. The answer to this analytic problem was first discovered by Newton. According to Newton's "law of cooling," the difference in temperatures (if not too large) will diminish over time at a rate proportional to the existing temperature difference at any instant. Mathematically, this relationship is expressed by the differential equation

$$\frac{dU}{dt} = -kU \tag{6-1}$$

where k is a positive constant (per unit time) that depends on the properties of the particular system involved. Equation (6-1) can be solved to give the temperature difference $U(t)$ as a function of elapsed time

$$U(t) = U(0)e^{-kt} \tag{6-2}$$

where $U(0)$ is the initial difference. The reason the temperature difference changes in this manner over time is because of the decreasing rate of heat flow between the two subsystems. As heat energy passes from one subsystem to the other the difference in temperatures begins to decrease. Since the rate of heat flow is proportional to the difference at any moment, the flow also diminishes over time, continuously lessening the rate at which the temperature difference decreases. When $U(t) = 0$ the flow of heat ceases and the subsystems are said to be in a temperature equilibrium. Newton was able to formulate this law two centuries before the nature of heat flow was established, however.[1]

Equations 6-1 and 6-2 are shown graphically in Figures 6-1 and 6-2. Equation 6-1 is a straight line beginning at the origin and decreasing at a slope of $-k$. Figure 6-2 shows that the difference decreases exponentially over time. If $t = 1/k$ then

$$U\left(\frac{1}{k}\right) = U(0)e^{-1} = 0.37U(0)$$

The quantity $1/k$ is referred to as the time constant for the system. After a length of time $1/k$ the difference $U(t)$ will always have been reduced to 37% of its value $U(0)$. After an elapsed time of $4.6/k$ the difference will be only 1% of its initial value.

Let us assume that a social flow or interaction exists between two regions of an isolated social system. For entropy to be considered an acrossvariable in social systems analysis, differences in entropy must follow the analogy to Newton's law, decreasing over time in proportion to the instantaneous difference. In other words, if a social system consists of two interconnected

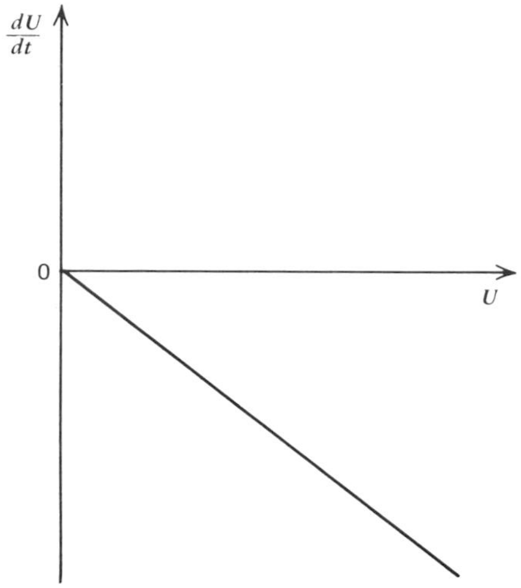

Figure 6-1. $dU/dt = -kU$. Rate of change is proportional to the difference.

subsystems at different entropy levels, and if each subsystem remains fairly homogeneous itself over time, the difference $U(t)$ between the entropy levels will decrease according to equation 6-2 for an initial entropy difference of $U(0)$. The constant k will depend on properties of the social system that determine the rate of flow or interaction between the two regions.

The equations 6-1 and 6-2 would be easy enough to verify for social systems if we find systems for which we can make accurate two-point entropy measurements over a period of time (Or if we might experiment with social systems under the ideal conditions of a physics laboratory.) Unfortunately, ideal cases are rarely found in the real world, and we must approximate the necessary experimental situation. The main experimental difficulties are of three kinds. (1) We must ordinarily consider the interactive effects of multiple social regions within the system. (2) We cannot ignore environmental effects; system entropy levels are frequently affected by external causes. And (3) instead of observing a single system or subsystem continuously over time, we must usually compare the relative changes in a set of cases over a single or synchronous time interval. The different cases for analysis have different initial entropy differences and the relative amounts of change in each are compared as a function of their respective initial differences.

Japan: a Study in System Relaxation. Even with approximating conditions, few social systems offer data for study that is both adequate and convenient. We are always constrained by our reliance on elections as entropy measurements. Moreover, the electoral data must pertain to systems where we can safely infer that interaction between regions at different entropy levels exists.

Data for Japan during the years before the Second World War, from about 1920 to 1937, is fairly well suited to the problem. (This data was cited earlier in connection with the entropy hypothesis test for Japan.) During this period, as we have seen, the main area of Japan was divided into 46 prefectures, which were further subdivided into election districts for national parliamentary (lower house) elections. The electoral districts are the regions or subsystems in which we will make entropy measurements. The prefectures are a convenient guide to whether we should expect a relatively high degree of interaction between districts. Districts in the same prefecture should have a much higher level of interaction with one another than with districts in other prefectures. The intraprefecture interaction can be rather firmly separated from the interprefecture in Japan, because prefecture boundaries frequently coincide with severe natural barriers such as mountain ranges and bodies of water. During this period of history, too, transnational electronic communication was still at a low level of development. In addition, the prefectures were the major subnational governmental units. Thus people living in the same prefecture shared a range of common interests related to local governmental activity, regardless of their electoral district.

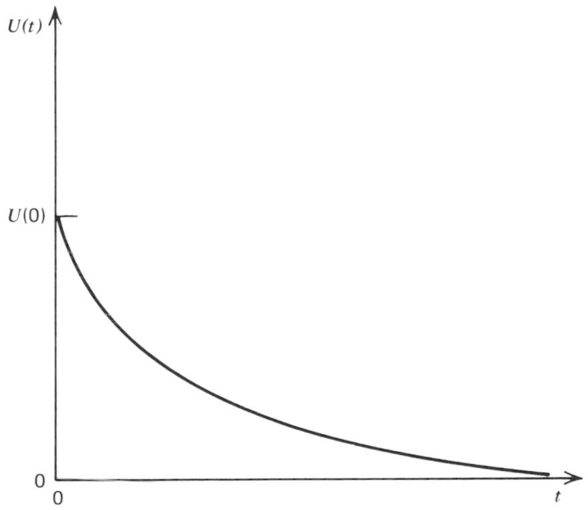

Figure 6-2. $U(t) = U(0)\, e^{-kt}$. The magnitude of the difference decreases exponentially over time.

The arrangement of electoral districts and prefectures in Japan enables us to infer that a high level of interaction or flow between districts within the same prefecture was possible. For short intervals of time, we can consider the prefectures as being isolated from one another, and disregard the effect of interaction between prefectures at different entropy levels. Interprefecture interaction will be subsumed in "errors" in the prediction of changes due to within-prefecture entropy differences.[2]

The total number of election districts was about 240 until 1925 when an electoral reapportionment reduced the number to about 120. We will be primarily concerned with those prefectures having only two districts. There were 19 of these in the post-1925 elections. Secondarily, we will examine all those prefectures with more than one district. The number of prefectures having two or more districts was 46 before 1925 and 39 after that date. The elections during this period occurred in: 1920, 1924, 1928, 1930, 1932, 1936, and 1937. The last five of these elections were held under the same electoral laws in the smaller set of electoral districts. The first two elections were for the larger set of districts. In addition to the variation in district number, the suffrage was greatly expanded after 1925 to include all males over the age of 25.

We will first analyze the electoral data for those prefectures containing only two districts; this concerns the last five elections only. We compute the entropy $H(P)$ values from the division of the political party vote in each district. The absolute value of the difference of the two entropy values in each prefecture of this set is then determined for each election. We plot the change in this absolute value between consecutive pairs of elections against the initial differences existing at the time of the first of each pair of elections. The change can be an increase or decrease. Hence, we compare for each pair of districts the amount of change that did occur with the magnitude of the entropy difference just prior to the change. This is done separately for each pair of consecutive elections.

If we were observing a single pair of districts over a period of time, we would expect the entropy difference to follow equations 6-1 and 6-2. But the observation of a set of prefectures over a single time interval involves a slightly different problem. Equations 6-1 and 6-2 show that, regardless of the initial difference existing in any prefecture, the resulting change will be a fixed percentage of the initial value for a given interval of time. That is, the same fixed percentage will apply to each prefecture for the observed time period. This holds as long as all prefectures have the same value of k (equation 6-1). Under the assumption of equal values of k, the constant percentage reduction of differences causes the prefectures to lie on a straight line when we graph changes against the initial differences for the whole set of prefectures. We shall show this mathematically.

Let Δt be the time interval between elections, measured in years. And let the magnitude of the initial difference in an arbitrary prefecture be $U(t)$ for an election at time t. The change in the difference will then be $U(t + \Delta t) - U(t)$, which should be a negative quantity. From equation 6-2

$$U(t + \Delta t) = U(t)e^{-k\Delta t}$$

Subtracting and dividing each term by $U(t)$ we obtain

$$\frac{U(t + \Delta t) - U(t)}{U(t)} = \frac{U(t)e^{-k\Delta t} - U(t)}{U(t)} \tag{6-3}$$

$$= e^{-k\Delta t} - 1$$

Note that the quantity on the right in equation 6-3 is independent of the value of $U(t)$, depending only on k and Δt. If k is constant for all prefectures and they are all observed over the same interval Δt, equation 6-3 implies that

$$m = \frac{U(t + \Delta t) - U(t)}{U(t)} \tag{6-4}$$

is a constant for all prefectures.

If we plot the change $U(t + \Delta t) - U(t)$ against the initial difference $U(t)$ for each prefecture, the quantity m of equation 6-4 is the ratio of the vertical to horizontal distance of each prefecture data point. (See Figure 6-3.) In other words, m is the slope of a line through the origin and point $[U(t), U(t + \Delta t) - U(t)]$ along which the prefectures will be distributed. Since m is a constant for all prefectures, under the assumptions made above, the prefectures must all lie along a straight line. The slope of the line depends only on the values of k and the length of time between elections Δt. If we fit a straight line to the set of prefecture data points for each pair of elections, we can estimate the value of m and then compute the value of k using equation 6-3. Since k is not likely to be equal for all prefectures, however, some error will be introduced. The severity of this error can be roughly assessed from how well the data fits a straight line.

As the actual results will show, the above equations cannot be applied directly in the case of Japan because of the effects of environmental forces on the district entropy levels. The general effect of the environment was to raise entropy levels in many election districts. Variations in the amounts of added entropy in the districts tend to show up as increases in the entropy *differences*. Although the resulting effect on differences is complex, we can estimate the nature of the error introduced. If the initial difference $U(0)$ is very small, that is, small compared to the variance of the amounts of entropy increase in the districts, $U(0)$ will become larger merely because of

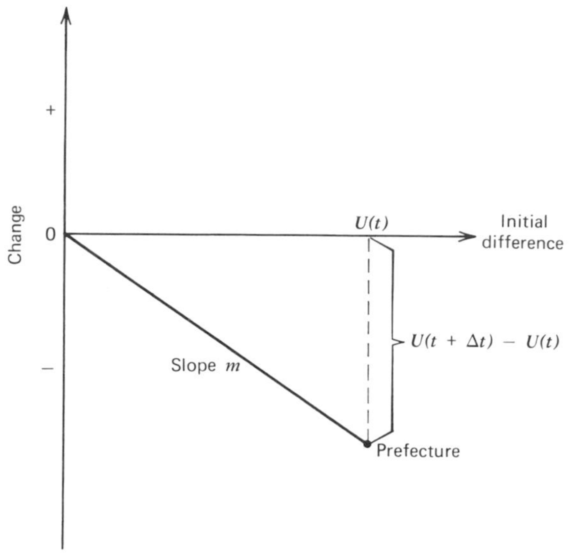

Figure 6-3. Prefecture location when predicted change in the entropy difference within the prefecture is plotted against the initial entropy difference there.

the variability of the added entropy in the districts. If $U(0)$ is very small, almost any change in the entropy levels of the pair of districts will tend to increase the difference; it is very unlikely that both districts would change their levels by the same amount, and the difference in the added amounts of entropy would probably be greater than $U(0)$ was. On the other hand, if $U(0)$ is very large compared with the variance of the added entropy, the difference will be just as likely to increase as to decrease. So on the average for a group of prefectures with large initial differences, the differences will be little affected by increases in district entropy. These same arguments apply to decreases in district entropy or to random unspecified changes. Thus, a bias is introduced to the entropy differences over time by the random change in district entropy levels. The amount of bias—the amount of spurious increase in the differences—decreases as the initial difference increases and tends to zero for large $U(0)$. This bias is shown schematically in Figure 6-4.

We can represent the effect of the bias on a pair of election districts over a short time as a constant force tending to increase the entropy difference. If the bias in a given prefecture is c, equation 6-1 would then be modified as follows

$$\frac{dU}{dt} = -kU + c \tag{6-5}$$

This differential equation has the solution

$$U(t) = \frac{c}{k} + \left[U(0) - \frac{c}{k}\right]e^{-kt} \tag{6-6}$$

The graph for equation 6-5 is a straight line, similar to Figure 6-1, but with the point of intercept on the vertical axis shifted to $dU/dt = c$. Equation 6-6 shows that if the initial difference is less than c/k, the entropy difference will show a net increase after a short period of time. But if $U(0)$ is greater than c/k, there will be a net decrease. We find an equilibrium point at $U(0) = c/k$ where the opposing tendencies of change exactly balance each other. If the force c were to continue at its same fixed rate for a sufficient length of time, all prefectures so affected would move toward the equilibrium point regardless of their initial differences; that is, in the limiting case of equation 6-6

$$\lim_{t\to\infty} U(t) = \frac{c}{k}$$

If we observe a group of prefectures over an interval Δt and all have the same value of c (and k), the set of prefectures would again be distributed along a straight line similar to Figure 6-3 but shifted in location. In this case, however, we must modify equations 6-3 and 6-4. If $U(t)$ is the initial difference in an arbitrary prefecture the change will be $U(t + \Delta t) - U(t)$.

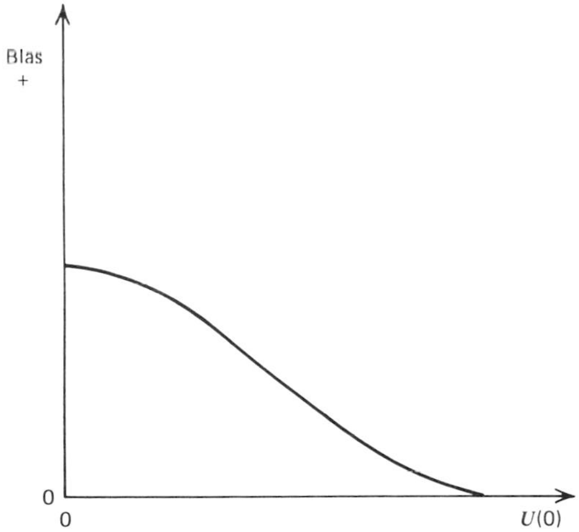

Figure 6-4. Bias or spurious change in the entropy difference because of change in the entropy levels over time, as a function of initial difference.

From equation 6-6 we have

$$U(t + \Delta t) = \frac{c}{k} + \left[U(t) - \frac{c}{k}\right] e^{-k\Delta t}$$

Transposing c/k and subtracting and dividing by $[U(t) - c/k]$ gives

$$\frac{[U(t + \Delta t) - c/k] - [U(t) - c/k]}{U(t) - c/k} = e^{-k\Delta t} - 1 \qquad \text{or}$$

$$\frac{U(t + \Delta t) - U(t)}{U(t) - c/k} = e^{-k\Delta t} - 1 \tag{6-7}$$

The quantity on the right of equation 6-7 is the same as for equation 6-3; the quantity on the left of the equality of equation 6-7 gives the slope m for a decreasing straight line crossing the horizontal axis at $U(t) = c/k$. The straight line of equation 6-7 varies in slope with k and intercepts the vertical axis at $-mc/k$, a positive number. The slope

$$m = e^{-k\Delta t} - 1$$

is negative and becomes increasingly negative (larger absolute value) as either k or Δt increases; it is independent of the constant c.

For a set of prefectures affected by the bias shown in Figure 6-4, the constant c decreases for prefectures with higher initial differences. Thus the distribution of prefectures will tend to curve as the changes are plotted against the initial differences. The net result is illustrated in Figure 6-5. As the initial differences in the prefectures become larger, c goes to zero and the curve approaches the straight line shown in Figure 6-3. The straight part of the curve is relatively error free and should give the best estimates of m, and consequently, of k as well.

The preceding discussion of change in entropy levels has consistently referred to differences between pairs of districts. It becomes much more difficult to derive an exact mathematical expression for the change when more than two districts or subsystems are involved. In such a situation, one must begin to pay more attention to relative geographical distances, varying rates of interaction, and so on, within each prefecture. Nevertheless, we must usually deal with multiple subsystem interactions in practice. We will see that this can be done fairly well, at least in the case of Japan.

Instead of the absolute value of the entropy difference as used above, we can adopt the standard deviation (*SD*) of the entropy within each prefecture as the measure of disequilibrium. This enables us to compare changes in the *SD* over time as a function of the initial prefecture *SD*. As the experimental results will show, the *SD* is a reasonably good choice as a measure of dif-

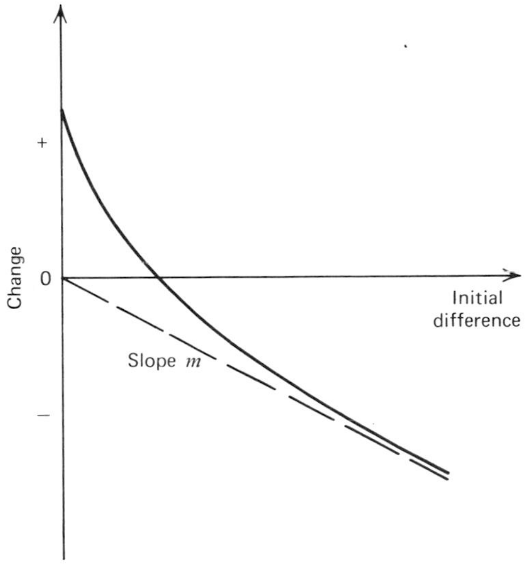

Figure 6-5. The expected distribution of prefectures.

ference or disequilibrium in multidistrict prefectures because the *SD* also fits a linear relationship of the form of equation 6-1.[3] As the *SD* approaches zero, the entropy in each district approaches the average prefecture value. This is the desired relaxation property for a heterogeneous system (Section 1-4). In applying this measure of disequilibrium to Japan, all prefectures with two or more districts are included in the sample.

In addition to the study of entropy differences and resultant change, we can also analyze the effects of differences in information variance across regions. The arguments concerning the information variance duplicate those on entropy. It is difficult to sort out the changes in the information variance that might be the result of a social effort to reduce information variance differences from those necessary with entropy change. Nevertheless, as in Chapter 7 there are cases of apparently independent information variance change. When more than two districts are involved, we can again resort to the use of the *SD* of the information variance in each prefecture as a measure of disequilibrium.

We will briefly summarize the results of the analysis of the Japanese data and then discuss certain features in greater detail. The results fit the expected pattern (Figure 6-5) with remarkable consistency. (See Tables 6-1, 6-2, and Figures 6-6, 6-7, and 6-8.) The curve fitting, and even visual inspection of the data, shows a decreasing, nearly straight line in all cases; the predicted pattern holds for all interelection periods, for the entropy as well

Table 6-1. Japan: Entropy Relaxation

Δt	n	m/Error	b/Error	Standard Error (bits)
		Entropy Differences Using a Linear Fit[a]		
1928–30	19	−.67/.18	.22/.07	.20
1930–32	15	−.53/.22	.04/.09	.18
1932–36	16	−.66/.34	.37/.09	.26
1936–37	18	−.90/.28	.30/.14	.28
		Entropy *SD* Using a Linear Fit		
1920–24	46	−.79/.10	.23/.03	.12
1924–28	39	−1.01/.16	.18/.05	.13
1928–30	39	−.58/.14	.10/.03	.11
1930–32	33	−.68/.16	.08/.03	.10
1932–36	34	−.71/.22	.20/.04	.13
1936–37	38	−.71/.17	.13/.05	.14

[a] Two district prefectures only.

as the information variance, and for both measures of disequilibrium (the magnitude of the difference and the standard deviation). The predicted relationships hold over a fairly wide range of initial differences and *SD*'s. For initial differences of entropy the range is about 0 to 1.0 bits; and the *SD* about 0 to 0.5 bits. For initial differences of the information variance the range is 0 to 1.5 bits^2; for the *SD*, 0 to 0.7 bits^2. As a guide, the *SD* values and changes run about half of the corresponding absolute differences and changes. The magnitude of the range of differences can be compared to the maximum possible range, judging from the psychological capacity, of about 3 bits. Some variation exists in the sample sizes (n) for the cases because of missing data and other idiosyncracies of the analysis; a few data points at the origin (no difference, no change) are lost.

The results of fitting straight lines to the data are shown in Tables 6-1 and 6-2. The line has the mathematical form

$$y = mx + b$$

where y is the change in the difference (or *SD*), x the initial difference (or *SD*), m the slope of the line, and b the intercept on the vertical or y axis. The values of m and b are computed for the fit lines. The estimates of the errors in m and b are also given in Tables 6-1 and 6-2 along with the standard error estimate for the fitting as a whole. (These errors were discussed in Chapter 3.) In almost every instance the coefficient errors are less than half the coefficient values, indicating a good fit; in a number of cases the errors are only a small fraction of the coefficients. (Percent of variance "explained" generally ranges from 30–60% for Table 6-1.) If we try second degree polynomial (parabolic) curve fitting and compare it to the linear, we find that the second degree curves usually bend slightly in the direction shown in Figure 6-5; but the distribution of the data is so close to being linear that there is virtually no reduction in the standard error estimates for the second degree fittings. To at least two or three significant figures the second degree standard errors are the same as the linear errors, as given in Table 6-1. The distribution is more linear than we might have expected considering that the value of *b* is significantly greater than zero in most cases. The relationships between the various constant factors may be more complex than anticipated. It may be that *k* increases somewhat when *c* increases, or that increases in the district entropy levels are more likely to be in those districts that already have the higher levels. In all cases the lines that are fitted to the data begin above the horizontal axis and generally extend well below the axis. Prefectures with fairly large initial differences almost invariably show some degree of reduction in their differences. The

Table 6-2. Japan: Information Variance Relaxation

Δt	n	m/Error	b/Error	Standard Error (bits^2)
Information Variance Differences Using a Linear Fit[a]				
1928–30	18	−.65/.32	.49/.14	.41
1930–32	13	−.65/.20	.09/.15	.29
1932–36	13	−.52/.26	.19/.12	.28
1936–37	18	−.66/.30	.36/.14	.35
Information Variance *SD* Using a Linear Fit				
1920–24	46	−.99/.13	.25/.04	.11
1924–28	38	−.68/.21	.13/.06	.16
1928–30	36	−.52/.28	.24/.08	.26
1930–32	30	−.94/.09	.17/.04	.13
1932–36	31	−.58/.26	.14/.06	.17
1936–37	37	−.69/.14	.16/.04	.14

[a] Two district prefectures only.

values of b show enough variation that it would not have been practical to aggregate the data for multiple elections or to follow change in individual prefectures over time.

The amount of reduction in the differences and the SD's is proportionately fairly high, as shown by the values of the slope of the fit lines. The values of m range from about -0.5 to -1.0 and average about -0.7. We can use equation 6-3 to calculate k from the values of m and Δt. Representative values of k (per year) for selected values of m and Δt are as follows:

m	$\Delta t = 2$ years k	$\Delta t = 4$ years k
−.5	.35	.18
−.6	.46	.23
−.7	.55	.28
−.8	.80	.40

The values of m found for the entropy changes appear to be somewhat larger for the four-year intervals than for the two-year periods. The 1936 to 1937 interval shows an exceptionally high value of m; for this period k = 2.3. We have reason to believe that this very high value of k was due to special conditions, the nature of which are discussed in Chapter 7. For the other election periods, k is usually between 0.4 and 0.55. Note that if the time constant were two years, we would have $m = -.63$ and $k = 0.5$, which is approximately the result found. The 1930 to 1932 entropy difference shows the smallest value of b and is perhaps a slightly better estimate of k despite the smaller sample size; for the 1930 to 1932 period $k = 0.4$. All but three of the 15 prefectures show a decrease in differences over this period.

At this point in the development of the theory the exact value or range of k is of less interest than the fact that all the observed values of k are fairly high. A value of $k = 0.5$ indicates an instantaneous rate of decrease of 50% and a reduction to 37% of the initial difference in only two years. If it were not for the recurrent and strong effects of the environment, as shown by the generally high values of b, the prefectures would have quickly attained uniform entropy levels within their boundaries. But the strength of the interaction within the prefectures seems to be much greater than that across the country as a whole. In previous case studies we found that a wide range of entropy levels persisted across the set of prefectures for long periods of time. Thus geographical proximity seems to be a strong factor in explaining the high values of k observed here. The consistently high values of k over the 1920 to 1937 period also show that the reapportionment of districts and the expansion of the suffrage in 1925 had no significant effect on the pattern of change. Furthermore, the expected pattern of entropy and information variance relaxation holds over a wide range of entropy levels. Averaging the entropy levels over the set of all districts for the elections, we get the following results:

Election Year	Average District $H(P)$ (bits)
1920	0.94
1924	1.09
1928	1.27
1930	1.27
1932	1.09
1936	1.47
1937	1.63

Note that the expected relaxation patterns hold just as well during periods of stationary, increasing, and decreasing system entropy levels. In view of the strength of these findings overall, other factors that one might have expected to play a role, such as the turnout level, the number of political parties in the districts (the orbit number), or the rankings of the parties in the districts must be of minor significance at best.

The empirical evidence presented here is enough to show that social entropy can be an intensive acrossvariable in social systems analysis. It would be desirable, of course, to compare these findings for Japan with other social systems, especially to better our understanding of the factors affecting the constant k. The strength of the findings here points to the existence of strong social forces at the micro level, notably when subsystems are close together or when there is a high degree of social interaction across a region of a system; but what the underlying social and psychological processes are remains unknown.[4] (Some further ideas on this are taken up in Appendix II.)

6-2. *Spatiotemporal Change of Social Entropy*

The experimental results of the previous section show that a system will act to reduce differences in entropy levels with the effect that the system becomes increasingly homogeneous over its area. The general problem in dynamic analysis is to determine the spatiotemporal distribution of entropy values throughout a system once the initial distribution of entropy values

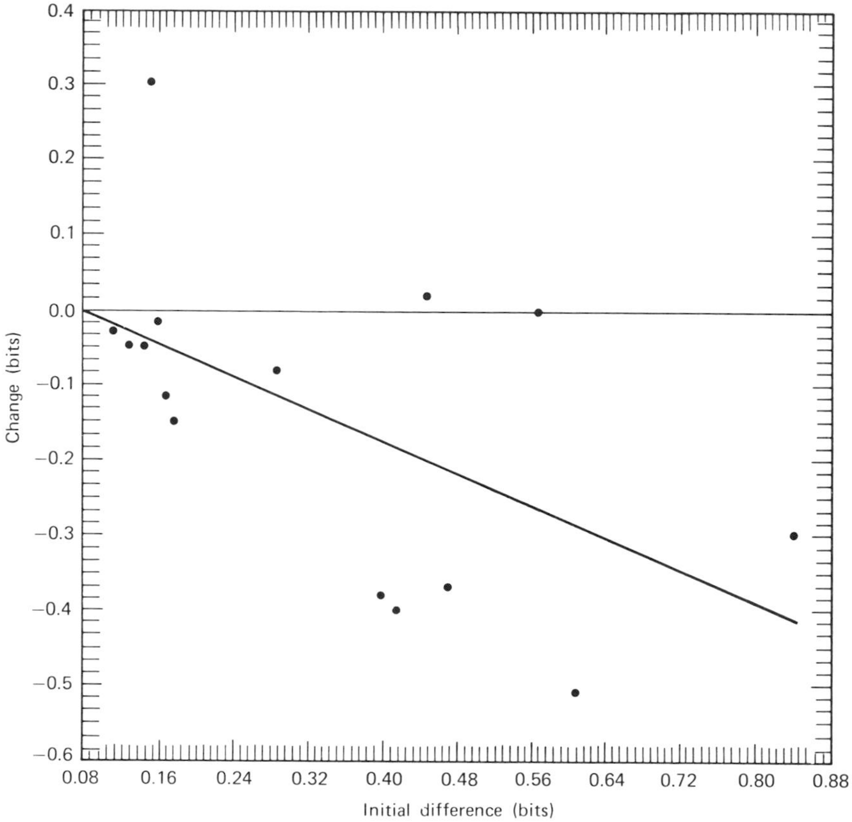

Figure 6-6. Entropy relaxation for entropy differences: Japan, 1930–32, with linear fitting.

has been specified. In other words, we want to know how the entropy values in a system change over time as a result of the initial system heterogeneity or disequilibrium. Since our knowledge of the state of a social system at this point is limited to what we can learn through entropy measurement alone, we are in a position similar to that of the early physicists who studied the properties of thermodynamic systems. Until the nineteenth century temperature was the primary quantitative measure for thermodynamic systems, and change was observed as change in temperature. Newton's law of cooling was the best quantitative expression of system dynamics. But even this limited knowledge of thermodynamics was sufficient for the construction of an analytic, mathematical theory having considerable scope and predictive power. This was accomplished in 1822 by J. B. Fourier in his *Theorie Analytique de la Chaleur.*[5] Fourier's theory allowed the prediction of temperature values across a system over time and required only a few simple assumptions about heat flow. Because of the analogy between the analysis of thermal systems and social systems, we can use Fourier's methods to develop a theory of social dynamics.

Let us review the problem in general terms. Suppose that we have an isolated social system composed of two homogeneous subsystems at different entropy levels H_1 and H_2, with H_1 greater than H_2. Suppose, too, that the system changes so that H_1 and H_2 converge in time to a single intermediate value representing the new equilibrium state of the system. (The final state is not necessarily between H_1 and H_2, however, if the system entropy levels are being raised or lowered by environmental influences.) In a naive interpretation of the observed system change one might reason as

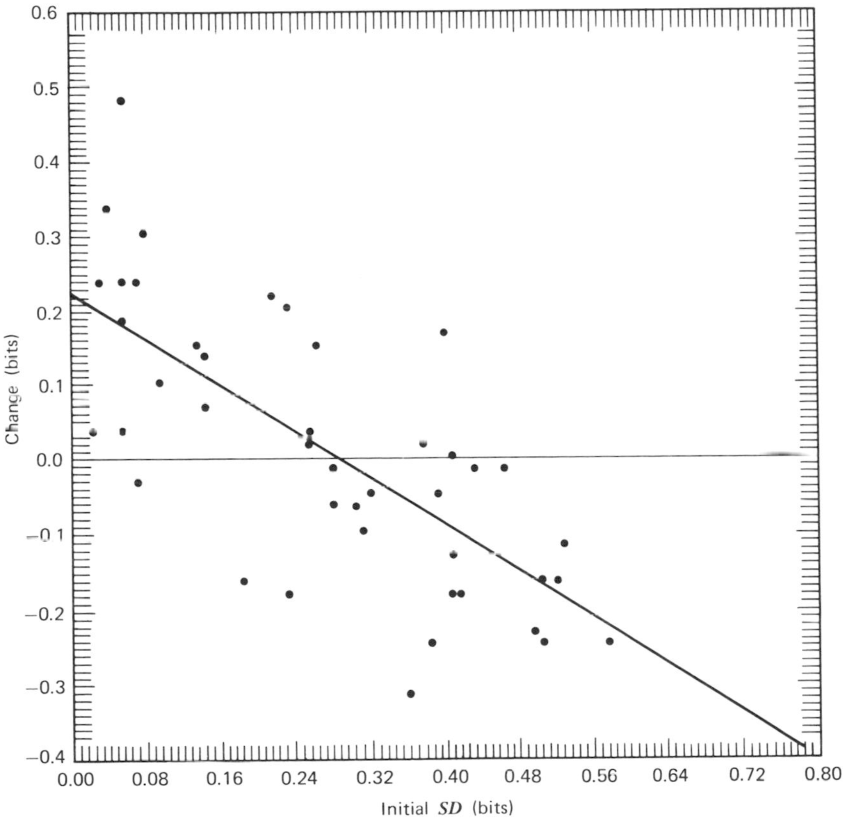

Figure 6-7. Entropy relaxation for the standard deviation *SD*: Japan, 1920–24, with linear fitting.

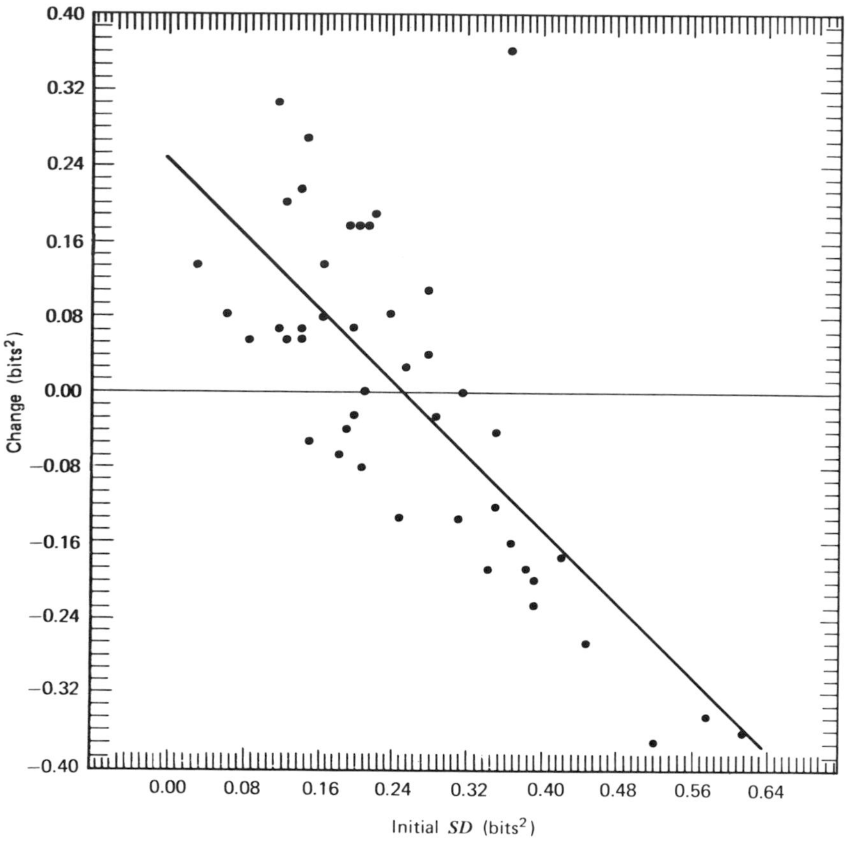

Figure 6-8. Information variance relaxation for the standard deviation SD: Japan, 1920–24, with linear fitting.

follows: The subsystem at H_1 initially had a quantity Q_1 of something that gave it that entropy level. But as a result of a flow of Q from the first subsystem to the second, the entropy level of the first decreased and that of the second, acquiring more Q, increased. Presumably, the amount of Q lost by one subsystem is equal to that gained by the other, and the net change in entropy levels is proportional to the amount of Q gained or lost by the subsystems, that is, the amount which flowed between the subsystems. (These assumptions are a conservation of Q law and the direct proportionality law for intensive variables.) This is exactly the reasoning that the early physicists used to explain changes in temperature; the quantity Q or heat was widely thought to be a real fluid, called caloric, which flowed between regions of unequal temperature.

The caloric theory of heat was eventually rejected in favor of the dual concepts of heat energy and thermodynamic entropy as it became known that no substantive flow or fluid is involved in the transfer of heat or entropy (by conduction or radiation). But for the purposes of an analytic theory, at least within a certain range of explanation, it does not matter whether the flow is real or not.[6] Thus Fourier was able to develop his analytic theory of heat at a time when the caloric theory was still widely believed, by relying on the known properties of temperature change and by making assumptions about heat flow that would be mathematically sufficient to "explain" the observed behavior of system temperatures. The sufficient assumptions are those just above in our naive interpretation of social change; they are properties we have come to associate with the two-variable measurement pattern. Systems one analyzes by analogous two-variable patterns have the same concepts of flow, even though sometimes there is no substantive flow.

In adapting Fourier's methods to the analysis of social dynamics, we can also use the primitive idea of a social quantity that can "flow" between social systems and cause the observed changes in entropy levels. This quantity can be labeled Q and its rate of flow dQ/dt, the time derivative. It is clear that no physical substance is involved in this social flow, and we are not concerned with a migration of people between social systems. (There may well be an important movement of people back and forth across system boundaries, however.) In effect, social flow is only a mathematical convenience—a notional flow—for predicting social entropy levels. It does not give any explanation of what social and psychological processes cause entropy levels to change as observed.

The quantity Q that we shall say is necessary for a social system to have an entropy level H can be called the social energy of the system. The term energy seems appropriate since it implies the ability to change the entropy level of another system at a lower entropy level. We can define the social energy in greater detail as we consider factors that would affect the final equilibrium entropy level attained by a heterogeneous system. It seems likely that the relative population sizes of interacting systems or subsystems would be of primary importance. If two regions of unequal population are involved, we would expect the larger to change its entropy level less than the smaller; or in other words, the majority will tend to prevail. Other factors affecting the final equilibrium might include population density, the number of different social event sets in the system, the frequency of events per person, and a factor related to the facility of social communication. We can combine some of these factors and write

$$Q = c\,P\,A\,H \qquad (6\text{-}8)$$

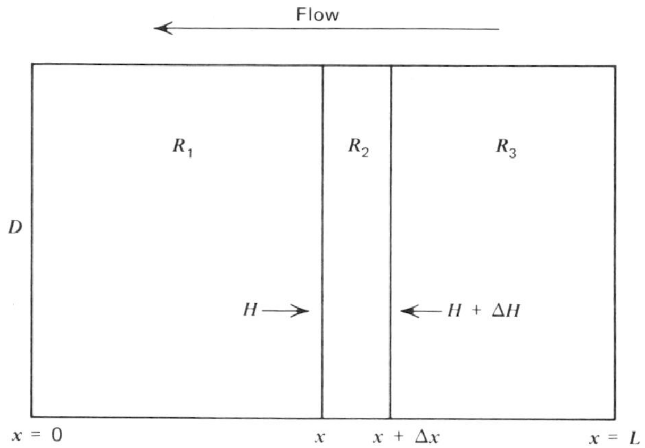

Figure 6-9. Hypothetical social system.

where Q is the social energy of a system of homogeneous population density P, of geographical area A, at entropy level H. The constant c represents a combination of other factors and should be interpreted as the amount of Q necessary to raise the entropy level of the system 1 bit per person. (The constant c is meant to be analogous to specific heat in thermal systems.) We must presume that c would vary somewhat from one social system to another. We will treat c as independent of the entropy level H in a system, although this may be only an approximation to actual systems. The units of Q can be called energy units. We could take the variables Q and dQ/dt as the throughvariables of the two-variable pattern, instead of N and dN/dt used previously; but we will not be measuring Q or dQ/dt in any case.

Let us next consider an idealized social system, as shown in Figure 6-9.[7] This system consists of two large regions R_1 and R_3 separated by a smaller region R_2. Over small areas at the edges of R_2 the values of entropy are H and $H + \Delta H$, respectively. The geographical dimensions are given by the width D and the coordinate x. Our problem is to analyze the change of entropy levels in this system along the single coordinate x. The population is assumed to be uniformly dense throughout the system.

We know (by assumption) that there will be a flow from R_3 to R_1 through R_2 because the entropy at the border of R_3 and R_2 is ΔH greater than at the border of R_1 and R_2. (See Figure 6-9.) We can find the amount of Q in R_2 at any moment from equation 6-8

$$Q_2 = c\, D\, P\, \Delta x\, \bar{H} \qquad (6\text{-}9)$$

where $\bar{H}$ is the average entropy in the interval $(x, x + \Delta x)$ which bounds R_2. We will also assume that the rate of flow through R_2 (Q per unit time) is

$$\text{(6-10)} \qquad \text{Rate of flow} \doteq -k \frac{\Delta H}{\Delta x} D$$

where k is a constant called the "conductivity" of the system (Q per unit time-bit entropy). The conductivity is a property of the system. We will assume, for simplicity, that conductivity is independent of direction of flow. Equation 6-10 states that as the distance between R_1 and R_3 increases, the rate of flow across R_2 decreases, or conversely, the resistance to flow increases. In social terms we would say that the greater the distance, and thus the more people, between R_1 and R_3, the longer it will take for the entropy change to propagate across the system. This is the effect observed in Japan where relaxation within prefectures is much more rapid than that due to interaction between different prefectures. But equation 6-10 also states that as the entropy difference $U = \Delta H$ increases, the rate of flow increases; this is a sufficient assumption for the "Newton's law" of entropy difference reduction to hold.[8] Equation 6-10 is analogous to Fourier's law in thermodynamics and Ohm's law in electrical theory. In the limiting case as $\Delta x \to 0$

$$\text{(6-11)} \qquad \text{Rate of flow} = \frac{dQ}{dt} = -k \frac{\partial H}{\partial x}$$

where $\partial H/\partial x$ is the partial derivative of H with respect to x.

Using either equation 6-9 or 6-11 we are able to calculate the amount of increase of Q in R_2 during a short interval of time $(t, t + \Delta t)$. We should, of course, obtain the same result from either equation 6-9 or 6-11. Therefore we have the equality

$$\text{(6-12)} \qquad c\,P\,D\,\Delta x[\bar{H}(x, t + \Delta t) - \bar{H}(x, t)]$$
$$= k\,D\,\Delta t \left[\frac{\partial \bar{H}(x + \Delta x, t)}{\partial x} - \frac{\partial \bar{H}(x, t)}{\partial x}\right]$$

where $\partial \bar{H}/\partial x$ is the average value of $\partial H/\partial x$ in the time interval $(t, t + \Delta t)$. Thus we have after a division

$$\text{(6-13)} \qquad \frac{c\,P[\bar{H}(x, t + \Delta t) - \bar{H}(x, t)]}{k\Delta t}$$
$$= \frac{[\partial \bar{H}(x + \Delta x, t)/\partial x] - [\partial \bar{H}(x, t)/\partial x]}{\Delta x}$$

And taking the limit as $\Delta x \rightarrow 0$ and $\Delta t \rightarrow 0$ we have the partial differential equation

$$\frac{\partial H}{\partial t} = \frac{k}{c\,P} \frac{\partial^2 H}{\partial x^2} \tag{6-14}$$

The equation 6-14 is solved to give $H(x, t)$, the entropy value at point x and time t. Thus we arrive at the spatiotemporal distribution of entropy values, not Q values, which is the desired practical result. To have a particular solution to equation 6-14 one must specify the initial or boundary values of entropy or its rate of change in the system. (The methods of solution are extensively covered in texts on partial differential equations and will not be discussed here.) The advantage in this method of analysis is that it lets us find entropy values when they may change continuously across a system over time. We are not restricted to viewing a system as a collection of homogeneous subsystems at discrete entropy values, as we have been previously. Alternatively, we can approximate a large number of small homogeneous subsystems distributed over a nearly continuous range of entropy values with the equations developed here.

For entropy change in more than one dimension, additional terms are added to equation 6-14. If x and y represent rectangular coordinates in two dimensions, the partial differential equation of change becomes

$$\frac{k}{c\,P}\left(\frac{\partial^2 H}{\partial x^2} + \frac{\partial^2 H}{\partial y^2}\right) = \frac{\partial H}{\partial t} \tag{6-15}$$

The Steady-State System. Many analytic problems involve finding a "steady-state" distribution of entropy values which is independent of time, that is, a distribution of values that will not vary with time. Such a case would arise if the initial entropy levels at points in the system were held constant in time, perhaps as a result of environmental interaction or constraints on the system. For a steady-state system the time derivative $\partial H/\partial t = 0$ and thus equation 6-14 becomes

$$\frac{\partial^2 H}{\partial x^2} = 0 \tag{6-16}$$

This is known as the Laplace equation (in one dimension). The solution of equation 6-16 gives $H(x)$, the entropy as a function of coordinate x alone. An important class of problems arises when we seek a solution to the Laplace equation that satisfies certain prescribed boundary conditions. That is, one must find a function $H(x)$ satisfying equation 6-16 and at the same time taking preassigned values on the boundary of the system. This problem, which was extensively studied by mathematicians in the last half of the nineteenth century, is known as the Dirichlet problem. In the multidimensional case it is known that this problem does not always have a solution, but if a solution does exist it is unique. In other words, the distribution of entropy values in a steady-state social system will be completely determined by the entropy values along the boundary of the system.

Before examining the implications of the Dirichlet problem for the analysis of social systems, we will solve the problem for a simplified one-dimensional case. Consider again the idealized one-dimensional social system of Figure 6-9. But suppose now that R_1 and R_3 are homogeneous regions at *fixed* entropy levels H_1 and H_3, with H_3 greater than H_1. We want to find the steady-state distribution of entropy values in R_2, a region of arbitrary width lying between x_1 and x_2. We must solve

$$\frac{\partial^2 H}{\partial x^2} = \frac{\partial H}{\partial t} = 0$$

for the boundary conditions $H(x_1) = H_1$ and $H(x_2) = H_3$. The solution is easily seen to be

$$H(x, t) = H(x) = c_0 + c_1 x$$

where c_0 and c_1 are two constant coefficients to be evaluated from the initial boundary conditions at x_1 and x_2. Solving for the coefficients we thus obtain

$$H(x) = H_1 + \frac{x - x_1}{x_2 - x_1}(H_3 - H_1) \tag{6-17}$$

for x in the interval (x_1, x_2) defining R_2. This solution is shown in Figure 6-10.

Figure 6-10 shows that the entropy increases linearly from x_1 to x_2, across R_2. The values of $H(x)$ in R_2 are completely determined by the values at x_1 and x_2. Since the values of entropy in R_1 and R_3 are assumed to be held constant in time, the distribution of entropy values across R_2 is constant in time once the steady-state distribution shown in Figure 6-10 is attained. Whatever the initial distribution of entropy values may be in R_2, the system will eventually reach the steady-state equilibrium of Figure 6-10, and there will be no further change in the system.

To study spatial distributions of entropy in actual social systems, we must use two geographical coordinates. The two-dimensional case is, of course, more complex mathematically than the one-dimensional case, but even so, the results shown in Figure 6-10 do express the main features of two-dimensional steady-state systems. The principal difference in the two-dimensional case is that instead of only straight lines, convex or concave curves, or both

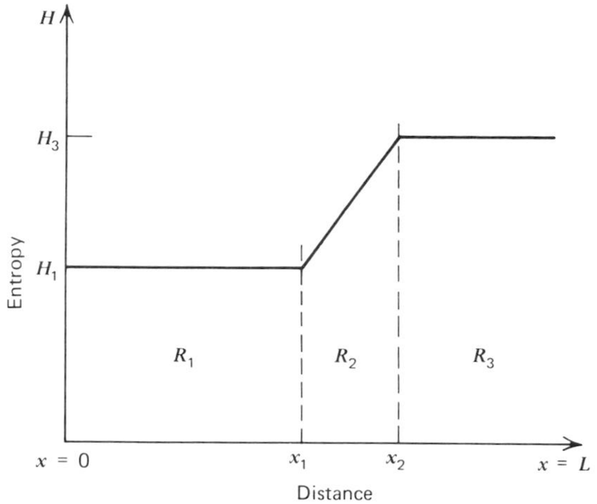

Figure 6-10. Spatial entropy distribution (equation 6-17) across region R_2 in the steady state, for fixed entropy levels in R_1 and R_3. The system will eventually attain this distribution regardless of the initial entropy distribution in R_2.

with an inflection point, may appear along a one-dimensional geographic cross section of the system.

Let us next consider the Laplace equation for two rectangular coordinates x and y and the spatial entropy distribution $H(x, y)$ or $H(x, y, t)$. Setting $\partial H/\partial t = 0$ in equation 6-15 we have

$$\frac{\partial^2 H}{\partial x^2} + \frac{\partial^2 H}{\partial y^2} = 0 \qquad (6\text{-}18)$$

A system with an entropy distribution satisfying equation 6-18 over its area is, again, a steady-state system.

A function $H(x, y)$ defined in a system or region of a system is said to be *harmonic* in the system or region, or alternatively, is called a potential function, if it is continuous together with its partial derivatives of the first two orders and satisfies equation 6-18.[9] Linear functions of the form $H(x, y) = ax + by + c$, where a, b, and c are arbitrary constants, are the simplest harmonic functions. A two-dimensional linear harmonic function is the simple extension of the one-dimensional results in Figure 6-10 and can be visualized as a plane tilted in one or both directions. A function of the form $H(x, y) = axy$ is also harmonic, but this function would be represented as a curved surface rather than as a plane. As one can easily verify (by differentiation), the product of a constant and a harmonic function is still a harmonic function, and the sum of any two harmonic functions is harmonic.

Several theorems about harmonic functions show this class of functions to have unique properties. In the first place, a (nonconstant) function that is harmonic on a closed region will always take its maximum and minimum values on the boundary of the region and never in the interior. The mean-value theorem for harmonic functions states that if a function is harmonic in a region, the average of values of the function around any circle in the region will equal the value of the function at the center of the circle. Thus averages around concentric circles must be equal. These theorems give a picture of how a harmonic function behaves, and consequently, also describe properties of steady-state systems. From these theorems we can also conclude that if a function is harmonic on a closed region, it is uniquely determined by the values the function takes on the boundary of the region. We have seen this to be true for the one-dimensional case where the region is a closed interval. In the two-dimensional case, however, the problem of determining the harmonic function that has certain known boundary values is considerably more difficult than in the one-dimensional case. In fact, we know that the problem does not always have a solution. But it has been shown that a solution does exist for a broad class of regions having sufficiently smooth boundaries; the boundary values need not be a continuous function around the perimeter of the region.

The properties of harmonic functions summarized above let us describe the distribution of entropy values that would occur in a steady-state social system, assuming that the macroscopic social processes are adequately represented by the mathematical assumptions implicit in equation 6-15. Analyzing the system as a collection of subsystems, we would expect to find the highest and lowest entropy values occurring in subsystems along the geographic boundary of the system. If one moved across the system from the highest to the lowest entropy region(s), the local entropy value in the intervening subsystems should decrease continuously (smoothly); however, the decrease need not be linear per unit distance. In the interior of the system there should be no regions or collections of contiguous subsystems that have uniformly higher or lower entropy values than the surrounding subsystems. In other words, if we think of the entropy distribution as a surface, there should be no "bumps" in it. Areas with local maxima or minima violate the conditions of a harmonic function. (The average entropy around a circle centered at the local extremum would not equal the value at that extremum.) We have also supposed that the population density is an important factor in the diffusion of social change across a system; in short, areas of higher population density should be more resistant to the propagation of change than lower density areas, if other things are equal. Steeper entropy gradients will be observed across regions of higher density.

If a political system or subsystem is relatively isolated from adjacent systems, yet uniformly conductive within its own borders, its entropy distribution may have the characteristics of a harmonic function over a closed region. This can come about despite the fact that we cannot hold the boundary values of a closed political system at fixed entropy levels, as through the action of exogenous entropy sources. Although the trend of change in a closed system will be toward increasing uniformity of entropy levels, the spatial entropy distribution will tend to approximate a harmonic function as the system relaxes to equilibrium.

Imagine that a system has been randomly disequilibrated so that one or more large regions of the system have higher than average entropy levels. Let us also assume that the cause of the disequilibrium was transient and no longer affects the system. The entropy distribution, as a surface over the system, will be uneven and there will be local maxima and minima. From the partial differential equation of system change (6-15), we see that the rate of entropy change in time is greatest where the sum of second partial derivatives of the entropy with respect to the spatial coordinates (the Laplacian) is greatest. This implies that the rate of system relaxation will be greatest in those regions of the system having local extrema and where the entropy level varies most unevenly (nonharmonically). Regions of the system where the spatial distribution is close to harmonic, in contrast, will have a much slower rate of change of entropy. We can state this more precisely, although we omit some steps necessary for complete mathematical rigor. Consider dividing the system into subregions of three kinds according to whether the entropy distribution is (1) approximately harmonic; or (2) greater than, or (3) less than the harmonic function that has those same boundary values for the subregion (or the system as a whole). It can then be shown that the Laplacian is approximately zero in subregions of the first kind, is negative in subregions of the second kind, and positive in the third. Thus from equation 6-15, the time rate of change of the entropy distribution in the three kinds of subregions will be zero, negative, or positive, respectively; the system will tend toward a harmonic distribution in each of the subregions and in the system as a whole.

The relaxation process can be approximated for theoretical or numerical purposes by a method of successive averaging. First, one determines the entropy values at a given time on the points of intersection of a grid on the system; these values will represent the entropy levels in corresponding subsystems. Then at each stage of the averaging process, each grid point value is replaced by a new value computed as the average of the four entropy values at adjacent grid points. (If the point is on the boundary, a three-point average may be used.) The successive averaging describes, approximately, the state of the system at intervals of time in the relaxation process; the time interval is proportional to the relaxation rate and the size of the grid pattern.

The overall distribution will continue to change throughout the relaxation period, of course, becoming increasingly uniform; but at any time it will still have the characteristics of a steady-state distribution once having reached that condition (approximately). Thus we can describe the system with a succession of harmonic functions, each approximating the entropy distribution over a period of time. This period of time could be fairly long, even without fixed boundary values, because the rate of change will be comparatively slow once the system is close to a steady-state distribution. (This is easily seen by applying the method of successive averaging to a suitable hypothetical case.) During the period of approximation, one could think of the system as being in a quasi-steady state. However, we cannot say *a priori* exactly when in its relaxation period a system will sufficiently resemble a steady-state system; this would depend upon the characteristics of the initial disequilibrium, the amount of random change during the relaxation period, and the conductivity of the system over its area.

If a political system has a harmonic entropy distribution, it would keep this characteristic despite various system-wide changes that might coincidentally occur. From the properties of harmonic functions we know that if a constant amount of entropy were added (or subtracted) uniformly throughout the system, the distribution would still be harmonic. This would also be the case if the entropy levels were increased or decreased by a fixed percentage of their existing levels, or in general, if the change itself could be represented as a harmonic function. Thus once a system attains a quasi-steady state, it is relatively "stable" in the sense that it will remain in a quasi-steady state despite subsequent changes that might affect entropy levels of the system as a whole in any of the ways just described.

Until now we have not considered in any way the effects on spatial entropy distributions of entropy or uncertainty sources (formally, Q sources) within a system. On the contrary, we have assumed their absence in the hypothetical systems analyzed previously. A mathematical treatment of the problem of entropy sources would be excessively complex at this stage of theory construction and would yield little more for a qualitative understanding of the problem than can be gained through simple reasoning. In any event, we have no direct method for quantitatively measuring the strength of entropy sources, apart from observing the net system entropy levels. As a practical matter, entropy sources such as urban, industrial centers are often located in boundary, and especially coastal, areas of political systems and thus may approximate fixed boundary conditions.

Fairly simple arguments have been given to suggest that during a relaxation period a closed political system may have at least temporarily and approximately the characteristics of a (nonhomogeneous) steady-state system, with a harmonic entropy distribution. In view of our limited knowledge of actual political systems, however, we cannot say *a priori* that quasi-steady-state political systems will occur frequently or have enough persistence in time to be readily observable with electoral entropy measurements. As desirable as a more comprehensive and mathematically rigorous analysis of the problem may be, we can only resolve these questions through an examination of actual systems.

The easiest way to investigate the properties of spatial entropy distributions is through a special kind of graphical analysis. A function that is harmonic over a two-dimensional region lends itself very well, because of its smoothness, to graphical analysis by isarithmic mapping: the plotting of contours of equal values of the harmonic function against the spatial coordinates. A familiar example of this technique is the isothermal weather map, where lines are drawn connecting geographical locations of equal temperature (or equal average temperature) at a given point in time. We can apply this method to the analysis of spatial entropy patterns across political systems; in this case the lines connecting points of equal entropy are termed "isentropic contours." This method of analysis does not offer a rigorous test of the underlying mathematical model, however, because it does not permit the time derivative of entropy change to be examined directly, as was possible in the case of Japan (Section 6-1). Nevertheless, the graphical method of analysis is a first step in establishing the existence of quasi-steady-state political systems. Moreover, as we will see shortly, it also yields a greater understanding of the dynamics of political systems that do not largely exhibit steady-state characteristics.

Spatial Entropy Distributions in the United States. Isentropic contour maps have been drawn for a number of American elections, including those for which data was used in testing the entropy hypothesis (Chapter 3). However, only the most important conclusions of this analysis will be presented here. We have used a simple, and easily duplicated, method for obtaining the contours. Entropy values for each state were rounded, in most instances to the nearest tenth of a bit, and contours were drawn along state boundary lines to separate regions at different entropy levels. This method is satisfactory for our purposes here, but a more sophisticated mapping procedure could certainly be used. (One could use smaller subsystems than states and some method of averaging or smoothing out minor variations over small two-dimensional regions.)

The map for the 1968 American election is shown in Figure 6-11, with contours drawn at increments of 0.1 bits. States lying between contours have entropy levels equal to that of the lower-valued contour, except where local extrema occur, as indicated. We can see immediately that the United States in 1968 had the characteristics of a (quasi) steady-state system; it is perhaps the best example of this among the elections studied. The entropy

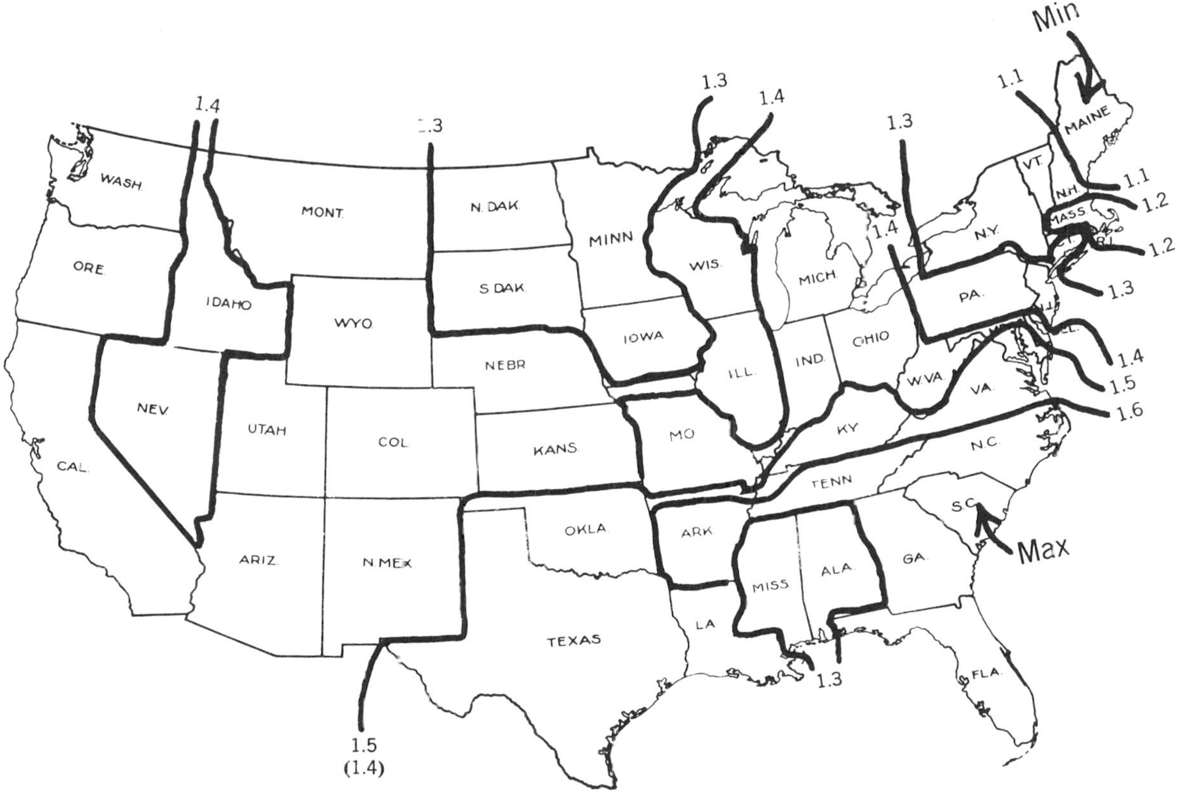

Figure 6-11. United States, 1968; isentropic contours, showing a near harmonic, steady-state distribution of entropy values.

maximum was located in South Carolina and the minimum in Maine, both boundary states.[10] The entropy level decreases gradually from the southeastern states toward the west or north. The greatest decrease in entropy level occurs from the maximum to minimum along the Atlantic coast; all intervening contours are crossed along this path. The greater decrease in entropy along the east coast in comparison with gradients toward the north-central or west may be due to the greater population density in the east. We see only a few minor departures from a harmonic entropy distribution. The states of Idaho and Nevada, together, form a local maximum 0.1 bits above the other western states. But if we consider the small populations of these states and their semi-isolation, the local maximum is not a surprizing occurrence. There are "missing" contours in several places; going west from Texas or north from Missouri or Arkansas, the entropy decreases by 0.2 bits instead of 0.1 bit. However, these missing contours might well be recovered if smaller subsystems were used in constructing the contours. The states of Alabama and Mississippi form a local minimum in the south; this is allowed for a harmonic distribution since they are boundary states. As an application of the mean-value theorem for harmonic functions one can compute the average entropy over concentric circles. In the case of the United States we can do this by calculating the average entropy for boundary states and again for the set of interior states. As would be expected from the theorem, these two averages are nearly equal for the 1968 election.

We can summarize the entropy distribution of 1968 as follows. Prior to the election there was a large but transient rise in entropy in the South, which was propagated throughout the system. The initial cause of the increased uncertainty was undoubtedly the civil rights movement of the 1960's and the related actions by the Federal government to alter behavior patterns, especially in the South. Although this source of uncertainty had a spatial orientation itself, we have no reason to believe that it had the smooth and graduated distribution observable in Figure 6-11. (There may also have been at the same time a more uniform but smaller entropy increase due to other causes, such as the Vietnam war and economic conditions, but this cannot be determined directly and it does not affect the observation of propagation effects.) The conclusion that the isentropic contours of 1968 do indeed represent a propagation or diffusion of entropy is reinforced by observation of earlier elections and the subsequent 1972 election. By the 1972 election the transient increase in entropy in the South had passed, and the South reverted to its normal, lower than national average, entropy levels. Nevertheless, the system again in 1972 had steady-state characteristics; in contrast to 1968, however, the slope of the entropy distribution decreased from west to east, and north to south.[11] The maximum state entropy in 1972 was in Oregon and the minimum in Georgia. One can imagine that the entropy distribution, as a continuous sheet over the country, had been lifted up by the southeast corner in 1968 and then dropped again in 1972 while the northern and western edges were held at almost the same levels during the whole time. Entropy levels of the intervening states rose and fell in proportion to their proximity to the Southeast.

The 1972 spatial entropy pattern of the United States is much more typical of historical distributions than is the 1968 election. The usual pattern is one of high entropy levels in the West and North and low entropy levels in the Southeast, with intervening states having intermediate values. As we have seen in other countries, entropy levels tend to be higher in areas of industrialization and urbanization. Thus a permanent tendency toward higher entropy levels in the North and in the Pacific coastal states of the United States seems to show again the effects of these factors. But urbanization and industrialization are not so evenly and gradually changing across the country to account completely for the observed spatial patterns having a nearly harmonic character. To explain uncertainty or entropy levels in the United States, we must include the effects of spatial propagation of entropy as well as the relatively fixed sources, such as industrialization, and other transient sources of uncertainty, which as in 1968 may even dominate or obscure the effects of fixed sources.

In earlier elections, as in 1920 or 1924, one also observes more local variability in the spatial pattern; local maxima and minima and steeper gradients between states are more common than in 1968 or 1972, especially in the South. This leads to the conclusion that the general course of social change in the United States has been in the direction of increasing the integration of the states and decreasing their isolation from one another. As a result, entropy changes are now more easily propagated across the system as a whole; the conductivity of the system has increased and become more uniform over its area. This situation can be contrasted with Japan, where there is still much greater isolation of prefectures from one another due to social, economic, or geographical reasons. In contemporary Japan, the effects of urbanization and industrialization play a much greater role in determining relative subsystem entropy levels than do spatial propagation effects. Only within the prefectures are high conductivity levels found, as reported in Section 6-1.

As a final comment on the strength of the steady-state patterns in recent American elections, especially in 1968 and 1972, we can call attention to the smallness of the increments between successive entropy contours. That is, it is still possible to draw isentropic contours with state data at intervals as small as 0.1 bits. This indicates a remarkable sensitivity to small entropy differences among the population, and correspondingly, the ability of the respective state populations to maintain equilibrium entropy levels to this degree, while controlling random subsystem variations in the level. Although not all elections or subsystems will show such finely separated isentropic contours, the fact that this can happen in a system where conductivity is high and there is sufficient variation across the system points to the high collective awareness of, or sensitivity to, local entropy levels by a population. This sensitivity also accounts for the strength of the results obtained for the study of relaxation in Japanese prefectures (Section 6-1), but it is perhaps more evident from the spatial mapping.

We can describe the entropy distributions in the United States during recent, twentieth-century elections as being close to quasi-steady-state over most of the country; the few states or regions that do not fit the pattern show instead the greater variability and discontinuity one associates with semi-isolated subsystems. This pattern of entropy distribution, which appears to be the normal state of the system now, has not always prevailed in the United States. The elections just prior to the Civil War show a sharply contrasting spatial entropy distribution. The pre-Civil War pattern can be characterized as being a fairly continuous entropy distribution across the system, but one that is distinctly *not* a harmonic function. It is highly instructive to contrast the 1860 election with recent American elections to get an insight into how a nonharmonic distribution may come into being and what its significance may be for a system. Entropy contours for the United States in 1860 are shown in Figure 6-12.[12] The country has been divided by the contours into regions of low, medium, and high entropy (**L,M,H**) according to whether the state entropy is (1) less than 1.1 bits; (2) between 1.1 and 1.3 bits; or (3) greater than 1.3 bits. The fairly wide contours smooth out the minor state variations and present the main features of the distribution more clearly.

As can be seen immediately in Figure 6-12, the entropy distribution, although reasonably continuous, fails to be a harmonic function for several reasons. In particular, the high entropy ridge extending in an arc across the system from Missouri to Pennsylvania violates the harmonic conditions; the high entropy regions in the South and New England are further departures from a steady-state pattern. On further inspection of Figure 6-12, however, we can imagine that if the system were divided along the more southern of the two east-west high contour lines, marked **AB** in the figure, the system would then consist of two separate regions each having a harmonic distribution. (One might also consider separating New England from the rest of the northern region, but the distance between their high entropy areas is relatively small.) In other words, we could view the United States in 1860 as a system consisting of two (or perhaps three) separate quasi-steady-state systems that happened to adjoin one another. Although the overall entropy

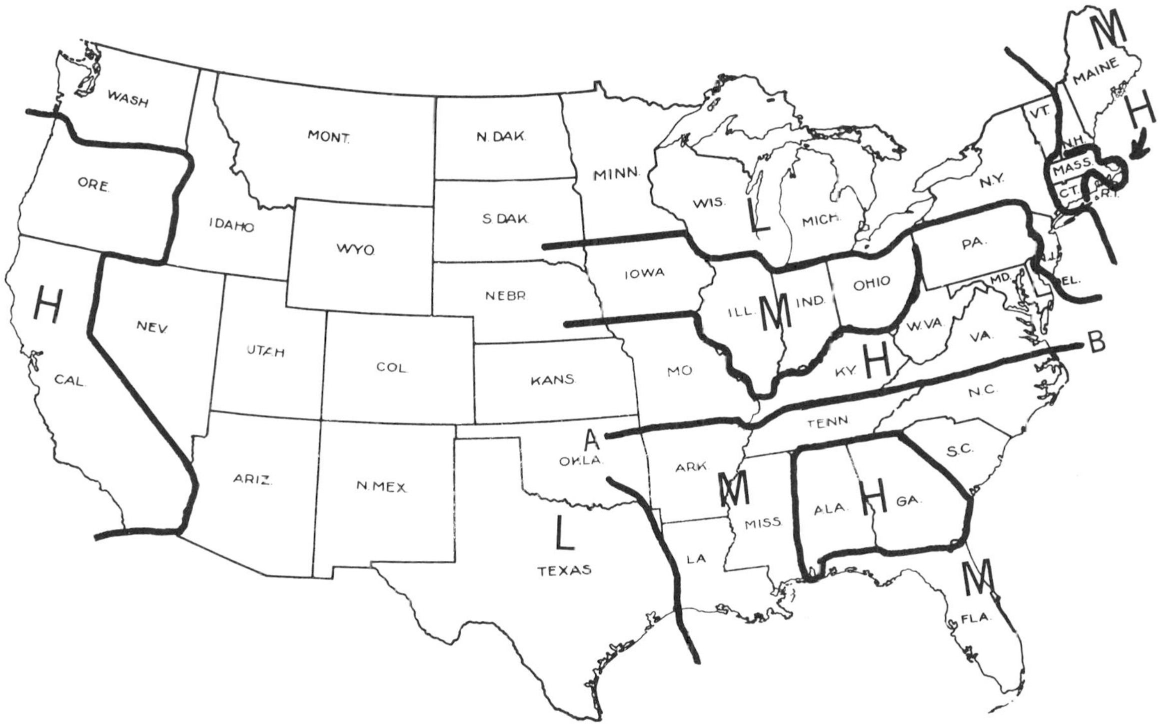

Figure 6-12. United States, 1860; isentropic contours (nonharmonic): **L**ow, **M**edium, and **H**igh entropy regions; a likely presecession or precivil war distribution.

distribution might be completely attributed to entropy sources having that distribution, we could also infer that the system had been for some time a union of semi-isolated regions each of which had taken on steady-state characteristics independently of the other and with little propagation of entropy change from one region to another. The secession of the South following 1860 supports this idea of pre-existing separate regions. Note that the contour line **AB** became the northern border of the Confederacy except for the addition of Virginia, which itself divided, leaving West Virginia in the Union. (Virginia is perhaps even less of an exception than Figure 6-12 indicates since the entropy in Pennsylvania was in fact substantially higher than in Virginia.)

In any case, whatever the cause of the 1860 distribution, our mathematical model of spatial entropy change, equation 6-15, indicates that the system would have had a rapid change in entropy levels if there had not been a secession and if there were a high degree of social interaction, or conductivity, in the central area of the country. Compared to a typical quasi-steady-state distribution, the pattern of 1860 is a potentially "unstable" condition that can persist only for a short time or in the absence of social flow or interaction across the system. Even had the United States had no secession and civil war, we can speculate that the magnitude of system relaxation, which must eventually have followed, might still have produced a great deal of social unrest. (One can reflect on the amount of civil strife that accompanied the transient rise of entropy in the United States prior to 1968.) But from the perspective of this analysis, the Civil War itself seems to have been the result of the secession and was not an immediate result of the nonharmonic distribution; it is the secession that we predict from the 1860 distribution, not necessarily the ensuing war. We see in Chapter 7 that other structural conditions and dynamic processes may also lead to civil strife or war, but without any partitioning of the political system.

The potentially unstable, nonharmonic, entropy distribution of the United States in 1860 occurred in a pre-existing national political system. The same kind of distribution could also come about through a different sequence of events, namely, by a political system being formed from previously separated quasi-steady-state systems. Or if the social interaction or conductivity between previously isolated systems were rapidly increased, it would very likely result in a nonharmonic distribution followed by a period of relaxation where there would then be considerable stresses due to the structural changes in the merging societies. An increased rate of interaction might be fostered by improved economic and technical conditions, or simply by a change in national boundaries. It is easy to think of nonharmonic distributions having occurred many times over in the past several centuries as nation-states in Europe and elsewhere developed from pre-existing aggregations of smaller, semi-isolated, political or social systems. In places where this process is still going on, as in many "developing" countries or in the European Economic Community, the methods of spatial analysis may prove useful in assessing how much integration or interaction there is between the subsystems or systems and thus what problems may later arise due to their prospective integration or merger.

6-3. *Conclusions on Acrossvariable Dynamics*

A numerical solution of the partial differential equations derived above may be quite difficult for an actual political system. One of the main advantages in developing the analytic theory is that a variety of general problems, or general classes of system phenomena, can be studied mathematically with only a minimal need of experimental data. This may lead to the prediction of regularities in system entropy distributions, such as the harmonic functions of steady-state systems. Or it may allow the study of hypothetical conditions that would produce dramatic, and perhaps unexpected, changes in entropy-measurable social structure. In this respect, we can also analyze the stability of solutions of the equations and the effects on the solutions of changes in initial entropy distributions or coefficient values. The most immediate difficulty in obtaining exact numerical solutions, however, is that the values of the coefficients, such as the conductivity k, are not known for actual systems. This was also a problem in Fourier's time for the analogous case of thermodynamic systems. It was several decades after Fourier's analytic theory first appeared before the values of the coefficients could be determined independently. Thus the quality of explanation and prediction within the social theory presented here is at about the same level as that of early or middle nineteenth-century thermodynamics and other physical theories of the period. The shared weakness of all these theories at this level of development is their nearly exclusive reliance on macroscopic properties and variables. Further progress and better explanation only became possible in physics when a greater understanding of microscopic system processes was attained. We can expect the same to be true of the social theory.

In this analysis of acrossvariable dynamics we have considered only unitary system models applied to national political systems. The extension of these methods to organizations presents a somewhat different analytic problem. Our primary concern in examining organizations is with the relationships between hierarchical strata and with the degree of control that one part of an organization may hold over another. (See also Section 4-2.) The degree of control, or power, can be expressed with an entropy-derived measure using conditional probabilities; the degree to which one person's behavior lets us predict the behavior of someone else describes the extent of control of the first person over the second. But an organization is an "unnatural" arrangement in the sense that this degree of control would not exist in the society at large. We can assume that persons in an organization have a tendency to reduce their dependence on, or control by, others. We must also expect the possibility of error or spontaneity in an individual's actions, going beyond expected role behavior in the organization. To maintain control or to correct inappropriate behavior there is a flow of communication in the organization in the form of instructions, orders, or correctives; this flow is essentially uni-directional (with an allowance for a feedback channel of communications, if necessary).

We can express the quantitative degree of control of one person over another by the distance function or metric cited in Chapter 2 (note 2): zero distance implies complete control; increasing distance (up to 1) implies decreasing or incomplete control. Thus, the analogy to acrossvariable dynamics and the equilibrium restoring property is that distance has a natural tendency to increase, and that a certain flow of communication is necessary to reduce the distance or hold it constant (a steady state). The amount and rate of communication flow will also depend on other, presumably constant, organizational factors. This tendency toward increasing distance is opposite the sense of change in relaxation patterns in other systems where the difference tends to decrease over time. So we could simply reverse our distance formula (subtracting it from 1) and then have a comparable formulation.

Since we can represent organizational strata in most organizations by a fairly small number of discrete points, we do not need the partial differential equation model of change, suited as it is to a range of entropy levels over a continuous system. Instead, in the analysis of an organization, the network model of systems analysis (Section 1-4) may be more appropriate for representing the relative location (control) of persons or strata and the lines of communication between them. The throughvariables of interest would likely be N and dN/dt (Chapter 2), not the virtual social quantity Q and its flow dQ/dt. (In certain cases we might also wish to consider feedback models, to analyze error-correcting procedures and their effects in organizations.) For some applications it might be desirable to consider, in addition, the absolute entropy levels of the organizational strata independently of their degree of control or dependence on one another. We can compare the absolute levels with one another or with the level in the society at large. Whether this might lead to the discovery of important dynamic properties of organizations is an open question. Rarely, one might also have occasion to model an organization with a large number of strata as a continuous, instead of discrete, system. To consider both within- and across-strata change, one might then use a three-dimensional partial differential equation model and spherical harmonic functions (which have the same properties as two-dimensional harmonic functions).

The tendency of a heterogeneous system to become increasingly homogeneous points to the existence of strong psychological motives for reducing entropy differences. There may well be an absolute quantity of psychological strain associated with an entropy difference or disequilibrium and proportional to it. Thus where a difference is maintained in opposition to the natural tendency to reduce it, system members may bear a continued psychological cost. On the other hand, the act of reducing entropy differences, and thus changing entropy levels and effecting changes in social behavior, may also cause psychological strain. Studies of the effects of social change on people show that change can cause both psychological and physiological maladies.[13] Sudden changes in entropy levels, entropy differences, or the rates of interaction between groups of people could lead to increases in the likelihood of psychological strain, violence, or social conflict.

We have seen that urbanization and industrialization, among other factors, can cause changes in local entropy levels in a national political system. These changes can be propagated to some extent across a system through the mechanism of acrossvariable dynamics. Thus people at a distance from the original source of uncertainty and entropy change may still be affected by the change and have to share in its costs. If the psychological effects of entropy change or maintenance of entropy differences could be quantified, it might then be possible to evaluate the true human costs (or benefits) of social, political, economic, or other change in a society.

A comparison of intensive and acrossvariable dynamics shows that traditional interests of political theory fit into the social theory in different ways. Intensive dynamics leads to conclusions about change in political party systems, voter participation, and their interrelationship. Acrossvariable dynamics brings out the importance of spatial interaction or communication across a political system. Acrossvariable dynamics is related to the definition and integration of national political systems, the partitioning of regional political units, and any spatial variations that may exist in governmental activities. In view of this, is seems feasible that political systems and governmental activity could be designed to achieve specific entropy related goals, as for example: to minimize the "side effects" of social or economic change, to reduce the likelihood of conflict, or to maintain desirable entropy levels (if there are such). We should also note that the existence of acrossvariable dynamic phenomena further contradicts the interpretation of electoral behavior as an individualistic decision-making rationale, a ranking of voter preferences, or an expression of popular will. The content-free nature of the entropy measure is especially apparent in dynamic processes.

CHAPTER SEVEN

Entropy Reduction

7-1. *Pathological Dynamics: Entropy Reduction*

In this chapter we conclude our study of macroscopic social phenomena by examining a third major type of dynamic behavior. Although this third variety of system behavior contains elements of both intensive and across-variable dynamics, it requires an explanation of additional factors that are not immediately related to the dynamics previously studied. The sociopolitical phenomenon we seek to explain is the mass authoritarian revolution, when an apparently democratic political system is transformed over a period of years into a dictatorial regime supported by a broad consensus among the population. This political change usually involves the emergence of a single dominant political party in place of an earlier multiparty system, as well as the suppression of or mass violence against minority groups in the population.

Instances fitting this pattern to a substantial extent are the transformation of Imperial Russia to become the Soviet Union, the fall of the Weimar Republic of Germany and the rise of the Hitler regime, and the demise of Sukarno's government in Indonesia in the 1960's and its replacement by military rule. We can distinguish these social transformations from other military coups and governmental changeovers in that the revolutions involved massive change in social and political behavior throughout the society. They were not simply the result of actions taken by small groups of conspirators or a social elite who seized control of the government. A military group or a revolutionary elite may very well take over the government, but this will inevitably be a consequence of prior, widespread social change. The new government may sometimes come to power through electoral success; the rise of the National Socialist party in Weimar Germany is an example of this.

Presumed causes for a revolution or its eventual outcome have included economic conditions, the effect of a revolutionary leader on the populace, the role of a revolutionary political party, the power of a revolutionary ideology on mass opinion, the failure of a democratic multiparty system, widespread change in psychological attitudes and needs, historical social class conflicts, and so forth. Since revolutions have often led to domestic violence or international warfare, we might also consider as causative factors the variety of explanations that have been offered for human aggression and violence. These range from violence as instinctual human behavior, to psychological motives, to immorality, and to the possibility that it is a completely learned behavior pattern. By and large, these explanations of revolution and violence all incorporate the idea of intentionality or goal-oriented activity on the part of the major social actors as the deciding force in bringing about the social transformation.[1] Since rationality or intentionality is a key assumption (often only implicit) of previous theories of revolution, we can use it as a point of comparison to the theory we shall propose here.

In our analysis of the authoritarian revolution we again use social entropy measurements, made with electoral data. This returns us to the question of rationality in social choice, which was discussed in the context of testing the entropy hypothesis (Section 3-4). An explanation of revolution might take several possible forms, with respect to rationality. (1) It could be a rational, intentional choice from among alternatives, with a widespread popular preference for a revolution or a revolutionary political party. (2) It could be a rational choice, preferred among alternatives, but involving a different basis from normal social conditions; people could change their personal utility scales or decision rules for perceived utility. For example, people might expect to gain more from violent action than they would in normal social conditions. (3) Revolution could be completely irrational or instinctive. Or (4), as the entropy measure would lead us to believe, revolution may have an entirely different, content free, basis of rationality and not imply anything about popular preferences or intentions to achieve a revolutionary transformation of society, or any subsequent violence or warfare. In this fourth case, however, we must be able to explain how such a massive change in entropy-measurable phenomena can develop when it is clearly not anticipated by the theory of social dynamics presented so far. We, in fact, introduce a theory of revolution that shows it to be a pathological variant of the normal dynamic processes. First, however, we examine in detail the empirical properties of an authoritarian revolution.

In judging from the empirical results to follow which of these, or other, explanations of the mass authoritarian revolution is most appropriate, the reader is invited to consider two points: First, whether the empirical findings, which are very complex, clear and distinctive, and involve entire national populations, fall in any way within the range of previous explanations of the historical events—even qualitatively, if not quantitatively. And, second, what degree or kind of intentionality and awareness about their society would have been necessary for large numbers of people to have acted collectively or individually so that the observed macroscopic patterns would occur. As a standard of comparison in reference to this second point, one can try to imagine how difficult it would be to organize a hypothetical society with the expressed purpose of producing the observed results, even with the full cooperation of the citizenry and under national guidance.

In the language of our method of analysis, a mass authoritarian revolution is best described as a rapid, spontaneous reduction in system entropy to a near zero level. In earlier case studies of national political systems we have observed a fairly wide range of entropy levels, extending from near zero to over 2 bits. We have also seen that the systems were able to keep relatively constant entropy levels over long periods of time. Where some change in entropy levels has taken place, it could be attributed to substantial socioeconomic forces such as urbanization and industrialization. In no instance have we observed continuous large changes or fluctuations in entropy levels. No systems oscillate over large entropy ranges from one election to the next. The ability of a system to maintain an equilibrium entropy level will be considered the normal or expected behavior of unitary systems. In this respect the social theory conforms to the two-variable theories of the physical sciences. Under certain conditions, however, the normal equilibrium properties of national political systems can be lost. Where this has happened, a dramatic period of entropy reduction or "revolution" has ensued, with system entropy falling rapidly to near zero levels. Once begun, this change is self-sustaining and is not a direct result of environmental influences. Such a change is not directly anticipated by the social theory or the social dynamics we have analyzed before. We might compare this unexpected or "pathological" form of system dynamics to economic phenomena like depressions, which are not explained by the standard equilibrium theories of macroeconomics. Apparently the most immediate cause for a period of entropy reduction is the attainment of excessively high levels of system entropy, approaching the psychological limit of human entropy capacity at 3 bits. As an example of this we consider in detail the Weimar era of German history, from the end of the First World War to the early 1930's.

Entropy Reduction in Germany. The years 1919 to 1934 in Germany saw a period of very high entropy levels throughout the country followed by a rapid decrease in system entropy, culminating in the fall of the Weimar Republic and the beginning of the Hitler period. The cause of the high entropy levels was very likely a combination of several factors. Industrial expansion prior to the First World War had been extraordinary, and economic expansion began again in the late 1920's. As the historical experience of other countries shows, the combined effects of industrialization and urbanization will usually raise entropy levels. In addition to this factor, there were also the effects of the war and a catastrophic economic inflation that followed it, reaching a peak in 1923–24. Although economic conditions began to improve after 1924, the depression of the 1930's again generated a great deal of uncertainty in the society. Unemployment rose to very high levels, with over five million being unemployed in 1932. Throughout this period Germany also endured a great deal of crime and political violence, which typified and no doubt contributed to the overall rise in social uncertainty and breakdown of expected patterns of social behavior. The severity of these combined factors may be unparalleled in modern times for any nation.

The high entropy levels also contributed greatly to governmental instability and ineffectiveness in dealing with the problems because of the multiplicity of political parties; as the entropy increased, the number of parties necessarily increased, and the parliamentary government became increasingly ineffective. It is not immediately clear what action the parliament or government might have taken to improve social conditions, but in the absence of decisive action the natural social dynamics ran their course, eventually bringing an end to parliamentary government.

To study entropy levels in Weimar Germany, we analyzed voting data for the last six parliamentary (*Reichstag*) elections: in 1924II, 1928, 1930, 1932I, 1932II, and 1933.[2] (In 1924 and 1932 there were two parliamentary elections.) The subsystems analyzed were the smallest for which electoral data is available and they range in size from rural districts and small towns to larger cities. These subsystems are referred to as constituencies, although they are only subunits of the national parliamentary constituencies (the *Wahlkreis*). Germany had over 1200 such subsystems, or constituencies, and their average population was about 60,000. In comparison with the subunits previously analyzed for other countries, the German constituency was on the average the smallest; and the total number of subsystems was the largest for any of the countries. The political party candidates of Germany were elected on the basis of national voting for parties, according to a proportional representation scheme. Germany, unlike other countries, had no individual constituency parties.

We carried out the analysis of the German election data in much the same manner as in the previous case studies. We plotted entropy $H(P)$ values against turnout values by constituency and applied second degree polynomial (parabolic) curve fitting. Although a lower limit of 1% of the party vote in a constituency was taken as the minimum to constitute a party choice, we aggregated fractional party votes and counted them as an additional choice if their total exceeded 1%. (We repeated this procedure with a

5% minimum and found essentially the same results; the overall entropy levels were somewhat diminished, however, as we would expect.) In some elections 12 choices were possible, but the maximum number was generally lower. Where there was a suspicion of error in the data, we dropped that constituency from the sample set for that election.[3] As a result of missing or faulty data, the number of constituencies in the final sample was about 10% less than the total possible for the country. Finally, we repeated this entire procedure for the information variance and turnout, instead of the entropy and turnout.

The analysis of the German data reconfirms the findings of our earlier case studies and gives some explanation of the period of entropy reduction. The principle observations from the analysis are as follows:

1. The entropy hypothesis holds for Germany during the Weimar era. The turnout values are over 50%, and the relationship between entropy $H(P)$ and turnout for the set of constituencies is about as expected. For example, in 1924II the parabolic curve fit to the data for all constituencies has a maximum at 67% turnout. The curve decreases from its maximum of 2.35 bits to 2.05 bits as the turnout reaches 95%. (See Figures 7-1 and 7-2, and Table 7-1.) If the constituencies are sorted according to their orbit number (the number of parties in each), the lower orbits generally show the same pattern: entropy decreasing as turnout increases. The highest orbits are much flatter, however, and show a considerable disequilibrium. The 1930 election is an exception to the rule. Although all other elections show entropy decreasing (almost linearly) with increasing turnout for combined orbit data, the 1930 election shows just the opposite trend. In 1930 entropy increases markedly with turnout. (See Figure 7-2 and Table 7-1.) This pattern of disequilibrium in 1930 was undoubtedly related to the onset of the depression at that time.

2. The level of entropy was very high on the average until the last elections of the Weimar period. (See Table 7-2.) The average constituency entropy was already at 2.26 bits in 1924II. In comparison, the average prefecture entropy level of Japan in 1949—the highest entropy election of any of the previous case studies—was only 2.24 bits. This figure had already been exceeded in Germany in 1924 and the German level continued to rise, reaching an unprecedented 2.55 bits in 1930. Moreover, the highest entropy level of any single prefecture in 1949 in Japan was 2.54 bits; yet hundreds of German constituencies exceeded this at some time during the Weimar period. (See Figures 7-1, 7-3.)

3. The greatest entropy values attained by German constituencies in any election were about 3.0 to 3.1 bits. Although a large number of constituencies had levels almost to 3 bits entropy, only a few were even slightly

Table 7-1. Germany: Parabolic Curve Fitting to $H(P)$-Turnout Distributions for Combined Orbits

Election	Number of Constituencies	Polynomial Fit a_0, a_1, a_2/Errors	Maximum at Percent Turnout
1924II	1199	.73, .048, −.00036 1.07, .029, .00018	66.7
1928	1162	3.11, −.010, .000020 .58, .016, .000110	[a]
1930	1181	.43, .048, −.00027 1.07, .027, .00017	88.8
1932I	1173	2.79, −.012, .000026 .84, .021, .000130	[a]
1932II	1113	3.21, −.023, .00011 .65, .017, .00011	[a]
1933	1110	5.29, −.077, .00043 2.55, .059, .00034	(min. at 89.0)

[a] Maximum or minimum outside range of data; data closer to linear.

over this value. Nevertheless, the number of choices would have allowed a significantly higher entropy level; the maximum possible for the 11 or 12 available choices was 3.46 or 3.58 bits. And hundreds of constituencies did have 11 or 12 parties in 1928 and 1930. (See Table 7-5.) We must, therefore, conclude that the upper limit for social entropy is in the range of 3.0 to 3.1 bits. This limit is approximately the same value found in psychological testing of individual capacity (see Section 4-2). The entropy maximum at 3 bits also appears to be independent of the turnout level of the constituency (Figure 7-3). The observed 3 bit limit may, perhaps, represent a restructuring of the set of alternatives by the population so that the voters actually perceived the election as an eight-choice event set (log 8 = 3). But this would again indicate that the society might have reached a maximum human or social capacity to structure alternatives. After the system attained its highest entropy levels, in 1928 and 1930, with many constituencies near the maximum of 3 bits, the period of entropy reduction began. Thus the immediate cause of the reduction was apparently related to the attainment of extreme, and perhaps intolerable, levels of social entropy.

4. The entropy decreased sharply after 1930, but there was a time lag

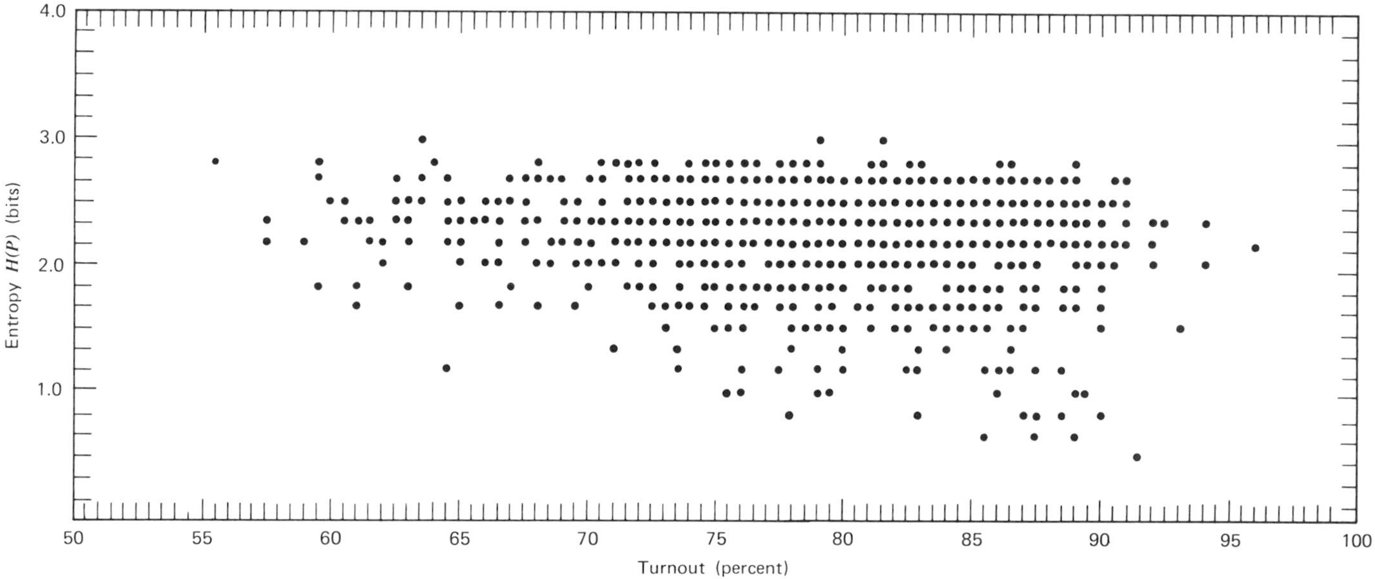

Figure 7-1. Germany, 1924II, the distribution for combined orbits.

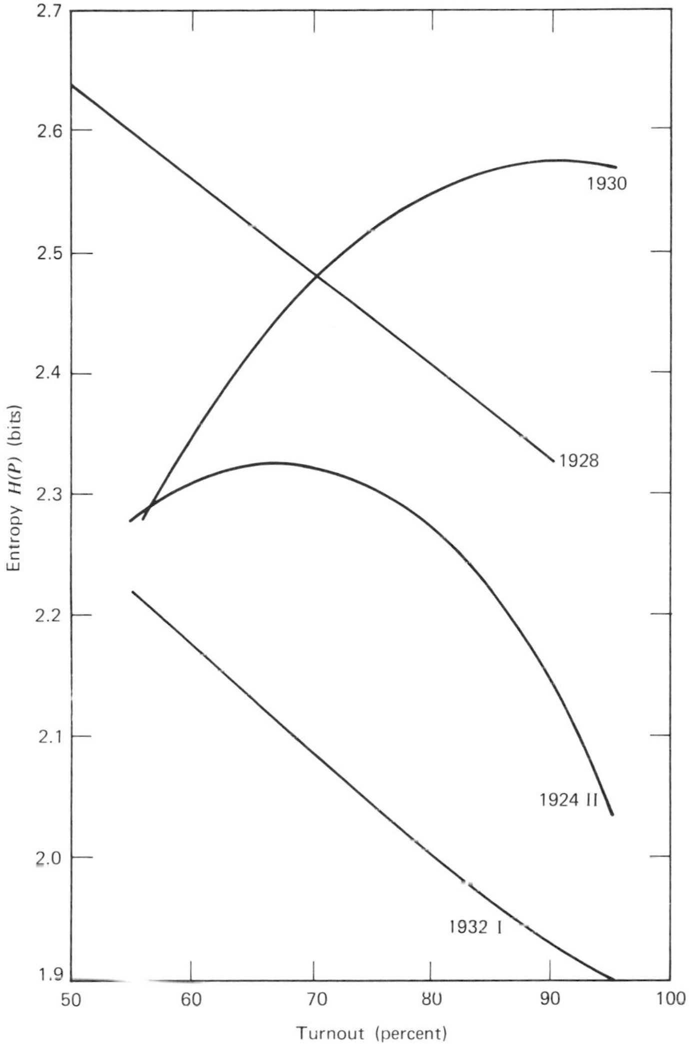

Figure 7-2. Germany, 1924II to 1932I, parabolic curve fitting for the combined orbits.

with respect to certain other variables—a finding that indicates that the trend toward entropy reduction had already begun before 1930, the year of greatest entropy.[4] The average constituency $H(T)$ started to decline after 1928, and a reduction in the variances of the entropy $H(P)$, turnout, and the information variance for the set of constituencies also began after 1928. (See Tables 7-2 and 7-3.) Moreover, a reduction in the variance of the in-

Table 7-2. Germany: Level and Dispersion of Entropy

Election	Average[a] $H(P)$	Variance of $H(P)$	Average Turnout	Variance of Turnout	Average $H(T)$
1924II	2.26	.14	79.1	44.5	.72
1928	2.44	.12	74.9	62.3	.79
1930	2.55	.11	81.1	39.0	.68
1932I	1.99	.074	83.8	35.1	.62
1932II	2.11	.074	80.1	46.0	.70
1933	1.88	.071	88.6	13.0	.50

[a] Averages and variances are computed over the entire set of constituencies.

formation variance for the set of constituencies was underway as early as 1924II, and it maintained a steady decline until 1932II. In short, there was a progressive contraction of the ranges of $H(P)$ and turnout for the subsystems so that the constituencies began to converge in entropy and turnout values even before the entropy level had started falling. The system became increasingly homogeneous over its area throughout the period of entropy reduction.

5. Even though entropy began to decline after 1930, the curve fitting shows that the system as a whole was not unusually disequilibrated after 1930. The overall distribution of data for elections after 1930 is similar to that for elections before 1930. Thus we cannot attribute the period of entropy reduction to disequilibrium and consequent system relaxation alone.

Table 7-3. Germany: Level and Dispersion of the Information Variance

Election	Average[a] Information Variance	Variance of Information Variance
1924II	1.63	.41
1928	1.89	.39
1930	1.69	.36
1932I	1.54	.20
1932II	1.41	.22
1933	1.44	.17

[a] Average and variance computed over the entire set of constituencies.

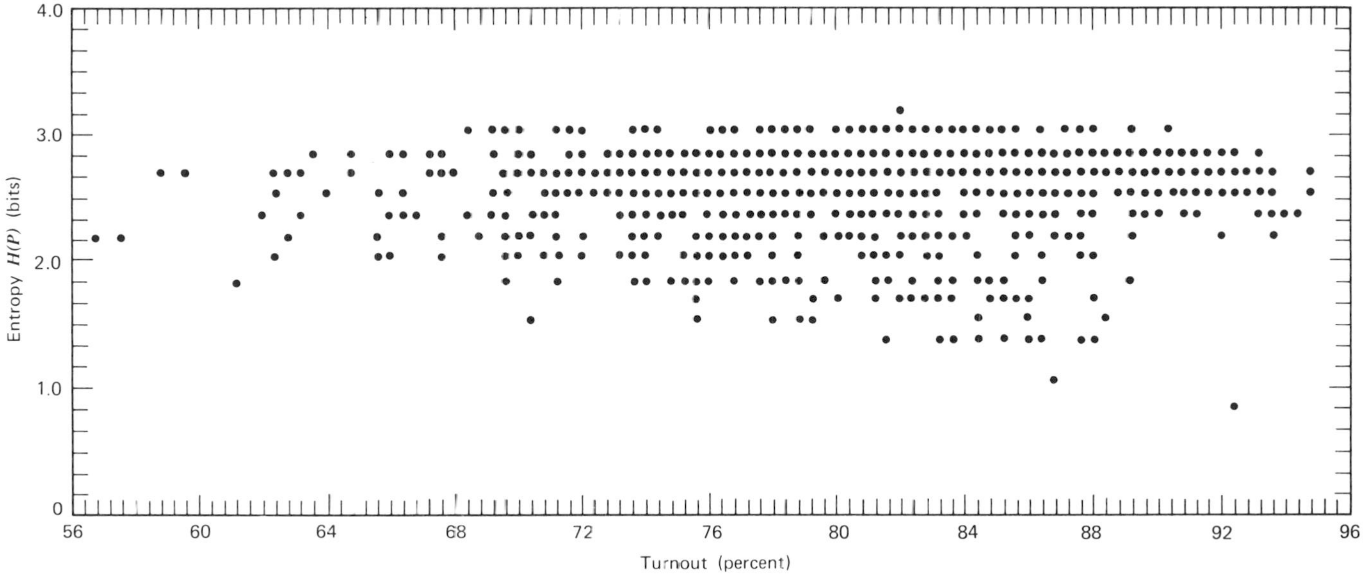

Figure 7-3. Germany, 1930, showing a limit for social entropy at about 3 bits.

6. In the sequence of elections, the distribution of constituencies plotted according to their information variance and turnout values becomes increasingly bounded above by an information variance curve after 1928. The subsystems increasingly shift their positions to be below a hypothetical curve that appears to be a multiple of the stereotypical information variance curve (Figure 2-2); the curve increases with turnout up to about 90% and then sharply decreases. (See Figures 7-4 to 7-6.) This trend is quite strong and easily visible in the data. Parabolic curve fitting to the information variance-turnout distributions for combined orbits also shows the predicted curve. Such a strong trend and stationary pattern were not observed for the information variance in any of the previous case studies. (Of the previous case studies, the prewar Japanese elections are most like the German in this respect.) The strong patterns, both for distribution averages and contours, indicate that the underlying social processes during the entropy reduction had not substantially changed, despite the disequilibrium that appears in the entropy-turnout distributions in some years. People were still able to link the two event sets together and were no less affected by the actions of other people. The social bonds tying people together in the society had not dissolved. Thus we must find an explanation for entropy reduction that is still consistent with normal social processes.

7. The end of the entropy reduction was a new equilibrium near zero entropy, which is shown by the *Reichstag* elections and national referenda after November 1933, that is, during the Hitler or National Socialist period. Entropy values for these elections are given in Table 7-4.[5] Even in these elections, however, the decline in $H(P)$ was lagging behind the decrease in $H(T)$ or increase in turnout, and $H(P)$ was still significantly greater than

Table 7-4. Germany: Post-Weimar Elections; Entropy Calculated from National Voting Statistics

Election	Turnout (%)	Vote for NSDAP %, or Referendum YES	Opposing NSDAP %, or Referendum NO	$H(P)$ (2 choices) (bits)
Nov. 1933	95.3	92.1	7.9	.40
1934[a]	95.6	89.9	10.1	.50
1936	99.0	98.8	1.2	.09
Apr. 1938	99.5	99.0	1.0	.08
Dec. 1938	98.9	98.6	1.4	.11

[a] Referendum; other dates are for *Reichstag* elections.

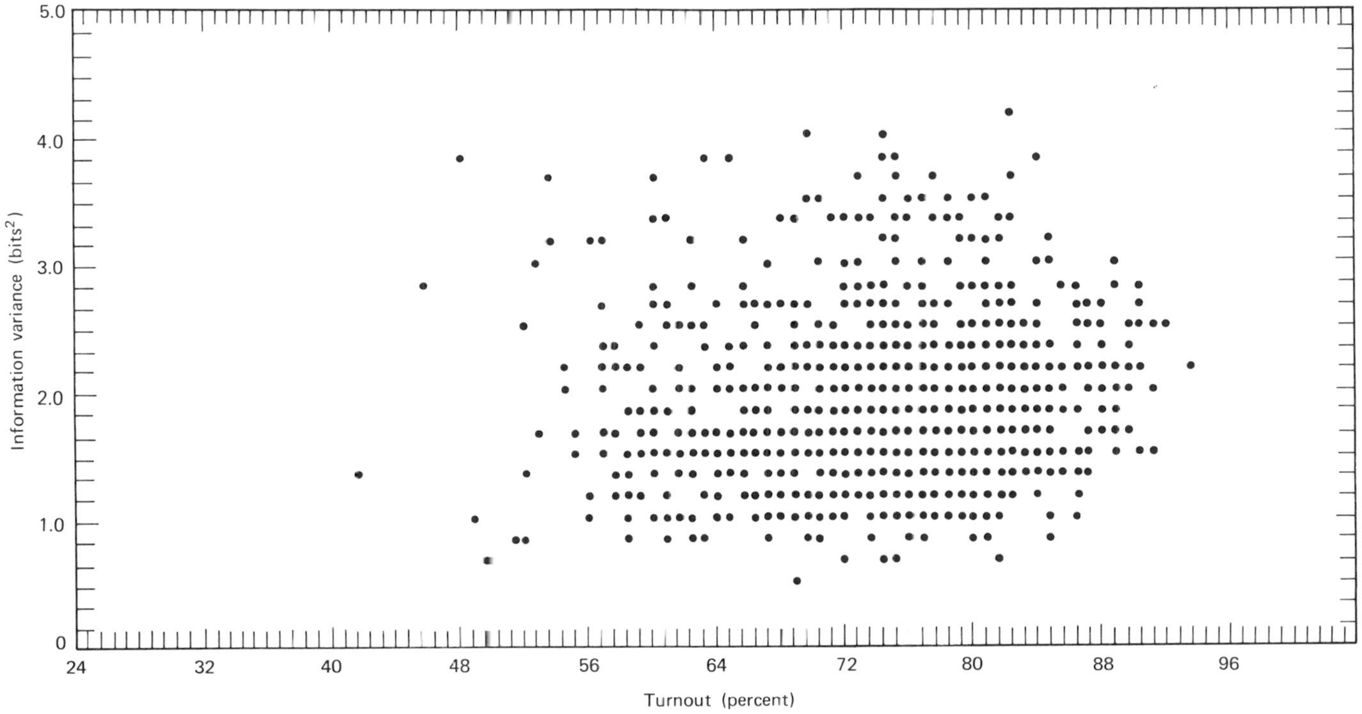

Figure 7-4. Germany, 1928, the distribution for combined orbits.

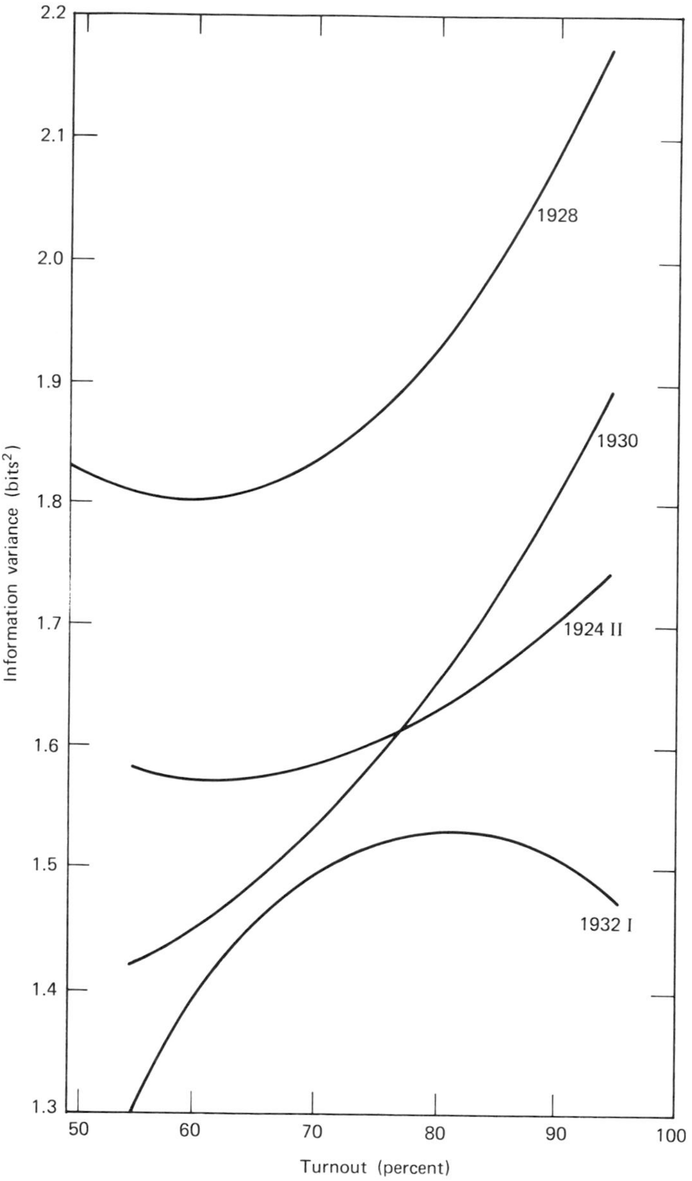

Figure 7-5. Germany, 1924II to 1932I, parabolic curve fitting for the combined orbits.

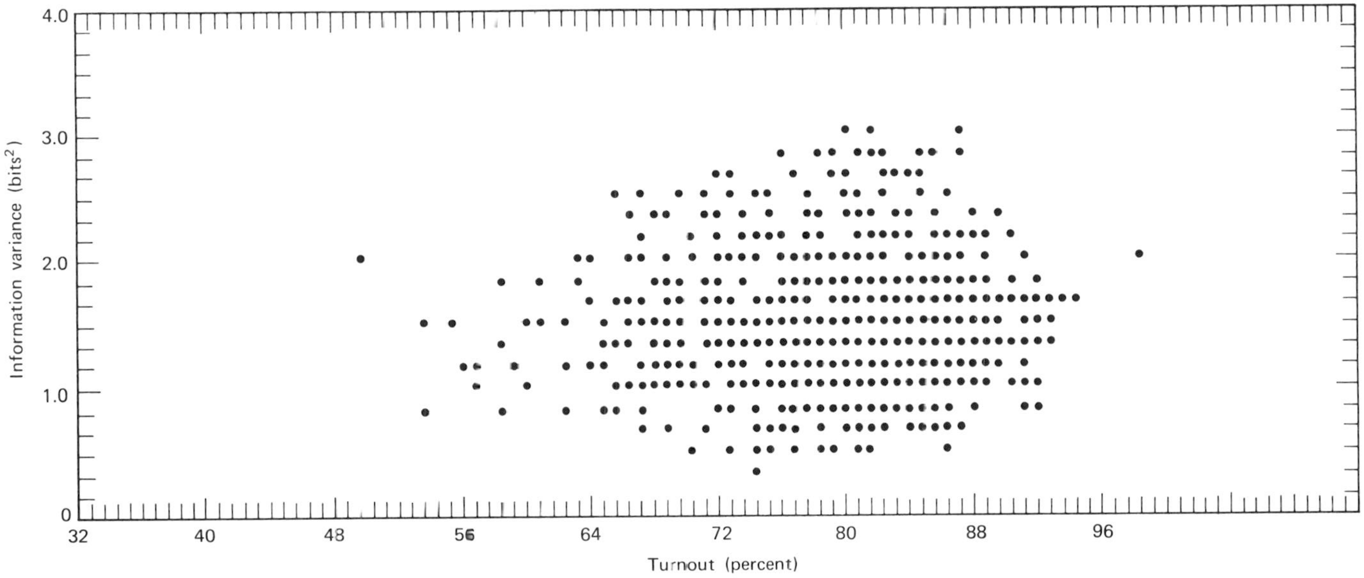

Figure 7-6. Germany, 1932II, distribution for the combined orbits showing the distinctive contour and the increasing system homogeneity.

zero up until 1936. Once a new equilibrium was established near zero entropy, there was little variation in entropy and no counterreaction to increase entropy levels.

Although the entropy reduction itself is an unexpected occurrence from our theoretical perspective, the behavior of the subsystems as a whole displays the familiar patterns of intensive and acrossvariable dynamics. The system behaves exactly as it would if it were to attain normally a zero entropy equilibrium near 100% turnout. Initially, the subsystems are distributed over very high orbits, but a sharp reduction of entropy in a high orbit requires a very high turnout, close to 100%. So turnout increases rapidly in the course of the entropy reduction. As we observed in the study of intensive dynamics (Chapter 5), the subsystems fall to lower orbits rather than staying in the same high orbits as turnout increases. (See Table 7-5, and compare with Figure 5-1.) Falling down through the lower orbits is the shorter relaxation path to zero entropy equilibrium, requiring less change in turnout.

The reduction of variance in entropy, information variance, and turnout during the entropy reduction can be attributed to the acrossvariable dynamics. The reductions in variance across the system indicate that the system had a strong trend toward homogeneity. What is remarkable in this case is the extent to which the whole system was becoming homogeneous; it was not just a case of adjacent constituencies becoming more alike. Thus one can say that the "conductivity" (the constant of equation 6-10, et al.) in the system, or the extent of interaction, was greatly increased over normal

Table 7-5. Germany: Distribution of Constituencies by Orbit

Election	Orbit Number (Number of Parties)							
	5[a]	6	7	8	9	10	11	12
1924II	0	34	210	525	366	58	0	0
1928	0	0	24	87	303	518	217	0
1930	0	16	49	86	200	437	367	23
1932I	97	345	382	378	66	0	0	0
1032II	45	260	401	292	108	0	0	0
1933	271	430	291	101	0	0	0	0

[a] Zero implies less than 15.

times and in comparison with other systems, such as Japan. The exceptionally strong trend of information variance reduction is apparently the cause of the bounding of the constituency distribution for information variance-turnout values. Such an upper bound would result from a reduction of information variance levels, or differences, to as great an extent as possible for the existing entropy levels. The trend toward uniformity of information variance appears to have been stronger and more rapid than the corresponding trend for entropy, however; this result points to the ability of population to adjust information variance levels semi-independently of entropy.

Why the entropy reduction should have continued to near zero entropy is a more difficult problem. We might infer from the high entropy levels attained that the population would take some action to return entropy levels, and social structure, to a tolerable range. But it is not clear that such a low final state was necessary. On the contrary, the entropy levels of other countries lead us to believe that some intermediate level of entropy would have been satisfactory in Germany as well. Thus it seems that the German case is one of overreduction or overreaction. Something may have gone out of control. We can reconstruct two alternative explanations of why an overreduction might have occurred.

Alternative Explanations of Entropy Reduction. The first explanation of entropy reduction assumes that the initial impetus for reduction was an intentional action by a large part of the population to reduce the entropy (and information variance) level. This is reasonable to infer from the fact that such high levels had been attained, but it is an extra condition that cannot be explained in terms of the theory proposed so far; it is an exception to the rule. Furthermore, this assumption still does not explain why the reduction continued to the zero point. As the population acted to reduce uncertainty, the economic system or other exogenous forces may have impaired the effectiveness of the attempted reduction by continually tending to increase entropy. This might have resulted in a cycle of increasingly stronger attempts to reduce entropy. It is also possible that the time lag in $H(P)$ reduction in comparison with other variables may reflect this or have had a part in it. The time lags could mean that the first movement to reduce $H(P)$ was temporarily ineffectual or that at least some time was needed for a relaxation to lower entropy to occur. Thus if people had later reacted to the observed $H(P)$ level instead of anticipating that it would decrease in time, and then had increased their efforts at entropy reduction, an excessive reduction was inevitable. Whichever variation of this explanation would be most accurate, the central idea is that a purposeful reduction of social uncertainty took place.

A quite different explanation of entropy reduction is also possible. This explanation does not require any assumption about purposeful entropy reduction. We can explain the entire phenomenon of entropy reduction within the theoretical framework of the "normal" theory of system dynamics. Recall that when entropy is estimated from observed relative frequencies of events, there is a negative bias error if the sample size is too small for the number of events in the event set. (See Section 3-2; equation 3-2.) An estimate of entropy will tend to become low if the sample size decreases or if the number of events in the event set increases. As the entropy level in Germany increased and the number of political parties multiplied, people would have increasingly underestimated the uncertainty level in their society. Suppose, furthermore, that the extreme uncertainty in the society led to a breakdown in social communication across the system in such a way that people had less knowledge available about other's behavior patterns; that is, suppose that the sample size for estimating entropy became much smaller. This deterioration of social communication could have been abetted by the psychological limit on entropy capacity being attained; as the social level approached 3 bits, it may have become increasingly difficult for people to discriminate variations in other people's behavior, with errors in judgment becoming increasingly likely. (In physical communication channels, error rates increase very rapidly as the transmission rate approaches the channel capacity.) Even though the system entropy level may have been increasing in Germany, from our macroscopic perspective, the combined effects of estimation error and limitation on entropy capacity might very well have led people in the society to believe that social uncertainty was *decreasing*. People would have believed that the level of conformity in their society was increasing.

To understand what may have happened in Germany, let us consider, as a hypothetical case, the effects of biased estimation error on two adjacent, interacting social subsystems R_1 and R_2. Let the actual entropy levels of the two subsystems be H_1 and H_2. Now suppose that people in one subsystem have an impaired knowledge of the other system causing them to underestimate its entropy level. That is, people in R_1 perceive the entropy level of R_2 as $H_2' < H_2$; and conversely, H_1 is perceived as $H_1' < H_1$ by R_2. We shall also assume that people in each subsystem can correctly estimate the uncertainty level of their own subsystem. (It would be enough, however, to assume that within-system estimation is better than between-system estimation.) Consider first the simple case where $H_1 = H_2 = H$ and $H_1' = H_2' = H'$. According to the principles of acrossvariable dynamics, each subsystem, perceiving the other as being at a lower entropy level than its own, will consequently try to reduce its own level. At a later time, the initial entropy levels of both subsystems will have been reduced. The estimated entropy levels will also have been reduced, however, and thus each subsystem will continue to reduce its own level. At any given time each subsystem will perceive the other as being at a lower entropy and the reduction will continue. A period of entropy reduction will go on for this hypothetical system as long as there is a negative bias in the estimate of entropy levels, that is, until zero entropy is reached.

Since the error bias should decrease as the number of events in the event set (the number of political parties) decreases, we would expect the error to become smaller as the entropy level falls; as we have seen, the number of parties usually decreases as the entropy level decreases. As an approximation we could write

$$H' = H - a\,H = (1 - a)\,H$$

where a is a positive fractional constant representing the magnitude of the error as a function of the actual entropy level. If the error estimate depends on H in this way, the rate of reduction will decrease as H becomes smaller. The rate of reduction depends on the perceived difference in entropy levls

$$U' = H_1 - H_2' = H_2 - H_1' = a\,H$$

Thus as the entropy levels of the subsystems fall to zero, the perceived difference becomes smaller and the rate of reduction will slow down.

One can also show that entropy reduction will occur even if only one of the two subsystems underestimates the other's entropy level, or if the initial difference is greater than zero and there is biased estimation. If one subsystem had an initial entropy level that was still estimated as being higher than the other subsystem's, despite the bias, there would be a temporary increase in the lower subsystem's level. But after the initial difference had diminished to some extent, the error in the estimation would again cause both subsystems to reduce their levels. An entropy difference will thus become increasingly smaller over time regardless of the initial value of the differences or the entropy levels of the subsystems; the system will become increasingly more homogeneous, and the relaxation rate may accelerate over normal rates because of the greater perceived difference.

An entropy reduction due to biased estimation, with the magnitude of the bias proportional to the entropy level, will always end in a period of simultaneous reduction of entropy levels *and* entropy differences to zero. This is exactly the pattern of entropy reduction observed in Weimar Germany. The continued, but temporary, increase in German entropy levels after the trend toward homogeneity had begun can be attributed to exogenous forces such as the coincident economic depression. The early and strong trend toward system homogeneity in Weimar Germany, despite later increases in entropy levels, supports very well this explanation of entropy reduction.

The German case, of course, presents considerably greater analytic difficulties than the hypothetical system studied here. Spatial properties of the entropy distribution would have to be taken into account, as well as the relative numbers of people at the different entropy levels and the magnitude of exogenous influences. Nevertheless, the potential for breakdown in equilibrium maintenance because of faulty entropy estimation is clear even in the simple example given above. In general, an increasing negative error bias that was not spatially uniform in a system could bring about a self-sustaining entropy reduction by leading people to believe that system uncertainty was decreasing. (A similar series of arguments could also be developed for individual behavior within a single subsystem where it was becoming increasingly difficult to estimate the ambient uncertainty level: everyone would begin acting as if the level were lower and still falling, and the reduction would then propagate to adjacent subsystems.)

Of the alternative explanations for entropy reduction in Germany, the second has the esthetic advantage of fitting into the theory we have devised thus far and requiring no ad hoc assumptions. But considering the apparent sensitivity of system dynamics to estimation errors, one must ask how it is that systems ordinarily avoid periods of uncontrolled entropy reduction. We are led to conclude that the various factors involved, such as rate of interaction, the entropy level, and human entropy capacity (and perhaps a threshold effect on error magnitude) combine to make large estimation errors and sudden increases in errors rare under normal conditions in societies. Beyond that we can only remark that the study of entropy reduction and the effects of estimation errors on dynamic processes opens a wide area to further theoretical and empirical research. (Further discussion of this is in Appendix II, where the micro-level aspects of entropy estimation are considered.)

We can also note in passing that many social scientists who have studied the conditions of prerevolutionary societies, such as Weimar Germany, have reported a high degree of anomie, alienation, individual isolation, or rootlessness among the population. In using such terms, however, one must carefully distinguish people's isolation and anomie caused by a deficiency in social communication or due to their lack of knowledge about the society from that which might presume a changed sensitivity to, or responsiveness to, others in the society. Our results here show the effects of isolation, but not in this latter sense; we see no sign of "randomness" or spontaneity in behavior in the population at large, as we might expect if everyone were going his own way. Even at the times of greatest social uncertainty, the existence of a social entropy maximum at 3 bits and the strong relationships between voter turnout and political party voting indicate that people were still acting collectively, out of social rather than individual motives. Similarly, one can say that "conformity" decreased in the high entropy years, but this only means a change in the quantitative level and in the number of groups a person might conform with; decreasing conformity does not imply a loss or change of the basic social bonds.

As we have seen, we can construct an explanation of entropy reduction that meshes with the social theory that we have previously developed. Of the two alternative explanations for entropy reduction—reduction caused by popular intention or by micro-estimation errors—the explanation of reduction as the effect of estimation errors seems the better in that it accounts for more of the observed phenomena and does not presume any radical change in the basic nature of social processes. From a strictly macroscopic view of society, however, we cannot completely resolve the question of what causes an entropy reduction. If high entropy levels are able to cause a breakdown in social communication, and thereby lead to a rapid increase in estimation errors, one would need microscopic data to prove it conclusively. Specifically, we would need a much greater understanding of the patterns of communication in a society and the extent of knowledge people have about others' behavior. A program of survey research would undoubtedly provide answers to these questions, but this would be an expensive undertaking. Simulation experiments with small groups of people might also be used to study the effects of very high entropy levels, which occur only rarely in national political systems. The best evidence we can provide now to support our interpretation of the German case and to indicate the universality of the entropy reduction phenomenon is the examination of further instances of entropy reduction from a comparative, cross-national, macroscopic perspective. The cases we shall use are Japan and Indonesia.

The Case of Japan. A less conclusive example of entropy reduction is provided by Japan during the 1930's. As seen in Chapter 6, entropy levels in Japan rose very rapidly until 1937. Further inspection of the data shows that in 1937 about one-sixth of the electoral districts had entropy levels over 2.0 bits, with values as high as 2.5 bits being attained. Following the 1937 election militarists seized the government, and by the next election in 1942 the entropy level had been greatly reduced.

The Japanese data shows that high entropy levels were attained prior to the reduction but it does not offer the detailed picture of the reduction that was shown in the German case. We can only observe that Japan had an extraordinarily high rate of entropy difference reduction from 1936 to 1937 in at least part of the country (Table 6-1) and also a high rate of information variance difference reduction (Table 6-2). This indicates that there was already a change in system properties and dynamics at that time; the accelerated trend toward homogeneity of system entropy and information variance levels began before the militarist government. Yet Japan is a contrast to Germany for two reasons. Although high entropy levels were attained in parts of Japan in 1937, the average district entropy (at 1.6 bits) was considerably below the corresponding German level at the onset of reduction. Furthermore, the extent of the reduction in Japan was not as severe as in Germany. In the 1942 Japanese Diet election, for example, the Japanese government's approved candidates won (only) 83% of the parliamentary seats. That nongovernment candidates were allowed to run for election contrasts sharply with the German elections of the National Socialist period.

The fact that less extreme entropy levels were reached in Japan than in Germany may help to explain why the reduction was less severe. The semi-isolation of the Japanese prefectures from one another (as described in Chapter 6) would also have had a moderating effect on a system-wide reduction. In summary then, the Japanese case points to the possibility of an entropy reduction occurring when entropy levels in a significant part of a country exceed 2.0 bits, even if they may still fall short of the 3.0 bit limit on human capacity. In general, the final outcome of a limited reduction would very likely depend on the relationship between the most strongly affected parts of the system and the central government or military, as well as the conductivity of the system. It is possible that estimation errors could have come about at lower entropy levels in Japan than in Germany, leading to an earlier reduction. But exactly what differences between the two societies could account for this is not clear. (One might investigate the effects of social stratification.)

The Case of Indonesia. Another example of an excessive national entropy level followed by an entropy reduction is Indonesia. The Republic of Indonesia was established in 1950. Judging from historical events and election data, we can infer that a period of very high entropy extended from 1950, or shortly thereafter, to about 1961, when signs of a reduction begin to appear. The events of the high entropy period and the subsequent reduction show a strong parallel to Germany between the two world wars. The Indonesian case is more like the German than is the Japanese case in the high levels of entropy attained and in the magnitude of internal civil strife and violence.

Only one parliamentary election took place in Indonesia during this whole period, which ended with the fall of Sukarno and the establishment of a military government in 1966. This election was held in 1955. Members of parliament were chosen under a proportional representation scheme for each of the 15 electoral constituencies, which varied considerably in population size. The number of eligible voters, under a universal suffrage, ranged from a few hundred thousand in the smallest constituencies to about ten million in the largest, those on the densely populated islands of Java and Sumatra. Turnout in the election was very high—about 90%. We have computed the entropy for each constituency for the 1955 election, and the results are given in Table 7-6.[6] The method of entropy computation with respect to party size was the same as used for the German data. The total number of political parties competing in most constituencies was at least 20 to 30; there were several major national parties, but none of them received a majority of the national vote.

The entropy levels in Indonesian constituencies in 1955 ranged from 2.0 to 3.0 bits (Table 7-6). The highest levels, at 3.0 and 2.9 bits, were in West Java and the urban Djakarta constituency (which is surrounded to the interior by the West Java constituency). These levels compare with the most extreme levels observed in Weimar Germany and exceed those of any other country analyzed here. Levels nearly as high also occurred in other areas of Indonesia, including the less densely populated and more remote islands.

The varieties of conflict and symptoms of social instability and uncertainty that plagued Indonesia in the high entropy years of the 1950's are particularly diverse, and we shall only list them generically. Among other miseries to rack Indonesia were: military rebellion and temporary control of separate islands, endemic civil guerilla warfare, banditry, paralyzing labor strikes, and deteriorating economic conditions and inflation. In external relations, Indonesia had shifting, unstable policies and was belligerent.

After 1960 several events signaled the beginning of an entropy reduction. Some of the civil guerilla warfare that had endured through the previous

Table 7-6. Indonesia: Entropy Levels in 1955

Electoral Constituency	Entropy (bits)
East Java	2.2
Central Java	2.3
West Java	3.0
Greater Djakarta	2.9
South Sumatra	2.6
Central Sumatra	2.3
North Sumatra	2.7
West Kalimantan	2.5
South Kalimantan	2.0
East Kalimantan	2.7
North Sulawesi	2.7
South Sulawesi	2.9
Maluku	2.4
East Nusatenggara	2.7
West Nusatenggara	2.4

decade came to an end. The government put increasing restrictions on the number and minimum size of political parties that it would legally allow, so that by 1962 it had outlawed all but eight or ten political parties while forcing the remaining parties to be in close agreement with its policies. In a collapse of civil rights, persecution of minority groups, such as the resident Chinese, increased, as did violence toward foreign establishments. In foreign relations, the territory of West Irian was joined to Indonesia after a long period of agressive foreign policy aimed at this objective, and in 1964 and 1965 Indonesia undertook military operations against Malaysia.

In short, Indonesians directed an increasing degree of violence at sources of uncertainty that were perceived by Indonesians to be the cause of their national problems. The final cataclysm followed an attempted coup by the Communist party in 1965. There was a short-lived civil war against the Communists (in Java), and throughout the country hundreds of thousands of alleged Communists were executed or massacred. Because the Communist party had been one of the largest groups in the country (although a minority party), its annihilation meant an immediate and substantial reduction in the social entropy level. Since the party had been a chief proponent of social change and modernization, its extinction also implied a return to more traditional, more predictable, social policies and activities. The period of reduction apparently ended shortly afterwards when a military government took control of the country under a broad consensus by the population.

Although there is no electoral data that can be used to analyze the Indonesian reduction after 1955, we can draw some parallels to the German case in the events that were to happen. Internally in both Germany and Indonesia (and more so than in Japan) there were the suppression, persecution, and massacre of minorities: religious, ethnic, or political. In foreign affairs the nations engaged in shifting alliances and military aggressions, as they attempted and achieved expansions of territory. The suppression of minorities in Indonesia, as in Germany, is directly associated with the decrease in entropy levels; decreasing entropy implies an increasing conformity to the majority groups in the society and a decreasing tolerance among the population of nonconformist or minority behavior. The international violence seems to have been more the result of decisions taken by political leaders than a mass phenomenon, although there was wide popular support for an aggressive foreign policy. Thus in international affairs a high entropy level or entropy reduction seems to have been more a contributory factor than a proximate cause in explaining violence and conflict.

The periods of entropy reduction in Germany, Japan, and Indonesia were of national scope, but we must also anticipate that reduction could occur on a local scale.[7] In such a case it would be more difficult to predict the system-wide effects. In a study of civil wars and revolutions, Wolf describes how a high level of social uncertainty in certain groups or regions of a country may lead to violent conflict.[8] He analyzes how various rural groups for whom economic modernization and the rise of capitalism led to increased social uncertainty were greatly responsible for the beginnings of civil war in Mexico, Russia, China, Viet Nam, Algeria, and Cuba. The wage labor system and the marketability of farmland introduced by capitalism displaced the traditional socioeconomic relationships and the interdependencies of social groups in traditional peasant societies; these relationships were usually of a reciprocal nature between social classes or groups and offered a good deal of stability and economic security to the population. As Wolf points out, the peasant was poor but had a guaranteed subsistence. Once the peasant became a farmer in a capitalist economy, he could no longer use the older social institutions to reduce his risks; yet the newer social, political, and economic structures did not compensate him for his loss of security. It is this situation of increased risk, which often turned to the disadvantage of the peasant, that Wolf sees as the likely proximate cause of rebellion and revolution.[9] We cannot determine from the historical evidence whether the subsequent efforts made by social groups to reduce their social uncertainty were purposeful entropy reductions, self-sustaining entropy reductions, or just trends toward increasing system homogeneity.[10] But the attempts by various peasant groups to reduce their social uncertainty usually put them in conflict with other segments of society.

Whatever the exact nature of entropy reduction, the incidence of violence associated with it is always high. Violence may be directed at putative sources of uncertainty either within a society or external to it. The greatest externally directed violence happened in the cases of Japan and Germany, perhaps because the reduction was so universal within the systems.

The most important finding of these case studies of entropy reduction is that we can observe certain phenomena *before* the entropy levels begin their rapid declines. A high and increasing entropy level is the most obvious warning of an entropy reduction. But a change in turnout or $H(T)$ levels may foreshadow a later change in $H(P)$ levels. And a rapid increase in the trend toward homogeneity of entropy and information variance levels across a society may also signal an entropy reduction. Since the early stages of an entropy reduction may be seen years before the main reduction itself, we have a good potential for preventing an overreduction of social uncertainty and the associated violence and conflict.[11]

CHAPTER EIGHT

Conclusion

If we judge by the success of the natural sciences, a key prerequisite in the development of a scientific theory is the discovery or establishment of a coherent set of measurement variables to describe and explain the phenomena of interest. Yet despite a great deal of research in the social sciences, measurement has remained a very difficult problem in the analysis of social behavior. The problem, however, does not lie simply in devising measures of social behavior; many different measurement variables have been proposed and used. The source of our difficulty is that it is not enough for us to quantify behavior in arbitrary ways. We must find measures that are necessary and sufficient (to an approximate degree) for the explanation of a significant class of social phenomena. But exactly how measurement and theory combine to give satisfactory explanations is not at all apparent; even the scientific theories in everyday use do not show us how to construct new sciences.

The best description we have of what constitutes the right kind of measurement variables seems to be the two-variable pattern of through- and acrossvariables found in a number of scientific theories. We have proposed an analogous set of measures applicable to a broad class of social behavior that is perceived statistically within a society. To a great extent the research presented here was designed to show that the proposed measures are uniquely appropriate to this class of behavior. The measures are appropriate not just because we can mathematically quantify social behavior, but because people themselves behave in a way that makes a specific mathematical form, the entropy function, uniquely necessary to an explanation of their collective behavior.

The reason the measures we use for social phenomena work so well is that people act and adjust their behavior (perhaps subconsciously) in response to the same conditions that we are measuring. When we compute the average uncertainty or entropy for a set of events in a social system, we are only duplicating with greater precision the same knowledge of the uncertainty of events that a person in the system would have acquired through his native statistical perception of what was occurring. It is hardly surprising that statistical knowledge forms the basis for our understanding of social phenomena, since it is also statistical knowledge that provides the basis for our understanding of physical phenomena in all the macroscopic natural sciences. A nondeterministic, statistical theory is the inevitable result of inherent limitations on human ability to perceive and comprehend phenomena. The regularities in structure and dynamics that we find in our societies are simply a product of these same limitations.

As a result of people's actions and our perception of them there is a level of uncertainty about social events in event sets. We can measure the average uncertainty in a society and follow its change over time. A significant finding is that an equilibrium level of average uncertainty can be maintained in a society for at least some event sets. This equilibrium in collective social behavior will be maintained despite changes in the specific "content" of the events, and despite changes in the behavior of individuals or in the composition and size of the population. The equilibrium level can accomodate some flexibility in the balance of more and less probable events as long as the average predictability remains about the same; the information variance is semi-independent of the average information. If there is a temporary loss of equilibrium, as implied by a lack of uniformity or equivalence in (unitary) system entropy values, we would anticipate a trend toward greater measurement uniformity, which is to say, a return or relaxation to a new equilibrium. But we also find that the average level of uncertainty can be forced to a new equilibrium as the result of such profound environmental forces as urbanization, industrialization, education, and economic catastrophe—forces that can alter the relationships between people, the kinds of behavior people must have, and the available choices of action. Only when excessive uncertainty prevails in a society, that is, when the entropy level approaches the psychological limit of about 3 bits, do we find evidence of a breakdown in equilibrium maintenance, as occurred in the dramatic entropy reduction of Weimar Germany.

Although uncertainty is a fairly intuitive measure, it was necessary to combine intuition with mathematical precision and logic to derive the entropy and information measures of uncertainty. The mathematical representation of uncertainty shows more clearly than our intuition could exactly what conditions must be satisfied for an entropy measurement to be possible. In particular, we found that elections can be used as entropy measurements. But, more generally, the problem in social measurement is to find all those social event sets that give valid entropy measurements. In other words, the problem in analyzing any social system is to learn how people categorize or structure their own choices and the events that they perceive to occur. Such an analysis would give us a comprehensive picture of the structure of a social system within the range of explanation of the measurement variables. For our immediate purposes, however, the use of elections as entropy measurements sufficed to show the validity of entropy as a social measurement variable, which was our first objective. The restriction to unitary social system models was a simplification taken with this same objective in mind. Only when we can establish the validity of entropy measurement for at least some social event sets does the general problem of determining the range of explanation in a society become realistic. The ability to measure entropy for national populations, besides being a significant finding in itself, strongly supports an extension of the same measurement variables to more complex system models of smaller social systems, such as organizations. The two-variable measurement pattern offers analogies that could direct research on measurement for complex social system models.

Quite apart from establishing the validity of entropy measurement, the discovery that *elections* are entropy measurements in (unitary) national political systems yields a number of conclusions of true importance to political theory. Paradoxically, we find that elections are very important to a social theory as entropy measurements, but are otherwise much less interesting than political theorists have long supposed. Electoral participation, the strength and number of political parties, and the mutual relationships of these phenomena have been the focus of many attempts at political theory construction. By reducing elections to the status of measurement, one sees that they are only a means to theory construction, and their explanation should not become, in itself, an end goal of political theory. Furthermore, we must discount the importance attached to elections by traditional democratic theory as expressions of the popular will and judgments on a party's or candidate's policies. Although the outcome of an election is not completely predetermined, it is greatly constrained by the existing equilibrium distribution; and even during periods of system change or system relaxation there are constraints on the kinds of change that are likely to occur in electoral distributions. Regardless of what desirability there may be in making "rational" decisions between alternative electoral choices, the observed electoral phenomena show that such behavior is infrequent and, in general, subsumed by the dominant collective processes. In making their voting choices, people rely mainly on their perceptions and expectations of the behavior of other people. The features of elections that stand in greatest contrast to the assumptions of democratic voting theory are the equivalence between the turnout and political party entropy measurements, $H(T)$ and $H(P)$; the content-free nature of elections as entropy measurements; and the importance of the event set, the set of electoral choices as a whole, over individual choices in a voter's rationale for choice selection.

Elections also bring out the dual nature of change in social systems. Change can be in discrete units, as when the number of electoral choices or political parties increases or decreases; or it can be continuous over a range of entropy values at a given number of choices. We must account for both varieties of change in social systems. We have been able to explain why certain changes in political party systems are more likely than others, the path of change depending upon the number of parties and the level of voter turnout. At times it may be possible to infer the recent dynamic history of a system or predict future changes from the distribution of subsystems in the entropy-turnout orbital model. Rapid social change may result in distributions different from slower change; or future system relaxation paths may be anticipated from orbital distributions.

The discovery of acrossvariable entropy dynamics lets us predict spatiotemporal changes in entropy levels across a heterogeneous unitary system. Whether by coincidence or hidden necessity, the pattern of change in a heterogeneous social system is analogous to dynamic processes in other sciences based on the two-variable measurement pattern. This enables us to develop an analytic theory of social change that is comparable to early dynamic theories in the physical sciences. Overall, the match between the social theory and the two-variable theories of the physical sciences is remarkable, extending from the pattern of measurement variables to the macroscopic system models and the mathematical formalization of dynamic processes. Beyond its implications for theory construction, the study of social dynamics may at last offer a better understanding of social conflict and the costs and benefits of social change.

Of all the conclusions reached in the foregoing research and analysis, one stands out in importance. It is the conclusion that we can study some kinds of behavior of large numbers of people in a society as an exact science, with accurate quantitative explanations.

APPENDIX I

Least-Squares Curve Fitting with the Entropy Curve

In testing the entropy hypothesis that $H(P) = \log n\, H(T)$, it was desirable to fit a curve of the form $aH(T)$ to the observed entropy values $H(P)$, where $H(T)$ is a function of the turnout rate. In curve fitting one seeks the value of the coefficient a that minimizes the total of the squared distances between the observed $H(P)$ values and those "predicted" by $aH(T)$ for the respective turnout values. We can also try fitting the variance of the information for the $H(P)$ event set against a multiple of the information variance curve for the two-event $H(T)$ set, with the latter again a function turnout rate. In general then, the problem is as follows: We assume that variable y can be expressed as a multiple of the function $f(t)$, where t is the voter turnout rate

$$y = a\,f(t)$$

Then given n pairs of data points (t_i, y_i), $i = 1, 2, \ldots, n$, we seek the value of the coefficient a that minimizes the sum of the n squared "errors" (or residuals), that is, the (vertical) distances between the fitted curve and the y_i values. The error sum

$$\begin{aligned} E &= \sum [y_i - af(t_i)]^2 \\ &= \sum [y_i^2 - 2y_i f(t_i)a + a^2 f(t_i)^2] \end{aligned}$$

To find the value of a where E is a minimum, we treat E as a function of a, differentiate E with respect to a, set the derivative equal to zero, and solve for a. The derivative

$$\frac{\partial E}{\partial a} = -\sum 2y_i f(t_i) + \sum 2f(t_i)^2 a$$

If $\partial E/\partial a = 0$

$$a \sum f(t_i)^2 - \sum y_i f(t_i) = 0$$

And then solving this equation for a we obtain

$$a = \frac{\sum y_i f(t_i)}{\sum f(t_i)^2}, \qquad i = 1, 2, \ldots, n$$

The standard error or estimate of the standard deviation of errors is

$$\text{s.e.} = [E/(n - 1)]^{1/2}$$

APPENDIX II

Microscopic Entropy Estimation

Heretofore our analysis of social systems has been concerned almost exclusively with macroscopic system properties. Still, the macroscopic patterns are inevitably the result of the actions of people in the society. And we must suppose that their choice of action depends upon their perception of society. We will develop here a hypothetical model of this perceptual process at the microsopic level of analysis. That is, we shall try to understand how persons in the society view their society.

Let us assume that people estimate the ambient entropy level of their society, and that they in turn use this knowledge as an immediate basis for determining their own actions in some particular respect. We do not have any direct evidence of the rules of action, or decision rules, people might have, and our model does not deal with this problem. (As a hypothetical decision rule one might assume that people act to adjust their behavior, in a probabilistic sense, in the direction of any change they perceive occurring in society: tending to take higher probability actions if the entropy is decreasing, and less probable actions if it is increasing.) The macroscopic observables give some information about the nature of the microscopic estimation process; and this can be the starting point for a model of microscopic social processes.

Recall that to compute the entropy of an event set we must first estimate the event probabilities from the relative frequencies of occurrence of the respective events. Since there will be some error in the estimation of the event probabilities, there will also be error in the entropy estimate. We shall tend to underestimate the probability of the least likely events; a small sample of events might not include events of low probability. This will lead to an underestimation of the event-set entropy because the less likely an event is, the more its occurrence contributes to the total entropy estimate of the event set. Event "information" varies with the logarithm of the inverse of the probability. Repeated estimates of the entropy of an event set based upon successive samples of events will, on the average, be lower than the true entropy.

If the entropy of an event set of s events is H, and if samples of N events are used to estimate the event probabilities, the average of the entropy estimates will be approximately

$$E(\hat{H}) = H - \frac{(s - 1) \log e}{2N} \tag{A-1}$$

And a collection of such estimates will have a variance of

$$Var(\hat{H}) = \frac{1}{N} (\sum p_i \log^2 p_i - H^2) \tag{A-2}$$

where p_i are the true event probabilities. (See also Section 3-2.) Equation A-2 expresses the fact that the variance of the estimates is a function of the variance of information $Var(I)$ for the event set. [See also Section 2-2 for a definition of $Var(I)$.] We can write

$$Var(\hat{H}) = \frac{1}{N} Var(I) \tag{A-3}$$

where $I = -\log p$.

A macroscopic system measurement gives us the exact values of H, or $E(I)$, and $Var(I)$ for the system population, since our knowledge of the probabilities is virtually exact. The members of the system, however, are restricted to much smaller samples of size N of the total population. Thus the equations A-1 and A-2 describe the distribution of perceived entropy values at the micro level. (As a simplification in the model we will assume that N is uniform among the population or that an average value of N can be used.) If N is fairly small, most people will perceive the system entropy level as being lower than it is from our macroscopic perspective. As the variance approximately indicates, however, there will usually be people in the society who perceive the entropy as higher than the macroscopic level. Observe also that equations A-1 and A-2 describe a "statistical equilibrium" of the microscopic distribution, since they are independent of time; although individuals may change their perception (and behavior) over time, the distribution of their collective estimates will be in a "steady state". The stability of the micro distribution is the source of the persistence and stability of the macroscopic entropy equilibrium.

Note the important difference in using equations A-1 and A-2 to describe the distribution of micro-level entropy estimates. The error between the micro-level estimate of H and the macroscopic H does not depend on either of the macroscopic obervables H or $Var(I)$, except as their values may presume a minimum value of s. Thus if we do not know N, we can say very little about the magnitude of the error. The $Var(\hat{H})$, on the other hand, varies directly with macroscopic information variance $Var(I)$. We would still have to know N to compute $Var(\hat{H})$, but for a given N—even if unknown—we can determine relative changes in $Var(\hat{H})$ directly for macroscopic observations.

It is instructive to work through a numerical example of what values may arise for $E(\hat{H})$ and $Var(\hat{H})$ in an actual population. From the analysis of American elections it appears that an error $E(\hat{H}) - H = -0.1$ bits might be a reasonable guess of how well a population is able to estimate the social entropy, on the average, under favorable conditions. One can argue, for instance, that if a population had underestimated the entropy by 0.1 bits and then had tried to bring the system into an equilibrium with turnout entropy $H(T)$ according to the entropy hypothesis, we would observe a macroscopic $H(P)$ about 0.1 bits above the predicted value. (There would also be a smaller error in the $H(T)$ estimate, tending to give a turnout value slightly closer to 50%.) If we consider just the 1968 American election (Chapter 3)—average errors and maximal values—it appears that a substantial number of subsystems were within these limits of accuracy. We must reiterate, however, that the variability of the macroscopic entropy measurements does not necessarily provide any information about the microscopic errors. In any case, it is important to see what sample size N would be necessary to achieve this level of accuracy. If a very large N were required, we would have to conclude either that our model of microscopic estimation were inappropriate or that macroscopic equilibrium errors would inevitably be large.

Consider then as an illustrative example the United States 1968 election, with $s = 3$ and an error of -0.1 bits in average entropy. If we substitute these values into equation A-1 we have

$$N = \frac{(s-1)\log e}{2[H - E(\hat{H})]}$$

$$= \frac{(3-1)(1.44)}{2(0.1)}$$

$$= 14$$

The value $N = 14$ seems to be small enough that we could in fact expect a high degree of accuracy in entropy estimation in actual social systems. Of course, this N must be a random sample of the population in order for this level of accuracy to be achieved. Since many persons in a society will undoubtedly have somewhat unrepresentative samples, a larger N would be necessary to give the same results under typical social conditions.

Taking the value of $N = 14$, we can also compute the variance of the micro-level estimates $Var(\hat{H})$. As a typical value of $Var(I)$ we will simply use the average value for the United States in 1968; $Var(I) = 0.42$ bits^2. Thus

$$Var(\hat{H}) = \frac{1}{N} Var(I)$$

$$= \frac{0.42}{14}$$

$$= 0.03 \text{ bits}^2$$

and the standard deviation

$$SD(\hat{H}) = (0.03)^{1/2} = 0.17 \text{ bits}$$

Comparing the $SD(\hat{H})$ to the average error -0.1 bits, and taking into account that the distribution of the estimates is asymptotically normal, we can conclude that roughly 25% of the population would overestimate H and 75% underestimate it.

Let us continue to work with $N = 14$ and compare how the error in the entropy estimate will increase in the higher orbits, as s increases. That is, one can imagine a system increasing its entropy level and increasing the number of alternative choices but continuing to operate with the same constraints on sample size, or with the same amount of social interaction at the micro level. The following table gives some representative values:

S	$E(\hat{H}) - H$ (bits)
3	$-.10$
4	$-.15$
6	$-.26$
8	$-.36$

Since the error increases substantially in higher orbits, we should expect greater equilibrium errors in higher orbits in testing the entropy hypothesis. This is a pattern observed previously in the case studies, although it does not necessarily explain the macroscopic errors.

The empirical case studies of the United States, India, Japan, and Germany show that the information variance also tends to increase as the entropy level H rises and the orbit number increases. Subsystem $Var(I)$ values as high as 4 bits^2 and average system values as high as 1.7 to 1.9 bits^2 are attained in Weimar Germany. But subsystem values under 1.0 bits^2 tend to be the rule in most systems, and ordinarily many subsystems will have very small values of $Var(I)$. For a value of $N = 14$ the following table gives some typical $Var(\hat{H})$ values:

$Var(I)$ (bits^2)	$Var(\hat{H})$ (bits^2)	$SD(\hat{H})$ (bits)
.20	.014	.12
.60	.043	.21
1.00	.071	.27
1.50	.11	.33
2.00	.14	.37
4.00	.28	.53

One can conclude that as the entropy level, orbit number, and information variance increase, substantial numbers of people will perceive their society as being quite different from its macroscopic state and also different from the average micro estimate. In so far as distinguishable behavior patterns could be associated with levels of perceived entropy, we would then expect to find a great diversity of behavior in societies with high information variance (other things equal). Everyone in the society might very well act under the same general decision rules, yet perceiving their society to be in quite different states would act quite differently. Whether societies would or could adapt to higher entropy and information variance levels by increasing N is an open question.

If, as we assume, people are estimating entropy from a sample of size N in a social system, we must also consider how the sample would come to be made over time. We can model the sampling process in two ways. Either we can treat the sample as occurring once, as once anew at each election; or we can think of the sampling as an ongoing process where the occurrence of each successive event brings about a readjustment of previously estimated event probabilities. The second of these hypothetical possibilities is the more interesting and, intuitively, it seems to be a more appropriate model; potentially it allows for a smoother change in system entropy levels over time, such as one observed in the spatiotemporal change of entropy values (acrossvariable dynamics).

The process of revising past probability estimates in the light of new data can be modeled as a "vector smoothing" operation.[1] Consider the set of s

event probabilities p_i and a constant c called the smoothing constant. The value of c will be between zero and 1. At the occurrence of the next event E_j at time t, one modifies the set of probability estimates previously made at time $t - 1$ as follows

$$\hat{p}_i(t) = (1 - c)\hat{p}_i(t - 1) \qquad \text{for} \quad i \neq j \tag{A-4}$$

$$\hat{p}_j(t) = (1 - c)\hat{p}_j(t - 1) + c \tag{A-5}$$

Thus, for example, if $c = 20\%$ the probability estimate associated with event E_j is increased by 0.2 minus 20% of its previous value; the values of all other probability estimates will be reduced by 20% of their previous values. Since successive estimates are adjusted for each probability by a constant percentage of previous value, the process is known as "exponential" smoothing. The actual readjustment process is more ragged than "smooth", however, since the probability estimates will change abruptly and fluctuate over successive estimates. On the average, this process of estimation will yield unbiased estimates of the event probabilities, but the variance of the estimate is a function c

$$Var(\hat{p}_i) = \frac{c}{2 - c}(p_i)(1 - p_i)$$

This relationship in turn leads to a dependence on the information variance in the entropy estimate, as before.

The effect of the coefficient c in equations A-4 and A-5 is to reduce the weight of earlier observations in favor of a correction by the most recent observation. If c is large, the estimate of the probabilities will adapt quickly to any change in the true values of the probabilities. If c is small, more weight will be given to past observation; and a change in the actual probabilities will only gradually lead to a revision in their estimates. In either case the rate of change of the estimates will increase as the difference between the present estimates and the actual values increases (again, the "exponential" smoothing). Note , however, that adaptability (a large c) also leads to a greater variance in the estimates when there is a steady state, that is, when there are no changes in the actual probabilities. Thus a small value of c will yield an estimation process that is relatively slow to adapt but which will give good estimates under steady conditions. A small value of c will also have the effect of reducing the sensitivity of the estimates to transients, temporary changes in the true entropy, such as a few sudden occurrences of some rare event. The transient would affect the system for a longer time with a small c but would not lead to a large, abrupt swing in estimated entropy as in the case of large c.

We can compare the exponential smoothing process with one in which only the most recent N observations are used, but where they are weighted equally. In this, c and N can be compared by the equation

$$c = \frac{2}{(N+1)}$$

Values of N and c related by this equation will give approximately the same rate of smoothing.[2] If $N = 14$, for instance, we would have $c = 0.13$ as the equivalent smoothing constant, a fairly low value.

If a large group of people are adapting to entropy change over time according to a smoothing model, the average of their estimates will change much more smoothly than that of any single person. The group average will move in a steady curve without abrupt fluctuations up or down as it adjusts to new values of the true probabilities; the group average will show virtually no variance in the steady state. (The variance of a group of random samples of estimates will decrease to zero as the number of samples, or people, in the group increases.)

As an application, take the case of interaction between two groups of people initially at different average entropy levels. Suppose that the interaction has the effect of individual members of each group including members of the other group in their sample. The interaction will cause members of one group to estimate that their entropy is increasing and the other that it is decreasing. If people in the respective groups then modify their collective behavior to more nearly approximate the perceived level of entropy, there will be a smooth convergence in the entropy levels of the two groups. The greater the initial difference in entropy levels, the more rapid the adjustment process, under the hypothetical estimation model. The net pattern of interaction is thus an exponential reduction of actual entropy differences over time. This is, of course, the observed macroscopic pattern of entropy difference reduction in acrossvariable dynamics. The larger the value of the smoothing constant c, or equivalently, the smaller the N value, and the greater the overlapping of the two groups in terms of inclusion in each other's sample, the faster will be the macroscopic relaxation rate and the greater will appear to be the macroscopic "conductivity" of the total system. (The rate of the sampling process or the rate of occurrence of events would also be an important factor, but how this might vary in an actual system is unknown.)

In general, the sampling process also has a spatial extent. Observe, however, that the overlapping or interaction of groups, over a spatial dimension, will only appear as increased conductivity if samples of some members of the groups include an increased proportion of members from the other groups; a change in N alone will not necessarily accomplish this. The visibility of spatially more remote people or groups, and thus their proportion of an individual's sample, might increase through public demonstrations and the like. In such a case sampling errors might increase, since public visibility does not necessarily imply representativeness or randomness in a sampling sense. The spatial distribution of sampling errors may be an important characteristic of a society.

The factors that affect microscopic entropy estimation will also affect the possibilities for a self-sustaining entropy reduction. The reduction could begin through an abrupt decrease in average perceived entropy levels in a system, at the micro level. The perceived "decrease" could then lead to changed behavior patterns commensurate with the lower entropy level; these might in turn yield a still lower perceived entropy. The reduction could then be propagated throughout the system by the mechanism of acrossvariable dynamics. A "spontaneous" (endogenous) decrease in perceived entropy may result from a decreasing sample size N, or equivalently, from an increase in the micro smoothing constant. As a second possibility the reduction could be brought on by a decreasing representativeness of the sample, possibly having a spatial bias as well. In the latter case, imagine people changing their sampling habits in relation to their own behavior or to their past samples, as in associating with people of like behavior to the greater exclusion of others. The preconditions for micro-level sampling errors or sampling changes would be especially fostered by high entropy levels or orbit numbers, and by adverse changes resulting from entropy levels near the maximum psychological capacity. Adaptive behavior by a system, by members of the system, could also produce these same effects in certain cases. If a system at high entropy were subject to rapid changes or fluctuations in entropy, as a result of exogenous forces for example, the result at the micro level might be an increase in the smoothing coefficient, or a reduction in N. Such a change would render the system more adaptive to sudden change but also cause increased estimation errors and increase the possibility of an entropy reduction.

Since the quality of a micro sample is a key to determining macroscopic system characteristics, it is important to know what social conditions affect the sampling process. In general terms, any social condition that restricts the likelihood of contact between individuals will be inimical to good sampling. Thus a society with diversive social stratification or social classes, or one in which people tend to associate in homogeneous groups, will show the effects of poor sampling. A society in which there is a high degree of freedom of association or in which people tend to have multiple affiliations in diverse associations or interest groups, will have characteristics of good micro sampling. These topics, of course, have been much discussed in the literature of political science, usually as conditions for stable and harmonious polities; but their relation to the macroscopic dynamics of social systems has a more immediate and explicit importance from the perspective of microscopic entropy estimation.

This discussion of entropy estimation has been mainly qualitative and hypothetical, but it gives some insight into the origins of the previously observed macroscopic phenomena. And it enhances the macroscopic theory when we can construct at least a partial model of microscopic processes which is both reasonable and supportive. The microscopic model is, however, still of a probabilistic nature and so does not offer an easy route to the verification of the macroscopic theory. The macroscopic laws, as they represent stable averages of large numbers of microscopic events, are more nearly deterministic than are the microscopic principles of action embodied in this model. The analysis and explanation of macroscopic phenomena remain essentially within the province of the macroscopic observables and the resulting social laws.

APPENDIX III

Table of −p *log* p *Values for Entropy Computation*

Probability p	$-p \log p$	Probability p	$-p \log p$
.005	.038	.26	.502
.01	.066	.27	.510
.02	.113	.28	.514
.03	.152	.29	.518
.04	.186	.30	.521
.05	.216	.31	.524
.06	.244	.32	.526
.07	.268	.33	.528
.08	.292	.34	.529
.09	.313	.35	.530
.10	.332	.36	.531
.11	.350	.37	.531
.12	.367	.38	.530
.13	.383	.39	.530
.14	.397	.40	.529
.15	.410	.41	.527
.16	.423	.42	.526
.17	.434	.43	.524
.18	.445	.44	.521
.19	.455	.45	.518
.20	.464	.46	.515
.21	.473	.47	.512
.22	.480	.48	.508
.23	.488	.49	.504
.24	.494	.50	.500
.25	.500		

Probability p	$-p \log p$	Probability p	$-p \log p$
.51	.495	.76	.301
.52	.490	.77	.290
.53	.485	.78	.280
.54	.480	.79	.269
.55	.474	.80	.258
.56	.468	.81	.246
.57	.462	.82	.235
.58	.456	.83	.223
.59	.449	.84	.211
.60	.442	.85	.199
.61	.435	.86	.187
.62	.428	.87	.175
.63	.420	.88	.162
.64	.412	.89	.150
.65	.404	.90	.137
.66	.396	.91	.124
.67	.387	.92	.111
.68	.378	.93	.097
.69	.369	.94	.084
.70	.360	.95	.070
.71	.351	.96	.056
.72	.341	.97	.043
.73	.331	.98	.028
.74	.321	.99	.014
.75	.311		

Notes

Chapter 1

1. Formalization is the reverse of operationalism as it has been practiced in much of social science research. Attempts at theory construction have usually begun with abstract models or theoretical constructs, and only subsequently were measurement problems considered, if at all.

2. The discussion of the two-variable measurement pattern follows that of A. G. J. MacFarlane, *Engineering Systems Analysis,* Addison-Wesley, 1964; and Ole Franksen, "Mathematical Programming in Economics by Physical Analogs, Part I," *Simulation* **12,** pp. 297–314 (June 1969). Original sources are cited by these authors. Also helpful was Fredric Bailey, "Large-Scale System Models," unpublished lecture notes, Department of Electrical Engineering, University of Minnesota, 1970.

3. This discussion of measurement is meant to be only an introduction. For more detail on measurement variables and scales and their dependence on empirical system properties, see the following authors as listed in the Bibliography: B. Ellis, Kaplan, Krantz, Pfanzagl, and Stevens, among others.

4. For rotational mechanical systems, instead of translational, a slightly different pattern is used: angular velocity is substituted for velocity and moment of inertia for mass in the translational pattern. In the thermodynamic system, entropy and entropy flow can be taken as the initial throughvariables instead of heat and heat flow; see MacFarlane, pp. 48–50.

5. The economic pattern is suggested by Franksen, p. 308.

6. For a more detailed description of energy and power, and the related functions co-energy, content, and co-content, see Franksen and MacFarlane.

7. The discussion of macroscopic systems and the definition of terms parallels L. D. Landau, E. M. Lifshitz, *Statistical Physics,* 2nd ed., Addison-Wesley, 1969, pp. 1–14. Other useful texts are Herbert B. Callen, *Thermodynamics,* Wiley, 1960; and Edward Shapiro, *Macroeconomic Analysis,* Harcourt, Brace, World, 1966.

8. Compare the discussion of "arc sine laws" and statistical equilibrium in William Feller, *An Introduction to Probability Theory And Its Applications,* Volume 1, 2nd ed., Wiley, 1961, pp. 38ff, 77ff, 356ff.

9. Landau and Lifshitz, p. 1.

10. This concept of equilibrium poses certain difficulties, even in well-established physical sciences. According to Laszlo Tisza, *Generalized Thermodynamics*, MIT Press, 1966; with regard to thermal equilibrium (page 92),

> ". . . there is no satisfactory empirical definition of equilibrium. The usual requirement that visible intrinsic processes should cease is only a necessary criterion that serves us well in simple situations, but we lack a practical sufficient condition to reassure us that equilibrium is actually established. . . ."

And see also page 119. Note that a statistical equilibrium is not "stable" in the sense that a system disturbed from an equilibrium will return to the *same* equilibrium, although it will return to an equilibrium.

11. See also Herbert Simon, Albert Ando, "Aggregation of Variables in Dynamic Systems," *Econometrica* **29** pp. 111–138, (April 1961); and L. T. Grujic, D. D. Siljak, "Exponential stability of large-scale discrete systems," *Int. J. of Control* **19,** pp. 481–491, (1974).

12. Network equations in electrical theory are formulated according to Kirchoff's laws. In a general form these laws state that: (1) the sum of all throughvariable rates incident at any point of the network model is zero; and (2) the sum of all intensive acrossvariable difference measurements around any closed loop of the network is zero. (See also MacFarlane, p. 53; and Franksen, p. 311, who states that the first law is a necessary condition and the second a sufficient condition for steady-state equilibrium in a dynamic system.)

13. Oscillatory behavior can only occur within a system if both extensive variables are found in the two-variable pattern; oscillatory behavior implies a transfer of energy back and forth from one kind of extensive storage to the other.

14. An extended study of energy is D. W. Theobald, *The Concept of Energy*, London: E&FN Spon, 1966.

15. For further information see MacFarlane, *op. cit.*, H. E. Koenig, et al., *Analysis of Discrete Physical Systems*, McGraw Hill, 1967, and J. Lowen Shearer, et al., *Introduction to System Dynamics*, Addison-Wesley, 1967. (All these authors use an interdisciplinary approach to systems analysis based on the two-variable measurement pattern.) Another interesting example of systems analysis with the two-variable pattern is J. B. Ellis, *The Description and Analysis of Socioeconomic Systems by Physical Systems Techniques*, Doctoral Dissertation, Michigan State University, 1965. The two-variable pattern is applied to biological systems by Douglas S. Riggs, *Control Theory and Physiological Feedback*, Williams and Wilkins, Baltimore, 1970. An early example of this kind of analogic analysis in economics is S. Enke, "Equilibrium among spatially separated markets: solution by electric analogue," *Econometrica* **19,** pp. 40-47, (1951).

Chapter 2

1. A. I. Khinchin, *Mathematical Foundations of Information Theory*, Dover, 1957. (An English translation of "The Entropy Concept in Probability Theory,"

Uspekhi Matematicheskikh Nauk, **8**, 3, 1953, pp. 3–20.) Khinchin's method is slightly different from Shannon's original derivation which is given in Claude E. Shannon, Warren Weaver, *The Mathematical Theory of Communication*, University of Illinois Press, Urbana, 1969. For details of the proofs refer to these sources.

2. As a result we also have for S_i the ith event of S and T_j the jth event of T; $i = 1, 2, \ldots, n$; $j = 1, 2, \ldots, m$; the conditional probabilities

$$P(S_i \mid T_j) = \frac{P(S_i T_j)}{P(T_j)}$$

and
$$H(S \mid T_j) = -\sum_{i=1}^{n} P(S_i \mid T_j) \log P(S_i \mid T_j)$$

and the result $H(S \mid T) = \sum_{j=1}^{m} P(T_j) H(S \mid T_j)$

A metric can be established on the space of all finite event sets. The functional

$$d(S, T) = 1 - \frac{I(S, T)}{H(ST)} \quad \text{for} \quad H(ST) \neq 0$$

is a distance in this space for any sets S and T and

$$I(S, T) = H(T) - H(T \mid S) = H(S) - H(S \mid T)$$

This is proven by C. Rajski, "A Metric Space of Discrete Probability Distributions," *Information and Control* **4**, pp. 371–377 (1961).

3. Robert M. Fano, *Transmission of Information*, MIT Press, 1961; this derivation can also be made from an axiomatic basis.

4. An algebraic derivation of entropy is also possible. See R. S. Ingarden, "Information Theory and the Thermodynamics of Light. Part 1," *Fortschritte der Physik* **12**, pp. 567-594 (1964) (Berlin GDR). Additional insight is provided by the derivation of entropy for the "fuzzy set" introduced by Zadeh; see A. DeLuca, S. Termini, "A Definition of a Non-probabilistic Entropy in the Setting of Fuzzy Sets Theory," *Information and Control*, **20**, pp. 301-312, (1972).

5. See Shannon and Weaver, pp. 87-91, for a complete discussion of entropy for continuous distributions.

6. Shannon and Weaver, pp. 90-91.

7. This method is adapted from a procedure used by C. E. Shannon, "Prediction and Entropy of Printed English," *Bell System Technical Journal* **30**, pp. 50–64, (1951).

8. Brian Ellis, *Basic Concepts of Measurement*, Cambridge University Press, 1966, pp. 48–51 and 160–182.

9. This is the subject of Chapter 6.

10. Note that entropy or average information as we use it here is not equivalent to the entropy of thermodynamics and statistical physics where it is an extensive throughvariable. (Cf. note 4, Chapter 1.) The entropy measures of information

theory and statistical physics have the same mathematical form but are not used for the same measurement purpose. The distinction between these two entropies is discussed by Frank Tillman, B. Roswell Russell, "Information and Entropy," *Synthese* **13,** pp. 233–241.

An extensive social entropy analogous to that of statistical physics could be derived from the probabilities of the set of possible combinations of people with respect to the events of an event set. (Alternatively, one might consider combinations of people with levels of perceived (micro) entropy; see Appendix II.) The number of possible combinations would increase with the size of the population, resulting in an extensive measure. There would also be questions of which combinations were to be considered distinguishable and of equal probability. The utility of such a measure is problematic, since we find no dynamic social laws involving the measure, in contrast to the analoguous case in physics.

11. Shannon and Weaver, p. 15.

12. Khinchin, p. 7.

13. An analogy is drawn from the measurement patterns for rotational and translational mechanical systems. (Cf. Fig. 1-1 and note 4, Chapter 1.) In the translational scheme the mass is used to find the momentum; in the rotational scheme, the moment of inertia to find the angular momentum. Computationally, the distribution of mass is averaged to find the center of gravity; the moment of inertia is the variance of mass about the average. Thus there is a mathematical parallel between the two social measurement patterns and the two mechanical system patterns, and we will consider the information variance as the initial variable instead of the information standard deviation or some other related function. We will not investigate higher moments of the information variable here, although they could be of potential interest in social systems analysis.

Chapter 3

1. It is not possible to make these kinds of intensive measurements in physical systems, since we have no way to measure an ensemble of interspersed particles without measuring the whole set; we cannot measure the set composed of every second or third molecule, for example. If a subset of the whole physical ensemble could be removed from the rest and measured separately, it would no longer be the same system.

2. The following values of log n are given for reference:

log 1 = 0	log 5 = 2.322
log 2 = 1.000	log 6 = 2.585
log 3 = 1.585	log 7 = 2.807
log 4 = 2.000	log 8 = 3.000

3. A sound introduction to methodology in social science research is, J. W. Tukey, M. B. Wilk, "Data Analysis and Statistics: Techniques and Approaches", in Edward R. Tufte, Ed., *The Quantitative Analysis of Social Problems,* Addison-

Wesley, 1970. A standard reference is Hubert M. Blalock, *Social Statistics*, McGraw-Hill, 1960. A good discussion of the role of curve fitting in the construction of explanatory models, which also deals with a related empirical context, is Adam Przeworski, G. A. D. Soares, "Theories in Search of a Curve: A Contextual Interpretation of Left Vote", *American Political Science Review* (*APSR*), **65,** pp. 51–68 (March 1971).

4. All curve fitting was done with the University of Minnesota CDC 6600 computer routine ORTHON by J. Carlson, et al., 1964. This routine allows a linear least squares approximation using orthonormalized arbitrary functions. See also, Philip J. Davis, "Orthonormalizing Codes in Numerical Analysis," in *Survey of Numerical Analysis*, John Todd, Ed., McGraw-Hill, pp.347 ff.

5. The standard error $S = [E/(M - N)]^{1/2}$ where M is the number of data points, N is the number of coefficients, and E is the sum of the M squared errors (residuals). The standard error of a coefficient is the standard deviation of the coefficient multiplied by S. Note also that the least squares method may give error estimates that exaggerate the extent of disequilibrium in the system when the fit curve is close to the predicted curve. The errors (residuals) are calculated from vertical distances between data points and the fit curve, but this distance may be farther than that from the data point to the nearest equilibrium point. The net error would usually increase with the steepness of the entropy curve. Thus the results that follow might generally be stronger if it were practical to use a curve fitting algorithm that computed the errors more appropriately. The "explained variance" (which is total sample variation minus E) will be used only infrequently as a measure of goodness of fit, since it does not relate directly to the prediction of specific point values; its sensitivity to variable (entropy) range can give misleading results.

6. For a study of the misconception and faulty explanation that can arise when goodness of fit is the sole criterion for curve fitting and the development of a theory, see William Feller, *An Introduction to Probability Theory and Its Applications*, Vol. 2, Wiley, pp. 52-53; or in greater detail, W. Feller, "On the Logistic Law of Growth and Its Empirical Verifications in Biology," *Acta Biotheoretica* **5,** pp. 51–66 (1940).

7. Symmetry has a key role in scientific theories, and mathematical formulations are often devised to bring out a natural symmetry. See Ole Franksen, pp. 306–307; and H. Weyl, *Symmetry*, Princeton University Press, 1952.

8. The distribution of extreme values in samples from a population can be computed with the order statistic and in general is not the same as the population distribution.

9. G. P. Basharin, "On a Statistical Estimate for the Entropy of a Sequence of Independent Random Variables," *Theory of Probability and Its Applications*, **4,** 3, pp. 333–336 (1959). This is a translation of the original article in the Soviet journal, *Teoriya Veroyatnostei i ee Primeneniya* **4,** pp. 361–364. The author also notes that the estimate will be most precise when the event probabilities are equal. Confidence intervals can also be computed using these formulas. The value of log *e* is about 1.44. Or see the derivation of George A. Miller, "Note on the Bias of Information

Estimates," in Henry Quastler, Ed., *Information Theory in Psychology*, Free Press, 1955.

10. Compare the findings of Angus Campbell, et al., *The American Voter*, Abridgement, Wiley, 1964, p. 152: " . . . it is the informal, extralegal barriers—not state legislation—that account for much of the variability in the turnout of the Southern Negro."

11. For statistical tests on coefficients and their errors see Blalock. These remarks apply to hypothesis testing for single cases.

12. *Report on the Third General Elections in India*, Delhi, Indian Election Commission, 1962; R. Chandidas, et al., Eds., *India Votes*, Bombay, Popular Prakeshan, 1968.

13. Nathaniel B. Thayer, *How the Conservatives Rule Japan*, Princeton University Press, 1969, pp. 111–116.

14. Japanese electoral data is available in the *Japanese Statistical Yearbook*, Bureau of Statistics, Tokyo, Japan (in serial volumes). The prewar election data used here was kindly made available to the author by Professor Roger Benjamin, University of Minnesota, in a cooperative study of comparative politics and political development. The postwar election data is available from the Inter-University Consortium for Political Research, Ann Arbor, Michigan.

15. Thayer, p.117.

16. Another confirming example is provided indirectly by Mark Kesselman, "French Local Politics: A Statistical Examination of Grass Roots Consensus," *American Political Science Review* (*APSR*) **60**, pp. 963-973 (1966); also in his *The Ambiguous Consensus*, Knopf, 1967. Using an entropy-like measure, he shows that "party competitiveness" (read entropy) decreases with increasing turnout, which was over 50%, in a large sample of French communes. He also discusses the high degree of social consensus associated with low entropy regions.

17. A good discussion of Soviet elections and the significance of abstentions and dissenting votes is by Jerome M. Gilison, "Soviet Elections as a Measure of Dissent: the Missing One Percent," *APSR* **62**, pp. 814–826 (1968).

18. China may not be a very low entropy system, however, despite popular impressions to the contrary. Townsend reports turnout at (only) 86% in the 1953–54 elections, when there was also a rudimentary multiple party system. See James R. Townsend, *Political Participation in Communist China*, University of California Press, 1969, pp. 132–134, 146, *et passim*. The periods of social upheaval and mass movements in the 1950's and 1960's may have been the result of system maintenance of (or relaxation to) relatively high entropy levels despite the intensive efforts of the government and Communist party to reduce the level much further. There is also the conflict between system models or varieties: the hierarchical party structure versus the unitary model or structure of the collective masses, as would be shown in the election data.

19. There is a vast literature on voting behavior. Many articles will be found in journals such as the *American Political Science Reveiw* (*APSR*), *Comparative Politics*, *Comparative Political Studies*, *Public Choice*, *Econometrica*, and so forth.

The reader unfamiliar with survey election studies may refer to the first major works in this area: Bernard R. Berelson, et al., *Voting,* University of Chicago Press, 1954; and Angus Campbell, et al., *The American Voter,* Wiley, 1960. Among more recent articles pertinent to the discussion here are, Arthur S. Goldberg, "Discerning a Causal Pattern Among Data on Voting Behavior," *APSR* **60,** pp. 913–922 (1966); and Norman H. Nie, et al., "Social Structure and Political Participation," *APSR* **63,** pp. 361–378, 808–832 (1969).

20. Kenneth J. Arrow, *Social Choice and Individual Values,* 2nd. ed., Wiley. 1963. Gordon Tullock, *Toward a Mathematics of Politics,* University of Michigan Press, 1967. Bengt Hansson, "Choice Structures and Preference Relations," *Synthese* **18,** pp. 443–488 (1968); "Group Preferences," *Econometrica* **37** (1969); "Voting and Group Decision Functions," presented at the Econometric Society, Brussels, 1969. There are numerous other published articles on the subject.

21. John von Neumann, Oskar Morgenstern, *Theory of Games and Economic Behavior,* Princeton, 1944. R. D. Luce, Howard Raiffa, *Games and Decisions,* Wiley, 1959. Hermann Chernoff, Lincoln Moses, *Elementary Decision Theory,* Wiley, 1959. Peter C. Fishburn, "Summation Social Choice Functions," *Econometrica,* **41,** pp. 1183–1196 (1971); *Utility Theory for Decision Making,* Wiley, 1970. Anthony Downs, *An Economic Theory of Democracy,* Wiley, 1957. William Riker, Peter Ordeshook, "A Theory of the Calculus of Voting," *APSR* **62,** pp. 25–42 (March 1968). John A. Ferejohn, Morris Fiorina, "The Paradox of Not Voting," *APSR* **68,** pp. 525-596, (1974). Richard G. Niemi, Herbert Weisberg, Eds., *Probability Models of Collective Decision-Making,* Merrill, 1972.

22. Patrick Suppes, "Behavioristic Foundations of Utility," *Econometrica,* **29,** pp. 186–201 (April 1961).

23. See Richard Schlegel, "Statistical Explanation in Physics: the Copenhagen Interpretation," *Synthese* **21,** pp. 65-82 (March 1970). Quoting Schlegel, p.66,

> "The major point of this paper will be to emphasize that in quantum physics the observation process creates the event or property that is the individual datum of statistical description. In a sense, of course, it is trivially true in all of science that it is observation that gives rise to information; but in quantum theory the presumption is forced on us that the event recorded exists *only* by virtue of the interaction-observation by which it is discerned." And on p. 78, ". . . existence in detail only arises with the measurement or observation."

An introductory text in quantum theory is Robert H. Dicke, James P. Wittke, *Introduction to Quantum Mechanics,* Addison-Wesley, 1960.

Chapter 4

1. This method is adapted from a procedure used by C. E. Shannon, "Prediction and Entropy of Printed English," *Bell System Technical Journal,* **30,** pp. 50–64 (January 1951).

2. See also Roger Benjamin, et al., *Patterns of Political Development,* McKay,

1972, pp. 149–150 and 169–170 for graphs of some of these results. Similar findings about the effects of urbanization and industrialization on the Japanese political system have been reported by a number of social scientists. See, for example, Scott Flanagan, "The Japanese Party System in Transition," *Comparative Politics* **3**, pp. 231–253 (1970).

3. See Benjamin, et al., pp. 30-80, especially graphs on pp. 49, 62.

4. Benjamin, et al.

5. Compare the findings of Daniel Lerner, *The Passing of Traditional Society*, Free Press, 1958.

6. G. A. D. Soares, M. A. C. deNoronha, "Urbanizacao e dispersao eleitoral," *Revista direito publico e ciencia politica* (Brazil), **3**, No. 2, pp. 258–270, July-December 1960.

Additional supporting examples which use less comparable methods of analysis are: (*a*) Benjamin, et al,. pp. 81–132, for Israel; (*b*) Chae-Jin Lee, "Urban Political Competition in a Developing Nation: the Case of Korea," *Comparative Political Studies*, **4**, pp. 107–116 (April 1971); (*c*) Kesselman, *op. cit.*., on France. The inadequacies of research on the United States in this area are reviewed by Philip Coulter, Glen Gordon, "Urbanization and Party Competition: Critique and Redirection of Theoretical Research," *Western Political Quarterly*, **21**, pp. 274–288 (June 1968).

7. David Butler, Donald Stokes, *Political Change in Britain*, St. Martin's Press, New York, 1969, pp. 144–150.

8. Stanley Milgram, "Nationality and Conformity," *Scientific American*, **205**, No. 5, pp. 45–51 (December 1961).

9. George A. Miller, "The Magical Number Seven, Plus or Minus Two: Some Limits on our Capacity for Processing Information," *The Psychological Review* **15**, No. 2, pp. 183–218 (1956).

This article reviews the experimental findings on the subject. The various experiments involve different human senses and give slightly different results. For visual perception, which shows the largest entropy capacity, the average of the limits from all reported experiments is about 2.8 bits. In a few experiments values over 3.0 bits are found; the highest value reported by any experimenter was 3.9 bits. Whatever the exact value should be—and it probably varies somewhat with the experimental context—human information or entropy capacity is definitely very small. Note, however, that this does not imply anything about capacity for memory. See also the similar findings of Siegfried Geiger, *Erkennen und Waehlen*, Kiepenheuer and Witsch, Cologne, Berlin; 1970.

10. Henry Miller, James Bieri, "An Informational Analysis of Clinical Judgement," *Journal of Abnormal and Social Psychology*, **67**, No. 4, pp. 317–325 (October 1963). They find a maximum group entropy averaging 2.86 bits, but the reliability of group judgment, indicated by agreement between individual judgments, decreases with increasing number of categories and increasing entropy. The maximum for reliable judgments is no more than 1 to 2 bits. Their experiments are restricted to eight categories or less. Comparable findings showing a group entropy

limit just under 3 bits and slightly less than individual capacity are reported by Virginia Senders, "The Effect of Number of Subjects on the Estimate of Transmitted Information," in Henry Quastler, Ed., *Information Theory in Psychology*, Free Press, 1955.

11. A. S. Eddington, *The Mathematical Theory of Relativity*, Cambridge University Press, 1960 (first edition 1923), p. 106.

12. Eddington, p. 238.

13. Michel Crozier, *The Bureaucratic Phenomenon*, University of Chicago Press, 1964; Chapter 6, "Power and Uncertainty," pp. 145–174, *et passim*.

14. A good study of the relation between an organization's communications and structure, although nonquantitative, is Franz Schurmann, *Ideology and Organization in Communist China*, 2nd. ed., University of California Press, 1970; especially Chapter 1, "Ideology," pp. 17–104.

15. For some simple examples on the relation between information theory and problem solving see Gordon Raisbeck, *Information Theory*, MIT Press, 1963.

16. An introduction to the possible connection between information theory and the adaptiveness of self-organizing systems is Henri Atlan, "Du bruit come principe d'autoorganisation," *Communications* **18** (French), pp. 21-36 (1972). See also, C. E. Shannon, J. McCarth, Eds., *Automata Studies*, Princeton University Press, 1956; H. Von Foerster, G. W. Zöpf. Eds., *Principles of Self Organization*, Pergamon, 1962; Marshall C. Yovits, C. Cameron, Eds., *Self Organizing Systems*, Pergamon, 1960; Heniz von Foerster, et al., Eds ., *Purposive Systems*, Spartan, 1969.

Much of this literature concerns biological systems and makes use of the thermodynamic concept of entropy and related thermodynamic laws, which are applicable to biological systems (being physical systems) but not to the social systems described here; the relevance of this literature to social systems remains to be proven.

17. A pertinent normative study is by Henry S. Kariel, *Open Systems: Arenas for Political Action*, F. E. Peacock, Itasca, Illinois, 1969.

Chapter 6

1. Relationships analogous to Newton's law arise in electrical theory for the decay of electrical current and voltage in an electrical circuit, as for example, when the circuit is broken. Such changes occur very rapidly in electrical circuits, however, and are not usually observable in detail.

2. See also Herbert Simon, Albert Ando, "Aggregation of Variables in Dynamic Systems," *Econometrica* **29**, pp. 481–491 (1961).

3. In determining whether a system will approach an entropy equilibrium over time, becoming increasingly homogeneous over its area, any of a large class of functions will serve as measures of disequilibrium, including the functions of entropy difference magnitude and standard deviation used here. It is not necessary that the function fit the linear differential equation 6-1, although it is a great convenience to the analysis if equation 6-1 holds reasonably well. One finds in fact that if a dy-

namic system has a stable equilibrium, its behavior near the equilibrium value (zero disequilibrium) can usually be approximated by a linear differential equation. The general class of functions that can be used to determine whether a dynamic system has a stable equilibrium at a point are known as Lyapunov (or Liapunov) functions. Sufficient conditions for Lyapunov functions and related problems of system stability are extensively covered in the literature on control theory. See for instance MacFarlane, Chapter 9, "Lyapunov Methods for the Investigation of Nonlinear System Stability"; or Joseph LaSalle, Solomon Lefschetz, *Stability by Liapunov's Direct Method*, Academic Press, 1961. Similar problems are also discussed in the theory of differential equations and in mathematical economics.

One can conclude that it is not necessary for social systems always to behave linearly in order for equilibria to exist in entropy levels. And there is also the implication that individual or collective behavior in response to perceived entropy differences need not be uniformly linear or consistent over time, or from one person to another, for the predicted macroscopic patterns to arise.

4. We can observe, however, that exponential change in time is a characteristic of physical systems where the action taking place at any instant of time is independent of the system's past history and depends only on the current state of the system, as the distance to equilibrium for example; such systems can be said to have no "memory." These conditions may also characterize the behavior of people in social systems at the micro level with regard to dynamic processes leading to a system entropy equilibrium.

5. Jean Baptiste Fourier, *The Analytic Theory of Heat*, Cambridge University Press, 1878; Dover, 1955.

6. Similar fluid theories were proposed in early versions of electrical theory. It was later discovered, of course, that electrical current involved a flow of electrons. The direction of flow assumed by early theorists (in the one fluid theory), as first proposed by Franklin, was from positive to negative. This direction is usually followed by convention even today, despite the fact that the electron flow is actually in the direction opposite to the "current." Thus not only the substantiveness of the throughvariable flow but also its direction is arbitrary for the purposes of a mathematical analysis of macroscopic system dynamics, within the framework of the two-variable system.

7. The derivation here generally follows that of I. S. Sokolnikoff, R. M. Redheffer, *Mathematics of Physics and Modern Engineering*, McGraw-Hill, 1958, pp. 455–458.

8. The analogy to Newton's law of cooling (Section 6-1) can be easily derived as an approximation to the conditions implied by equations 6-9 and 6-10 together.

From equation 6-10 we have the rate of flow

$$\frac{dQ}{dt} = -k' \, \Delta H = -k' \, U \tag{A-6}$$

for some constant k' and the difference in entropy U. From equation 6-9 we also have that the change in Q is proportional to change in H. Thus in R_1 we have

$$\frac{dQ_1}{dt} = a_1 \frac{dH}{dt}$$

and in R_3 we have

$$\frac{dQ_3}{dt} = a_3 \frac{d}{dt}(H + \Delta H)$$

where a_1 and a_3 are constants.

For a constant flow (i.e., over a short time interval) the flow out of R_3 is approximately equal to the flow into R_1. Thus

$$\frac{dQ}{dt} = \frac{dQ_1}{dt} = -\frac{dQ_3}{dt}$$

(One must also assume that no Q is lost in the process.) So we have

$$\frac{dQ}{dt} = \frac{1}{2}\left(\frac{dQ_1}{dt} - \frac{dQ_3}{dt}\right)$$

$$= \frac{1}{2}\frac{d}{dt}[a_1 H - a_3(H + \Delta H)]$$

We can consider two cases:

(1) If a_1 and a_3 are approximately equal to $2a$ (which should be the case in the Japanese districts analyzed above)

$$\frac{dQ}{dt} \doteq -\frac{1}{2}a_3\frac{d}{dt}(\Delta H) = -a\frac{dU}{dt}$$

(2) If a_1 is much larger than a_3

$$\frac{dQ}{dt} = \frac{1}{2}\frac{d}{dt}[(a_1 - a_3)H - a_3\,\Delta H]$$

$$= \frac{a_1 - a_3}{2}\frac{dH}{dt} - \frac{a_3}{2}\frac{dU}{dt}$$

But in case (2) H would be relatively constant over a short time compared to the change in ΔH because of the relatively larger value of a_1; thus $dH/dt \doteq 0$ and $dQ/dt = -a\,dU/dt$. Comparing with equation A-6 we see that

$$\frac{dQ}{dt} = -k'\,U = a\frac{dU}{dt}$$

and

$$\frac{dU}{dt} = -k\,U$$

9. For a thorough discussion of harmonic functions and proofs of the theorems

cited here see: Lars Ahlfors, *Complex Analysis*, McGraw Hill, 1953, pp. 175–199; Oliver D. Kellog, *Foundations of Potential Theory*, Dover, 1953 (original edition, Springer, 1929); I. S. Sokolnikoff, R. M. Redheffer, *op. cit;*or P. R. Garabedian, *Partial Differential Equations*, Wiley, 1964.

10. Since about two thirds of the American states are boundary states, the probability of finding both the maximum and minimum in boundary states in any one election is about one-half; thus the occurrence of the extreme values in boundary states does not become an interesting or significant finding, by itself, until the same is observed in several elections. For the five elections cited in Chapter 3 and the 1972 election, the following results were obtained:

Year	Maximum in	Minimum in
1920	Washington	South Carolina
1924	Arizona	South Carolina
1940	Wisconsin	Mississippi
1948	Florida	Mississippi
1968	South Carolina	Maine
1972	Oregon	Georgia

11. The 1972 election campaign was confused with respect to the "third party" candidacy because of the withdrawal of George Wallace as a possible candidate. Nevertheless, the American Independent Party—the major "third party"—was able to get on the ballot with a secondary candidate in most states. The data for the election gives rather consistent and expected results in terms of a steady-state distribution, except for those states where this party was not on the ballot; in the spatial map several of these states appear as local minima, 0.1 bits below the level of their surrounding states.

12. The maximum in 1860, at over 1.8 bits, occurred in Missouri, and the minimum was in Texas; both of these states were boundary states in 1860. South Carolina was not included in this analysis because there was no popular vote for the presidency. Data for Virginia includes the area later to become West Virginia.

13. There is a rapidly growing literature on the relationship between change in a person's life and the subsequent occurrence of psychological illness or psychologically induced physiological illness; the stress of a change may lower the resistance to disease, for example. In many instances, change in a person's life will be part of broader changes in the society which are in turn related to the social entropy level or changes in the entropy level. The deleterious physiological effects of change in an individual's life, and the relative impact of various kinds of change, have been extensively studied by Dr. Thomas H. Holmes and his colleagues at the University of Washington School of Medicine. Among other published articles by this group are: R. H. Rahe, et al., "Social stress and illness onset," *Journal of Psychosomatic Research*, **8,** 1964; T. H. Holmes, R. H. Rahe, "The social readjustment rating scale," *J. Psychsom. Res.*, **11,** pp. 213–218 (1967), T. S. Holmes, et al., "Short term intrusions into the life style routine," *J. Psychosom. Res.*, **14,** pp. 121–132 (1970), T. S.

Holmes, *Adaptive Behavior and Health Change*, Medical Thesis, University of Washington, 1970, A. R. Wyler, et al., "Magnitude of life events and seriousness of illness," *Psychosomatic Medicine*, **33**, pp.115–122 (March-April 1971).

Various psychological problems have also been studied (less extensively and with less success) in the framework of epidemiology, in terms of their spatiotemporal distribution in a society. For an introduction to the subject see: E. H. Hare, J. K. Wing, Eds., *Psychiatric Epidemiology*, Oxford, 1970; Richard J. Plunkett, John E. Gordon, *Epidemiology and Mental Illness*, Basic Books, New York, 1960; Charlotte Silverman, *The Epidemiology of Depression*, Johns Hopkins Press, 1968.

Although medical problems such as physical or mental illness may be the pernicious side effects of social change, there are other sociomedical concerns that should not be viewed as side effects but as operating by means of the social dynamics analyzed in this book. This class of phenomena, of which drug usage may be one example, involves the learning and diffusion of behavior patterns through a society by means of the mechanisms of social choice and pressures of conformity. These phenomena are very likely in the class of entropy-measurable phenomena, and thus may be analyzed directly with the methods developed here.

Chapter 7

1. There is a very large literature on revolutionary change, mass violence, and authoritarian political systems. Although many of these works deal only with specific nations, some recent works attempt to study the problem from a comparative, cross-national, theoretical perspective, often incorporating empirical data. Among these are: Chalmers Johnson, *Revolutionary Change*, Little, Brown, 1966; Anthony Wallace, "Revitilization Movements," *American Anthropology* **58** (1965); Lewis Coser, *The Functions of Social Conflict*, Free Press, 1956; Ralf Dahrendorf, *Class and Class Conflict in Industrial Society*, Stanford University press, 1959; Barrington Moore, *Social Origins of Dictatorship and Democracy*, Beacon, 1966; John V. Gillespie, Betty Nesvold, Eds., *Macro-Quantitative Analysis*, Sage, 1971; S.J. Woolf, Ed., *The Nature of Fascism*, Vintage Books, 1969; Samuel Huntington, *Political Order in Changing Societies*, Yale University Press, 1968. A good review of the literature on violence in various contexts of social change is Henry Bienen, *Violence and Social Change*, University of Chicago Press, 1966. Also of interest here is the older work of a psychological nature on German fascism, Erich Fromm, *Escape from Freedom*, Avon, 1965.

2. This data was made available by the Inter-University Consortium for Political Research, Ann Arbor, Michigan. There were also presidential elections in the Weimar Republic, but these were two-stage elections, the second a run-off for the candidates receiving the most votes in the first election. To calculate entropy we would have to take into account both elections, since voters could change their choice between them. We would have to know the conditional probabilities associated with different voting combinations for the two elections, but these cannot be determined for individuals from aggregate election data. There was universal suffrage during this period.

3. Data errors in party voting percentages can be checked by summing to 100%; voter turnout errors can be checked by comparing with the maximum turnout range of about 40–100%.

4. The early onset of the reduction process can also be judged from the record of serious crime in Germany during the prewar years: arrests and convictions reached a peak in 1923 and declined fairly steadily thereafter, falling to about one third of the 1923 level by 1940. This data is provided by C. Johnson, *op. cit.*, p. 133, who makes a similar observation.

5. Dolf Sternberger, Bernhard Vogel, Eds., *Die Wahl der Parlemente*, Walter de Gruyter, Berlin, 1969, p. 365.

6. Indonesian election data is from Herbert Feith, *The Indonesian Election of 1955*, Cornell University Press, 1957, 1971. This data is not complete for the smallest parties, which are merely aggregated in the analysis here.

7. An example of a more localized entropy reduction may be Brazil in the 1960's. Entropy had risen rapidly through the 1950's but then decreased from about 1960 to 1964 when there was a military revolution. In this case the turnout, which had been less that 50%, was reduced to zero. The period of reduction was especially marked by an increasing occurrence of party coalitions during elections, with little regard for the ideological differences between the parties. Judging from the data of Soares and deNoronha for the 1954–55 municipal elections (Section 4-1, note 4-6), entropy levels were approaching 3 bits in at least two regions of the country, the Northeast and the largely urbanized Sao Paulo-Rio di Janeiro area. Among the states included in the data, the maximum of 3.14 bits (average) was in the most urbanized parts of Sao Paolo state, and the minimum of about 1.2 bits was in the least urbanized sector of the western border state of Mato Grosso.

8. Eric Wolf, *Peasant Wars of the Twentieth Century*, Harper & Row, 1969.

9. Wolf, p. xv.

10. Fairly good data is available for the Russian election just prior to the revolution and civil war; see Oliver Henry Radkey, *The Election to the Russian Constituent Assembly of 1917*, Harvard University Press, 1950. An analysis of the spatial entropy distribution at this election shows a distinctly unstable, nonharmonic distribution with several regions at high entropy levels, over 2 bits. There was an interior minimum at about 1.2 bits in the Central-Black Earth region with exceedingly steep gradients toward the Ukraine in the west and the Kama-Ural region in the east, the latter having an interior maximum of about 2.3 bits. We cannot determine from this single election whether an entropy reduction was in progress, but the Russian case shows the possibility of a combination of the nonharmonic, precivil war pattern (as observed in Section 6-2) with a reduction due to excessive entropy levels in some regions.

11. Another example of the role of excessive entropy in producing conflict situations is given by Charles A. McClelland, "Access to Berlin: The Quantity and Variety of Events, 1948–63," in J. David Singer, Ed., *Quantitative International Politics*, Free Press, 1968, pp. 159–186.

McClelland categorizes 18 types of internationally perceived actions (i.e., for an international system of nations) relating to Berlin. He computes entropy levels over time intervals between 1948 and 1963. He finds a crisis threshold exists at 70% of the maximum entropy of 4.14 bits, that is, at an entropy of about 3 bits (page 183). As in the examples studied here, excessive levels are apparently attained before the actual conflict.

Appendix II.

1. Robert Goodell Brown, *Smoothing, Forecasting and Prediction of Discrete Time Series*, Prentice-Hall, 1963; pp. 199–201.
2. Brown, pp. 97–122.

Bibliography

Adams, Ernest W., "On the Nature and Purpose of Measurement," *Synthese* **16,** pp. 125–169 (1966).

Ahlfors, Lars, *Complex Analysis*, McGraw Hill, New York, 1953.

Alford, Robert; Eugene Lee, "Voting Turnout in American Cities," *American Political Science Review* **62,** pp. 796–813 (1968).

Allardt, Erik, "Types of Protests and Alienation," in Erik Allardt, Stein Rokkan, Eds., *Mass Politics*, Free Press, New York, 1970.

Arrow, Kenneth J., *Social Choice and Individual Values*, Wiley, New York, 1963.

Atlan, Henri, "Du bruit comme principe d'autoorganisation," *Communications* **18** (France), pp. 21–36 (1972).

Basharin, G. P., "On a Statistical Estimate for the Entropy of a Sequence of Independent Random Variables," *Theory of Probability and Its Applications*, **4,** pp. 333-336 (1959).

Basic Statistical Analysis of India, Government of India, Delhi, 1962.

Bellman, R., et al., "Abstraction and Pattern Classification," *Journal of Mathematical Analysis and Applications*, **13,** pp. 1–7 (1966).

Benjamin, Roger; Alan Arian; Richard Blue; Stephen Coleman, *Patterns of Political Development*, McKay, New York, 1972.

Benjamin, Roger W., et al., "Modernization and Political Change: A Comparative Aggregate Data Analysis of Indian Political Behavior," *Midwest Journal of Political Science* **15,** pp. 219–261 (1971).

Berelson, Bernard R., et al., *Voting*, University of Chicago Press, Chicago, 1954.

Blalock, Hubert M., *Social Statistics*, McGraw-Hill, New York, 1960.

Bohannan, Paul, "Extra-processual Events in Tiv Political Institutions," *American Anthropologist* **60,** pp. 1-12 (1958).

Brown, Robert G., *Smoothing, Forecasting and Prediction*, Prentice-Hall, Englewood Cliffs, New Jersey, 1963.

Butler, David; Donald Stokes, *Political Change in Britain*, St. Martin's Press, New York, 1969.

Callen, Herbert B., *Thermodynamics*, Wiley, New York, 1960.

Campbell, Angus, et al., *The American Voter*, Abridgement, Wiley, New York, 1964.

Census of India, Government of India, Delhi, 1962.

Chandidas, R., et al., Eds., *India Votes*, Popular Prakashan, Bombay, 1968.

Chernoff, Hermann; Lincoln Moses, *Elementary Decision Theory*, Wiley, New York, 1959.

Churchman, C. W., P. Ratoosh, Eds., *Measurement: Definition and Theories*, Wiley, New York, 1959.

Coleman, Stephen, *Measurement and Analysis of Political Systems*, Doctoral Dissertation, University of Minnesota, 1972; and University Microfilms, Ann Arbor, Michigan.

Coser, Lewis, *The Functions of Social Conflict*, Free Press, New York, 1956.

Coulter, Philip; Glen Gordon, "Urbanization and Party Competition," *Western Political Quarterly* **21,** pp. 274–288 (1968).

Crozier, Michel, *The Bureaucratic Phenomenon*, University of Chicago Press, Chicago, 1964.

Dahrendorf, Ralf, *Class and Class Conflict in Industrial Society*, Stanford University Press, Stanford, California, 1959.

Daugherty, Charles, et al., Eds., *Brazilian Election Factbook 2*, Operations and Policy Research, Inc., Washington, D.C., 1965.

Davis, Philip J., "Orthonormalizing Codes in Numerical Analysis," in John Todd, Ed., *Survey of Numerical Analysis*, McGraw-Hill, New York.

DeLuca, A., S. Termini, "A Definition of a Nonprobabilistic Entropy in the Setting of Fuzzy Sets Theory," *Information and Control* **20,** pp. 301–312 (1972).

Dicke, Robert H., James Wittke, *Introduction to Quantum Mechanics*, Addison-Wesley, Reading, Mass., 1960.

Downs, Anthony, *An Economic Theory of Democracy*, Wiley, New York, 1957.

Eddington, A. S., *The Mathematical Theory of Relativity*, Cambridge University Press, New York, 1960.

Ellis, Brian, *Basic Concepts of Measurement*, Cambridge University Press, New York, 1966.

Ellis, J. B., *The Description and Analysis of Socioeconomic Systems by Physical Systems Techniques*, Doctoral Dissertation, Michigan State University, 1965.

Fano, Robert M., *Transmission of Information*, MIT Press, Cambridge, Mass., 1961.

Feller, William, *An Introduction to Probability Theory and Its Applications*, Vol. 1, 2, 2nd ed., Wiley, New York, 1957, 1971.

Feith, Herbert, *The Indonesian Election of 1955*, Cornell University Press, New York, 1957.

Fer, Francis, "Impossibilite de definir une entropy par une function de point ou similaire pour un system hamiltonian en transformation quelconque," *Comptes Rendus*, **265,** Series B, pp. 205–208 (1967).

Ferejohn, John A., Morris Fiorina, "The Paradox of Not Voting: A Decision Theoretic Analysis," *American Political Science Reveiw* **68,** pp. 525–596 (1972).

Fishburn, Peter C., "Summation Social Choice Functions," *Econometrica* **41,** pp. 1183–1196 (1973).

Flanagan, Scott, "The Japanese Party System in Transition," *Comparative Politics* **3,** pp. 231–253 (1970).

Floyd, R. W., "Nondeterministic Algorithms," *J. Assoc. Comp. Mach.,* **14,** pp. 636–644 (1967).

Fourier, Jean Baptiste, *The Analytic Theory of Heat,* Cambridge University Press, 1878; Dover, New York, 1955.

Franksen, Ole, "Mathematical Programming in Economics by Physial Analogs, Parts I, II, and III," *Simulation* **12, 13** (June, July, August, 1969).

Fromm, Erich, *Escape from Freedon,* Avon, New York, 1969.

Garabedian, P. R., *Partial Differential Equations,* Wiley, New York, 1964.

Garner, Wendell R., *Uncertainty and Structure as Psychological Concepts,* Wiley, New York, 1962.

Gebhart, Benjamin, *Heat Transfer,* 2nd ed., McGraw-Hill, New York, 1971.

Geiger, Siegfried, *Erkennen und Waehlen,* Kiepenheuer and Witsch, Berlin, 1970.

Gilison, Jerome M., "Soviet Elections as a Measure of Dissent, *American Political Science Review* **62,** pp. 814–826 (1968).

Gillespie, John; Betty Nesvold, Eds., *Macro-Quantitative Analysis,* Sage, Beverley Hills, California, 1971.

Goldberg, Arthur, "Discerning a Causal Pattern Among Data in Voting Behavior, *American Political Science Review* **60,** pp. 913–922 (1966).

Grujic, L. T.; D. D. Siljak, "Exponential stability of large-scale discrete systems," *International Journal of Control* **19,** pp. 481–491 (1972).

Hansson, Bengt, "Choice Structures and Preference Relations," *Synthese* **18,** pp. 443–488.

Hansson, Bengt, Group Preferences," *Econometrica* **37** (1969).

Hansson, Bengt, "Voting and Group Decision Functions," presented at the Econometric Society, Brussels, 1969.

Holmes, T. H.; R. H. Rahe, "The social readjustment rating scale," *J. Psychosom. Res.,* **14,** pp. 121–132 (1967).

Huntington, Samuel, *Political Order in Changing Societies,* Yale University Press, New Haven, Conn., 1968.

Ingarden, R. S., "Information Theory and Thermodynamics of Light. Part I," *Fortschritte der Physik* **12,** (Berlin, GDR) pp. 567–594 (1964).

Japan Statistical Yearbook, Bureau of Statistics, Tokyo.

Japan Year Book, 1942–1943, Japan Times Press, Tokyo.

Jeans, James, *An Introduction to the Kinetic Theory of Gases,* Cambridge University Press, New York, 1960.

Johnson, C. D., "State over-description and uncontrollability of dynamical systems," *International Journal of Control* **19,** pp. 225–249 (1974).

Johnson, Chalmers, *Revolutionary Change,* Little, Brown, Boston, 1966.

Kaplan, Abraham, *The Conduct of Inquiry*, Chandler, San Francisco, 1964.

Kariel, Henry S., *Open Systems: Arenas for Political Action*, Peacock, Itasca, Illinois, 1969.

Kellog, Oliver D., *Foundations of Potential Theory*, Dover, New York, 1953.

Kesselman, Mark, "French Local Politics: A Statistical Examination of Grass Roots Consensus," *American Political Science Review* **60,** pp. 963–973 (1966).

Kesselman, Mark, *The Ambiguous Consensus*, Knopf, New York, 1967.

Khinchin, A. I., *Mathematical Foundations of Information Theory*, Dover, New York, 1957.

Koenig, H. E., et al., *Analysis of Discrete Physical Systems*, McGraw-Hill, New York, 1967.

Krantz, David H., "Measurement Structure and Psychological Laws," *Science* **175,** No. 4029, pp. 1427–1435 (1972).

Krantz, David H., et al., *Foundations of Measurement*, Academic Press, New York, 1971.

Lacey, William N.; Bruce H. Sage, *Thermodynamics of One-Component Systems*, Academic Press, New York, 1957.

Landau, L. D.; E. M. Lifshitz, *Statistical Physics*, Pergamon Press, 2nd ed., Addison-Wesley, Reading, Mass., 1968.

LaSalle, Joseph; Solomon Lefschetz, *Stability by Liapunov's Direct Method*, Academic Press, New York, 1961.

Lee, Chae-Jin, "Urban Political Competition in a Developing Nation: The Case of Korea," *Comparative Political Studies*, **4,** pp. 107–116 (1971).

Lerner, Daniel, *The Passing of Traditional Society*, Free Press, New York, 1958.

Luce, R. D.; Howard Raiffa, *Games and Decisions*, Wiley, New York, 1959.

MacFarlane, A. G. J., *Engineering Systems Analysis*, Addison-Wesley, Reading, Mass., or George Harrup & Co., London, 1964.

Margenau, H., et al., "The Present State of Operationalism," *Scientific Monthly* **79** (1954).

McClelland, Charles A., "Access to Berlin: The Quantity and Variety of Events, 1948–63," in J. David Singer, Ed., *Quantitative International Politics*, Free Press, New York, 1968; pages 159–186.

McGill, W. J., "Multivariate Information Transmission," *IEEE (IRE) Transactions on Information Theory*, **1,** pp. 93–111 (1954).

Milgram, Stanley, "Nationality and Conformity," *Scientific American*, **205,** pp. 45–51 (1961).

Miller, George A., "The Magical Number Seven, Plus or Minus Two: Some Limits on our Capacity for Processing Information," *The Psychological Review*, **63,** pp. 81–97 (1956).

Miller, Henry; James Bieri, "An informational analysis of clinical judgment," *Journal of Abnormal and Social Psychology*, **67,** pp. 317–325 (1963).

Moore, Barrington, Jr., *Social Origins of Dictatorship and Democracy*, Beacon Press, Boston, 1966.

Nie, Norman, et al., "Social Structure and Political Participation," *American Political Science Review* **63,** pp. 361–378, 808–832 (1969).

Niemi, Richard; Herbert Weisberg, Eds., *Probability Models of Collective Decision Making,* Merrill, Columbus, Ohio, 1973.

Petersen, Svend, Ed., *A Statistical History of the American Presidential Elections,* Ungar, New York, 1968.

Pfanzagl, Johann, *Theory of Measurement,* Wiley, 1968.

Pinsker, M. S., *Arbeiten zur Informationstheorie V, Information und Informationsstabilitaet zufaellinger Groessen und Prozesse,* VEB Deutscher Verlag der Wissenschaften, Berlin GDR, 1963 (translated from the Russian); English edition: Holden Day, San Fransisco, 1964.

Przeworski, Adam; G. A. D. Soares, "Theories in Search of a Curve," *American Political Science Review* **65,** pp. 51–68 (1971).

Quastler, Henry, Ed., *Information Theory in Psychology,* Free Press, Glencoe, Illinois, 1955.

Radkey, Oliver, *The Election to the Russian Constituent Assembly of 1917,* Harvard University Press, Cambridge, Mass., 1950.

Rahe, R. H., et al., "Social stress and illness onset," *Journal of Psychosomatic Research,* **11,** pp. 213–218 (1964).

Raisbeck, Gordon, *Information Theory,* MIT Press, Cambridge, Mass., 1963.

Rajski, C., "A Metric Space of Discrete Probability Distributions," *Information and Control* **4,** pp. 371–377 (1961).

Renyi, A., "On the dimension and entropy of probability distributions," *Acta Math. Sci. Hung.,* **10,** pp. 193–215.

Report of the National Advisory Commission of Civil Disorders, Bantam, New York, 1968.

Report on the Third General Election in India, II, Indian Election Commission, Delhi, 1962.

Riggs, Douglas S., *Control Theory and Physiological Feedback,* Williams and Wilkins, Baltimore, 1970.

Riker, William; Peter Ordeshook, "A Theory of the Calculus of Voting," *American Political Science Review* **62,** pp. 25–42 (1968).

Rokkan, Stein; Jean Meyriat, Eds., *International Guide to Electoral Statistics,* Mouton, The Hague, 1969.

Runyon, John H., et al., Eds., *Source Book of American Presidential Campaign and Election Statistics, 1948–1968,* Ungar, New York, 1971.

Scammon, Richard, Ed., *America at the Polls (1920–1964),* University of Pittsburgh Press, Pittsburgh, 1965.

Schlegel, Richard, "Statistical Explanation in Physics: The Copenhagen Interpretation," *Synthese* **21,** pp. 65–82 (1970).

Schlesinger, Arthur, Ed., *History of American Presidential Elections,* McGraw-Hill, New York, 1971.

Schoenbaum, David, *Hitler's Social Revolution,* Anchor, New York, 1967.

Schoultz, Lars, "Urbanization and Political Change in Latin America," *Midwest Journal of Political Science* **16,** pp. 367–387 (1972).

Schurmann, Franz, *Ideology and Organization in Communist China,* 2nd. ed., University of California Press, Berkeley, 1970.

Shannon, C. E., "Prediction and Entropy of Printed English," *Bell System Technical Journal,* **30,** pp. 50–64 (1951).

Shannon, C. E., J. McCarth, Eds., *Automata Studies,* Princeton University Press, Princeton, New Jersey, 1956.

Shannon, C. E., Warren Weaver, *The Mathematical Theory of Communication,* University of Illinois Press, Urbana, Illinois, 1969.

Shapiro, Edward, *Macroeconomic Analysis,* Harcourt, Brace & World, New York, 1966.

Shearer, J. Lowen, et al., *Introduction to System Dynamics,* Addison-Wesley, Reading, Mass., 1967.

Simon, Herbert; Albert Ando, "Aggregation of Variables in Dynamic Systems," *Econometrica,* **29,** pp. 111–138 (1961).

Smith, Stephen A., "A Derivation of Entropy and the Maximum Entropy Criterion in the Context of a Decision Problem," *IEEE-Transactions on System, Man, and Cybernetics* **4,** pp. 157–163 (1974).

Soares, G. A. D., "The New Industrialization and the Brazilian Political System," in James Petras, Maurice Zeitlin, Eds., *Latin America, Reform or Revolution?,* Fawcett, Greenwich, Conn., 1968.

Soares, G. A. D.; M. A. C. DeNoronha, "Urbanizacao e dispersao eleitoral," *Revista de direito publico e ciencia politica* (Brazil), **3**(2) July–December 1960, pp. 258–270.

Sokolnikoff, I. S.; R. M. Redheffer, *Mathematics of Physics and Modern Engineering,* McGraw-Hill, New York, 1958.

Steiner, Henry; David Truber, "Brazil—All Power to the Generals," *Foreign Affairs* **49,** pp. 464–479 (1971).

Sternberger, Dolf; Bernhard Vogel, *Die Wahl der Parlemente,* Walter de Gruyter & Co., Berlin, 1969.

Stevens, S. S., "On the theory of scales of measurement," *Science* **103,** pp. 667–680 (1946).

Suppes, Patrick, "Behavioristic Foundations of Utility," *Econometrica* **29,** pp. 186–201 (1961).

Symon, Keith R., *Mechanics,* Addison-Wesley, Reading, Mass., 1960.

Thayer, Nathaniel B., *How the Conservatives Rule Japan,* Princeton University Press, Princeton, New Jersey, 1969.

Theil, Henri, *Economics and Information Theory,* Rand McNally, Chicago, 1969.

Theobald, D. W., *The Concept of Energy,* E&FN Spon, London, 1966.

Tillman, Frank; B. Roswell Russel, "Information and Entropy," *Synthese* **13,** pp. 233–241 (1961).

Tisza, Laszlo, *Generalized Thermodynamics,* MIT Press, Cambridge, Mass., 1966.

Townsend, James R., *Political Participation in Communist China,* University of California Press, Berkeley, 1969.

Tukey, J. W.; M. B. Wilk, "Data Analysis and Statistics: Techniques and Approaches," in Edward R. Tufte, Ed., *The Quantitative Analysis of Social Problems,* Addison-Wesley, Reading, Mass., 1970.

Tullock, Gordon, *Toward a Mathematics of Politics,* University of Michigan Press, Ann Arbor, Michigan, 1967.

Van Duijn, P., "A Model for Theory Finding in Sciences," *Synthese* **13,** pp. 61–67, (1971).

VonFoerster, H.; G. W. Zopf, Eds., *Principles of Self Organization,* Pergamon, New York, 1962.

VonFoerster, H., et al., Eds. *Purposive Systems,* Spartan, East Lansing, Michigan, 1969.

VonNeumann, John; Oskar Morgenstern, *Theory of Games and Economic Behavior,* Princeton University Press, Princeton, New Jersey, 1944.

Walker, E. L.; R. W. Heyns, *Anatomy of Conformity,* Prentice-Hall, Englewood Cliffs, New Jersey, 1962.

Wallace, Anthony, "Revitilization Movements," *American Anthropologist* **58,** pp. 264–281 (1956).

Woolf, S. J., Ed., *The Nature of Fascism,* Vintage Books, New York, 1969.

Wyler, A. R., et al., "Magnitude of life events and seriousness of illness," *Psychosomatic Medicine,* **33,** pp. 115–122 (1971).

Yovits, Marshall C.; C. Cameron, Eds., *Self Organizing Systems,* Pergamon, New York, 1960.

Zadeh, L. A., "Fuzzy Sets," *Information and Control* **8,** pp. 338–353, (1965).

Zadeh, L. A., "Fuzzy Algorithms," *Information and Control* **12,** pp. 94–102, (1968).

Index